Teachers: The Culture and Politics of Work

Teachers: The Culture and Politics of Work

Edited by

Martin Lawn and Gerald Grace

The Falmer Press
(A member of the Taylor & Francis Group)
London, New York and Philadelphia.

UK   The Falmer Press, Falmer House, Barcombe, Lewes, East Sussex,
            BN8 5DL

USA   The Falmer Press, Taylor & Francis Inc., 242 Cherry Street,
            Philadelphia, PA 19106–1906

© Selection and editorial material copyright M Lawn & G Grace
1987

First published 1987
Reprinted 1990 and 1993

British Library Cataloguing in Publication Data

Teachers: the culture and politics of work.
1. Teaching—Social aspects 2. Educational
sociology
I. Lawn, Martin II. Grace, Gerald
371.1   LB1025.2
ISBN 1–85000–216–9
ISBN 1–85000–217–7 Pbk

Library of Congress Cataloging-in-Publication Data

Teachers: the culture and politics of work.

Bibliography: p.
Includes index.
1. Teachers—Social conditions—History.
2. Teachers—Political activity—History. 3. Women
teachers—Social conditions—History. I. Lawn, Martin.
II. Grace, Gerald Rupert.
LB1775.T418 1987   371.1   87–14875
ISBN 1–85000–216–9
ISBN 1–85000–217–7 (soft)

Jacket design by Caroline Archer

Typeset in 10/12 Garamond by
Mathematical Composition Setters Ltd, Salisbury

Printed in Great Britain by
Redwood Books Limited, Trowbridge, Wiltshire

Contents

Introduction

The study of the culture and politics of teachers' work is currently emerging as an important field of social and educational inquiry. For too long teachers have been largely taken for granted both in theoretical analysis and in empirical investigation in education. As Connell (1985, p2) remarks

> 'The 'new sociology of education' that emerged in the 1970s made giant strides with problems like the schools' relation to the economy and the class bases of educational knowledge but had curiously little to say about teachers. In the most influential text of the decade, Bowles and Gintis' *Schooling in Capitalist America*, teachers hardly figure as a problem at all; they were assumed to be more or less well-controlled agents of the capitalist system'.

The reasons why teachers and teachers' work have not featured significantly on the agenda of educational and sociological inquiry are too involved to be dealt with adequately here. However a number of preliminary observations must be made. In the first place, it has to be noted that whether the theoretical framework of social and educational study is conservative functionalism (as in role theory), radical relativism (as in the new sociology of education) or structuralist analysis (as in recent Marxist work) teachers are seen as being socially constrained. This has had the effect of implying that an understanding of the teacher's position can be largely read off from an understanding of these wider constraints, whether these are expressed as role expectations, dominant cultural and pedagogic codes or as the social relations of schooling and the economy. In all cases, a relatively autonomous cultural and political space for teachers has been omitted from the analysis.

This theoretical tendency has been reinforced by a substantive emphasis in the study of teachers (at least in Britain) which has concentrated upon particular interpretations of professionalism. Until recently, much of the work on teacher professionalism has been of the type which Johnson (1979) refers to as 'trait theory' ie, the abstracted consideration of claimed professional criteria which rarely includes 'any systematic treatment of the general social conditions under which professionalisation takes place' (p 30). The study of teachers has very largely been appropriated into this sort of professional paradigm. This paradigm has either lacked an appropriate socio-historical framework for the study of professionalism or it has presented a partial view of that history. It has muted the consideration of the teacher's work as *work*, rather than as vocation, and has not encouraged close study of the conditions of the workplace. Above all the study of teacher professionalism has been constructed over and against notions of teacher unionism and at a distance from political and class relations and even (incredibly) from gender relations.

As a result of these theoretical and empirical limitations we still know comparatively little about how teachers experience and organise their work situation. We know little about their ideological and pedagogical commitments, how these are influenced and formed and what effects they have upon teachers' work in schools and upon their occupational satisfactions. In short, our understanding of the culture and politics of the workplace, *from the teacher's perspective*, is still at an elementary level.

At a wider historical level and structural level we still have relatively few studies which have looked in detail at the formation of teachers' organisations; their socio-historical origins; internal groupings and divisions; struggles and conflicts; occupational ideologies and relations with the state and other agencies. Crucial questions about the nature of teacher professionalism and teacher unionism and of their history, culture and politics have remained underdeveloped. Studies of the ways in which teachers are themselves judged, appraised and evaluated and of how these processes are related to the wider socio-political and economic context, are in their early stages (see Grace 1985).

There are now signs that just as the 'hidden curriculum' has emerged into the field of analysis so too have the 'hidden teachers'. The recent appearance of sources such as *Teachers' Lives and Careers*; *Teacher Careers: crises and continuities*; *Teachers' Work*; *The Politics of Teacher Unionism* and *Teachers and Texts* confirms this development and begins to place the study of teachers centrally within cultural, organisational and socio-political analysis in education.

There are a number of strands present in the recent work focusing on teachers. In Britain, one of the most productive approaches, ethnography, has been important in generating essays and accounts of the work of teachers in schools and classrooms. It has enabled others to recognise the ways in which teachers organise their work, how they come to make assumptions about children and the learning process and how they see their own commitments and careers in teaching. Ethnography has moved into life history which promises to be a fruitful source for understanding the 'experience of being a teacher'. While the strength of these developments has allowed the focus of the educational process to be drawn to the teacher, the weakness has been the way in which an ahistorical and too narrowly focused school-based picture of the teacher has emerged. It is clear that teaching is more than a series of activities and assumptions operating within an insulated school or classroom. Teachers, in their teaching, incorporate social and political projects of one sort or another, whether that is consciously recognised or not. Ethnographic work has to attempt to illuminate the unintentional and the intentional aspects of teachers' educational work with a broader framework which recognises the personal, the political and the structural relations of the labour process.

What is perhaps still too implicit in much ethnographic work on teachers has been made explicit and visible in feminist work on teachers. As part of a wider project to recover and reinstate the history, consciousness and experiences of women, for so long marginalised in academic and policy studies, feminist writers and researchers (such as The Boston Women's Teachers' Group (1983); Hoffman (1981) and Purvis (1981)) have focused upon women teachers. In doing so they have underlined the fact that although women constitute the great majority of teachers in most societies, the significance of gender relations and women's experience of patriarchal structures and practices within the occupation have been scarcely commented upon. Contemporary feminist work is making explicit both the history of women's struggles within teaching and the nature of their experiences within the occupation. The sexual division of labour in teaching is a category which must now be central to any understanding of the culture and politics of teachers' work.

While feminist work represents a new awareness in the study of teachers, older categories of explanation such as class and professionalism are being reinterpreted. Existing influential texts on teachers and professionalism (such as Tropp, 1957) are being challenged. Such texts have constructed a view of organised teachers as making steady historical progress towards a clear set of professional goals. Their analysis has been located within liberal versions of social mobility theory, premised upon an essentially benevolent (or rationalist) view of the state and a sense that expertise, aspiration and responsible behaviour will ultimately be rewarded. In effect, this liberal, evolutionary, social mobility view of organised teachers has failed to illuminate the actual class and gender relations of teaching; the contradictions which have arisen for teachers in particular socio-political periods or the complexities and contradictions of teacher–state relations.

These relations and these contradictions are now being brought into sharp focus by the work of writers such as Harris (1982), Ozga and Lawn (1981) and Apple (1986). A powerful thesis is also being constructed which suggests that teachers are increasingly caught up in processes of de-skilling, of 'proletarianisation', and of loss of control of work and the workplace. Teachers' labour, from this perspective, begins to have more of the correlates of work than of professional vocation. Indeed the whole notion of teaching as a profession insulated from class, economic and political relations is under critical review. Socio-historical analysis within a framework of conflict theory begins to demonstrate that teacher professionalism is a complex ideology and strategy capable of various interpretations and appropriations by different sectors of teachers and by different sectors of the state, local and central. Professionalism is not an innocent, non-political, occupational concept. It is deeply implicated in the politics of teachers' work and in the wider politics of teacher–state relations. Contemporary critical scholarship and socio-historical inquiry is increasingly throwing light upon the politics of teacher professionalism.

The essays in this collection represent a number of these approaches to the culture and politics of teachers' work. They cover new ground in the exploration of teacher–state relations; the changing context of work and teachers' responses to these changes; the experience of being a teacher and the experiences of groups of teachers; union organisation and struggles and the history of women in teaching. The perspective from which teachers are viewed differs among the writers and the collection includes conflict theory, socio-historical analysis, feminist analysis, diary-based ethnography and interview-based research. The nature of the inquiry means that understanding teachers and their social, economic and political relations in society requires a comprehensive approach, an approach which goes beyond the one-dimensional view. If there are tensions and contradictions between some of the essays these may be regarded as just as important to our appreciation of the culture and politics of teachers' work, as are the insights and original material which they present. Among the many audiences to whom this book is addressed, that of the teachers and those preparing to teach is crucial. It is our contention that teachers and student-teachers have insufficient opportunities (and until recently, sources) for systematic reflection about the nature of their own occupation and the nature of their work. They have little opportunity to develop an informed appreciation of the history, culture and politics of the work, which by its nature under present conditions, absorbs them into constant practical 'busyness'. As one of us wrote in the conclusion of a study of inner-city teachers, 'the particular irony of the situation is that members of an occupational group who are by their own rhetoric, engaged in explaining the world critically and in a relational sense, are to an important extent precluded from doing this in relation to their own situation' (Grace 1978, p 218).

Teachers' leaders in England in the 1950s argued that if greater centralisation of state control over education was to take place, then it would be necessary for teachers to create their own alternative sources of research and policy. This book is offered as a contribution to that process in that it is part of a movement to restore the collective memory of teachers; to encourage a wider range of questions about their work and to encourage them, through the formation of their own research networks, to add to the story of teachers' work.

Martin Lawn
Gerald Grace

References

APPLE, M. (1986) *Teachers and Texts*, New York, Routledge and Kegan Paul.

BALL, S. and GOODSON, I. (1985) (Eds.) *Teachers' Lives and Careers* Lewes, Falmer Press.

BOSTON WOMEN'S TEACHERS' GROUP (1983) 'The Other End of the Corridor: The Effects of Teaching on Teachers' *Radical Teacher*, (23) pp 2–23.

CONNELL, R. W. (1985) *Teachers' Work*, Sydney, Allen and Unwin.

GRACE, G. (1978) *Teachers, Ideology and Control*, London, Routledge and Kegan Paul.

GRACE, G. (1985) 'Judging Teachers: The Social and Political Contexts of Teacher Evaluation', *British Journal of Sociology of Education*, (6) No 1 pp 3–16.

HARRIS, K. (1982) *Teachers and Classes*, London, Routledge and Kegan Paul.

HOFFMAN, N. (1981) *Women's 'True' Profession: Voices from the History of Teaching*, Westbury, Feminist Press.

JOHNSON, T. (1979) *Professions and Power*, London, Macmillan.

LAWN, M. (1985) (Ed.) *The Politics of Teacher Unionism*, London, Croom Helm.

OZGA J. and LAWN, M. (1981) *Teachers, Professionalism and Class*, London, Falmer Press.

PURVIS, J. (1981) 'Women and Teaching in the Nineteenth Century' in R. Dale et al (Eds.) *Education and the State: Vol 2: Politics, Patriarchy and Practice*, Lewes, Falmer Press.

SIKES, P. et al. (1985) *Teacher Careers: Crises and Continuities*, Lewes, Falmer Press.

TROPP, A. (1957) *The School Teachers*, London, Heinemann.

Part One
Recovering History

1
'Lady Teachers' and Politics in the United States, 1850–1930

Geraldine J. Clifford

'Women will bless and brighten every place she enters, and she will enter every place.'

—Motto of the Woman's Christian Temperance Union

Introduction

When Frances Merritt was a 'normalite' at the all-female Framingham Normal School in Massachusetts in 1855, the class one day discussed the vexing 'Woman Question' with the instructor. We cannot trust her diary entry fully because keeping a journal was a requirement of the School and it was occasionally examined by the faculty, but this is what Frances Merritt wrote about her feelings on the subject:

> There is so much truth in what Mr. Stearns said to-day of women's mission. His view seems to be just the right one.
>
> Better exercise the influence God has given her over the heart, mind and will of all mankind in the most lovely and becoming manner, than to speak about women's rights, or to step out of her Heaven-ordained sphere.
>
> I am glad these rights have been talked of, nevertheless, for I think that true women, after seeing a few experiments tried, will rejoice more heartily in the lot to which God has appointed them, and be more awake to its high and holy requirement[1].

Like countless others of her sex in the nineteenth century, and since, Frances Merritt admirably fulfilled her 'God-appointed lot': retiring from the schoolmistress's platform in her late twenties to marry a 'Good Man' (the

Reverend A.J. Quick) and assume the duties of 'the school that is the family'. Indeed, in the middle classes the whole weight of girls' schooling was bent to imparting the message that, in the words of an undated catalogue of the Girls Seminary in Winona, Minnesota, 'A woman's influence is best exerted not at the polls or on the rostrum, but in the Christian home'. Somewhat ironically, however, such female seminaries flourished and proliferated in the United States in the nineteenth century because they educated girls for work *outside the home*: to become teachers first and wives and mothers later, if at all.

By outfitting them with an education beyond that given in the common schools, seminaries and normal schools introduced a young woman to more opportunities to teach than could be found in her home community. Although such positions were intended to represent only brief prologues to a domestic career, in fact the personal networks of graduates which were formed eased the way to teaching in the larger towns, in distant communities in the South and West, in exotic places like Indian reservations and the foreign mission field[2]. Moreover, in the process of pursuing the independent life of an unmarried schoolmistress, often far from home influences, a significant number of women teachers came to different conclusions than their mentors intended about woman's God-given nature and her proper place in society. It turns out that her personal odyssey also greatly enlarged the pool of political activists who would agitate the 'woman question' until female suffrage and the other goals of the 19th-century women's rights movement were achieved.

This chapter will first sketch the place of teaching in women's labor force participation from the mid-nineteenth century to the present. Second, it will indicate, in brief, the influences that women's numerical dominance of teaching in the United States had in shaping the character of the nation's still unique public education system. Third, it will explore the effects of women teachers' experiences on their own fitness and readiness for political engagement. Next, the perhaps surprising role of women teachers in electoral politics in the twentieth century will be described, beginning with two case studies that demonstrate the new possibilities open to women teachers to form a political agenda and to assert their own claims to expertise in matters of public policy and governing. The chapter will conclude with speculations about the less visible role that former teachers may also have played in helping to turn public opinion in favor of expanding women's rights and opportunities, as put forward by the multi-faceted political movement of organized feminism.

Women in Teaching in the United States of America

For the century before World War II, women's participation in the labor force was comprised chiefly of women who were, variously, poor, single, childless, or highly educated professionals. Teachers were by far the largest part of that latter group; teaching dominated the Department of Labor's category of 'professional and technical occupations'[3]. Teachers were also a significant part of the total female labour force. According to the United States Censuses, at no time between 1870 and 1980 did teaching drop below fifth place among the leading occupations for all women workers.

Moreover, teaching recruited surprising widely among the social groups of an increasingly polyglot society. The daughters of farmers and small businessmen were a majority of the nation's teachers, but the largest proportions of the graduates of elite colleges who were employed were also included among those keeping the nations schools[4]. Additionally, by 1920 there were 30,000 black women teachers in the United States, when teaching ranked seventh in the distribution of all black women workers. Their opportunities came with the racially segregated school systems that existed, by law, everywhere in the southern border states[5].

Between 1830 and 1920, the United States admitted 35.3 million immigrants. Early on and increasingly often, immigrants' daughters were found as teachers: among the Scandinavians and Germans in the middle western states, the Irish of Boston, Chicago, New Orleans, and Buffalo, the Irish and Jews of New York City. They included immigrants Kate Kennedy and her sisters who moved from doing embroidery in New York City to teaching school in San Francisco, where Kate became a militant in the campaign to secure wage equality for women teachers. To United States-born Irish, schoolteaching became what domestic service had been to their immigrant mothers: the most popular and important means of their self-support[6]. Using Census data, Lotus Coffman reported in 1911 that the native-born daughters of foreign parentage were twenty-seven percent of the nation's teachers, a disproportionately high representation[7].

Although many women sought employment for the same reasons that motivated men and were hired because of the need for ever more teachers to staff the nations rapidly expanding school systems, social moralists preferred to think otherwise. Educational theory stressed woman's ordained usefulness for social service. Its founder, Mary Lyons, consistently preached to the students at the Mount Holyoke Female Seminary in Massachusetts that 'education fits one to do good'. To the extent that women educated for duty did not or could not teach, or found in teaching too small an arena in which to exercise their ambition 'to do good', education for a useful life could breed discontent with traditions presupposing feminine passivity. The American novelist Pearl Buck undoubtedly spoke for many earlier women when she complained, 'A man is educated and turned out to work. But a women is educated — and turned out to grass'.[8]

The righteous cause of female education and the *vocation* of teaching were being closely linked, among both liberals and conservatives on the 'woman question'. For example, the professed anti-feminist, Catharine Beecher, raised funds to send Protestant women to teach and civilize the West, lest Catholic influence spread unimpeded in places like Missouri and Michigan. Along with exhortations of Christian duty, economic and demographic factors pushed women into work outside the home[9]. As families grew progressively smaller and the home less important as a center of domestic manufacture through the nineteenth century, the 'Christian Schoolroom' increasingly competed with the 'Christian Home' for the time of the daughters and sisters of the United States. Married women, including mothers, were also employed as teachers in certain circumstances, more commonly in undesirable rural areas or where hardship, death, or desertion imposed the necessity of self-support[10]. As early as the 1830s the under-employed and unmarried daughters of New England farmers were prominent in the work force of the textile mills of the region. With the growth of immigration from Ireland, however, and changes in the social and cultural arrangements of industrial capitalism, many families sought 'cleaner' and more respectable employment. Prosperous families like the Curriers of New Hampshire consented to their daughters' plan to leave their community with its lack of eligible men, but dashed their hopes of entering the Lowell Mills; in 1845 they consented, however, to their keeping school[11].

The common school, rooted in Protestant millenialism, furnished a broadly acceptable alternative in nineteenth-century America. With the reforms of the 1840s and '50s associated with Horace Mann, improved working conditions and a lengthened school year made schoolkeeping competitive with factory work in earnings and preferable for the exercise of independence. With the passing years, schoolteaching increased its advantages. Thus, when she left her cousin's house in 1879 to live with her guardian George Nye, orphaned Mary Bartlett revealingly reported that 'Mrs. Nye said if she couldn't get a school she would have to work in the factory'[12].

Available data for Massachusetts before 1860, the state which led both in educational advance and the employment of women teachers, suggest that as many as one woman in four taught at some time in her life[13]. By 1895, women were reported to be 90.5 percent of all Massachusetts public school teachers. And as Yankees moved west, they took their social practices with them. Thus, by the end of the century, women were a half or more of teachers in all Northern and Western states, except Kansas and Indiana where men held a tenuous two percent lead[14]. Despite its late start in building public school systems, the South followed suit. On account of her sex, it was difficult for Hattie Lake to secure a teaching position in East Baton Rouge, Louisiana in 1877; the intervention of her widowed sister, the town's largest payer of school taxes, overcame the objections[15]. Necessity prevailed: single women already outnumbered single men in sixteen of the states bordering the Atlantic seaboard and Gulf of Mexico. By the turn of the twentieth century, therefore, the leading occupation among Southern women of the 'betterclasses' was teaching, and the men of the region rapidly lost their numerical advantage on school staffs. The trend continued everywhere into the next century. By the 1930s American men were only 11.4 per cent of elementary teachers and 40 per cent of secondary teachers, contrasted to men's share of 41.5 per cent and 71.8 per cent of elementary and secondary teachers respectively, everywhere else in the world[16].

The Consequences for Public Education

In a nation where over ninety percent of the students were enrolled in public schools, women were two-thirds of all public school teachers in the United States in 1900. The cities were the particular bastion of the lady teacher: in twelve cities in seven states, only women were hired. In Los Angeles, women were two-thirds of the city's high school teachers. In San Francisco, 967 of the city's 1070 teachers were women. Nationally, in the urban high schools in 1907, fifty-seven per cent of the students and fifty-three percent of the teachers were female[17].

Educationally, the United States was unique among western societies on two counts: women's prominent place among high school teachers and the early and rapid growth of secondary schools. The two facts are related, for without women teachers and the ability to employ them at lower wages than men commanded, the nation could not have popularized secondary education more than a generation before this happened in Europe. Upwards of ten percent of the age group was attending secondary schools in the United States by 1910; in Europe this happened only after 1945, the thirty percent mark was exceeded in the United States in the early 1920s, in Europe in the 1960s. On the eve of the Great Depression the proportion of the age group attending general or academic secondary schools was already five times higher in the United States than in Europe[18]. The academic culture of the schools changed in the process. As high school attendance became more widely available, the once-common entrance examination was eliminated for almost all high schools, and curricular and behavioural expectations were gradually altered to bring secondary schools into alignment with mass, unselective primary education. Their traditional associations with higher education were greatly weakened as a consequence[19].

Compared to European nations, where secondary schools had a per capita cost up to five times that of primary schools, the spending ratio in the United States was close to 2 : 1. As a consequence of hiring women, and later of economies of scale, local school districts could more easily accede to the wishes of middle class constituents for tax supported high schools. This subsidization of the schooling of a social and academic elite, in advance of the interests of the working classes in secondary schooling, secured in most communities the loyalty of the leading families to the public school system[20]. Its supporters believed that this development would realize, in these places, what was intended in the very concept of the

7

common school: educating all of the children of all of the people in a public institution, in a school comprehensive with regard to social class, culture, and academic aptitude. It also became more difficult for Catholic bishops to denounce the godlessness of the public schools when, as a parishioner publicly reminded a cleric in 1890, 'thousands of Catholic girls . . . had graduated from being pupils of public schools into becoming teachers, and reflect credit alike on the race that produced them, the church to which they belong, and the country which afforded them and their Irish-Catholic parents the splendid opportunities which culminated in their education'.[21]

The high schools themselves led easily into teaching careers. Besides the academic course, whose graduates could easily secure teaching positions in the elementary (primary) schools of outlying communities, many big-city high schools offered a 'normal course' by the late nineteenth century; some reserved city teaching positions for those who completed this local curriculum. Girls' High School, the second high school established in Philadelphia, was a normal school. Catholic parochial schools in big cities also added a high school department to prepare their young women for teaching[22]. These facts encouraged girls to persist in high school. By 1900 young women were about two-thirds of high school graduates nationally. At a time when most working class males left for unskilled industrial and service jobs, this female persistence in school furthered the demand for teachers. When the schools of St. Louis, Missouri enacted a policy permitting the city's black schools to employ teachers of that race, the immediate result was growing enrollments of black students and higher graduation rates among young women, most hoping to become teachers[23].

A still largely unexplored subject in the history of education in the United States, and one which appears to be related to teacher gender, concerns the mechanisms by which coeducation triumphed as the model for American schooling at all levels. Because of low population density, the rural elementary schools of the nineteenth century were unable to practice sex segregation, except in superficial forms like maintaining separate cloakrooms and play yards or seating the sexes on different sides of the schoolroom. In the larger towns, Yankee thriftiness usually precluded sex-specific schools. Even in the nation's largest cities, however, only the earliest public high schools were reserved for one sex and most of these disappeared in the wave of coeducation. The common pattern found elsewhere in the world of limiting women to teaching young children and girls broke down in the United States as secondary schooling detached itself from the ungraded rural schools and abandoned the private academy for the public high school model. Girls as students and women as teachers swept into these schools, firmly lodging coeducation in the process.

Because of the prevalence of coeducation in the high schools, it eventually dominated higher education as well, again assisted by economic considerations. The early flurry of founding women's colleges subsided and, by 1900, three quarters of the women attending colleges and universities were in coeducational institutions. It was at the coeducational University of Minnesota that a Miss Knox became conscious of her performance in relation to the other sex. In 1882 when she learned the amount she was offered to teach in the Austin (Minnesota) High School, she wrote to a fellow woman teacher, 'that a class mate whom I . . . invariably left in the rear in Greek should get twice what I receive and do half the work makes me righteously indignant. I think I shall put on pants and go west'[24]. In the process of raising this kind of feminist consciousness, coeducation in tertiary education also greatly increased the numbers of institutions in which women could be employed as professors, since women were almost never selected to teach in an exclusively male school, at any level of schooling[25].

In coeducational schools the girls had ample opportunity to 'leave in the rear', 'spell down' or otherwise outperform the other sex, as the records show they often did. This was contrary, of course, to what Barbara Berg calls the 'woman-belle ideal' and to the lessons of school books that 'girls should be taught to give up their opinions betimes, and not pertinaciously to carry on a dispute, even should they know themselves to be in the right'[26]. When Claude Bowers celebrated his graduation from the high school of Indianapolis, Indiana in 1898, the class honors went to three pupils, all girls. Claude vented his chagrin in his dairy, thus: 'Like most honor people, they are more than ordinarily commonplace — mere drudges'[27]. Regardless, many a Claude Bowers learned to play academic second fiddle to a Martha Allerdice.

Securing a 'Wider Sphere of Usefulness'

Tens of thousands of nineteenth-century women began and ended their teaching careers in those schools in which they had themselves been educated, or in nearby counterparts.[28] Untold numbers went father afield, however, escaping family control and parochial concerns. From Mount Holyoke Seminary alone, scores went forth to work with Indians in the Oklahoma and Oregon territories. Some four thousand women travelled South during and following the Civil War, to teach a quarter-million black children and vast numbers of adults. A well-educated, self-selected band of 'do-gooders' — reviled by white Southerners as 'horse-faced', Yankee 'nigger lovers' — were those teachers sent by the American Missionary Association. Using teachers' letters from Georgia in the Association's files, Jacqueline Jones demonstrates how some of these women, enlisted to further Negro rights, came to consider their own situations as needing remediation; they experienced the sex discrimination and oppressive paternalism that prompted many earlier women abolitionists to become feminists. Jones finds that, to the moral self-righteousness which motivated their teaching, they also brought a 'strong sense of professionalism to produce forthright challenges to their male

9

superiors in the areas of both educational policy and mission home management'[29]. Some of these women never returned home and, among those that did, it is doubtful that they could settle comfortably into the role of submissive and dutiful daughter or wife.

Nor could countless other women teachers who had ventured no father from home to teach than the next county. I have examined hundreds of letters of nineteenth-century teachers — written to family, friends, other teachers, suitors — and found rising expressions of assertiveness, self-determination, and ego[30]. Some teachers voiced their enlarged sense of independence and self-worth in quiet ways, choosing, for example, not to return to a given school district but to seek a better situation. Others became more openly the 'strong-minded woman' so disliked and feared by conservatives. The prominent feminists, like teacher Lucy Stone, placed a great store on their independence. But so did quite ordinary women teachers.

Economic Independence and its Effects

Teachers' diaries and letters clearly indicate that women teachers wished to be neither a financial burden nor otherwise indebted to anyone. They wished to pay their own way, to gain an initiative and advantage not likely to be experienced in their parents' home or as the unmarried 'auntie' in the homes of their brothers. Speaking for many, Flora Davis Winslow wrote on her way from Maine to Michigan in 1852, 'I teach school because I wish to be independent and not beholden to my friends for a livelihood'[31].

> The ability of women to earn their own living has put out of existence a class of people whom we meet in the novels of fifty years ago, 'the poor relation', 'the indigent female', 'the elderly spinster', who works for her board in the home of some prosperous relative, treading softly, echoing the opinions of those who feed her, wearing decent shabby black, as become her humble condition. That sort of dependence is not good for the woman who takes it, or for the one who gives it[32].

Historian Mary Ryan interprets the low wages paid to women teachers as restraining their independence and assertiveness. She writes, 'Preferences, aside, young unmarried women were not capacitated by the meagre wages of schoolteachers to challenge the hegemony of fathers, brothers, and grooms'[33]. Teaching wages *were* low, but the ability to earn even a small wage, especially in cash-poor rural and small town America where most of the population still lived, made young women, many girls in their teens, economically important to their families. The wages of teachers, mill hands, domestics, and later, office girls, might make the difference between keeping or losing the farm in a bad year, between renting or buying a house, between sending a brother to learn telegraphy in a proprietary school or to study natural philosophy in a college. V. F. Calverton even contended, in 1929, that 'women's economic independence has been a far more important item in her emancipation than her political enfranchisement'[34]. The ability to contribute economically is, we are told by modern-day feminists, a desideratum of social and political equality.

In her own autobiographical novel, *Country Schoolma'am* (1941), Della Lutes had her young heroine, Delly, recount her satisfaction and pleasure at receiving her first teaching wages:

> My father was a little touchy about the whole thing. The idea of girls at sixteen earning their own living didn't appeal to him in the first place. In fact he had been against it from the start and only my mother's tactful handling had kept the matter from becoming an issue. The pride my mother had in her daughter's ambitious achievement was, I am sure, shared by him, but it was not allowed expression or even openly recognized ... He did not relish these new and lawless ways[35].

As this father intuitively recognized, the fact that a young woman, hardly more than a girl, could begin teaching in a local school without anything more than a common schooling, *without an investment in a specialized education or in tools or in career ambitions*, had the potential for unsettling effects upon both herself and the observant girls in her classroom. That so many such teachers subsequently used their scant savings from teaching, perhaps augmented by loans or gifts by relatives, to purchase more schooling for themselves suggests rising self-confidence and self-interest; a certain risk-taking was required.

One such young woman was eighteen-year-old Sarah Jane Christie. After only a few weeks at a female seminary in Wisconsin, she wrote home in 1862 that, if her father could not support her studies beyond the present term, she supposed she would come home,

> and teach again in our District if they will give me enough wages, for I want to get as much as possible and I will then teach till I get enough to pay you and to give me a start to come up here again. I suppose that you will laugh at the idea of me saving money to go to school with. But I can tell you I am *determined* on having an education and if I keep my health I *will* have one if it takes me *ten years* or more to earn money for it .... Education gives me power for good which money can not give and as God has given us these intellectual powers it is our duty to cultivate them to their utmost extent and to use them for the means of doing the greatest good to our fellow creatures. I think therefore it is *my* duty as well as the duty of others to improve as much as possible and to cultivate my mind, to be a Teacher to others[36].

Sarah had already disregarded her father's wishes that she limit her studies, deciding to add the Normal Class so she could prepare herself to pass the state teacher's examination.

Parental doubt or ambivalence is a common theme in the personal documents I have examined. It reflects the unsettling effects of a transition in family and social relations. In distant Washington territory, Carrie White was distressed to recall that she had turned down a teaching position in Whitman College at her parents' request, to continue with them at home. In 1884, in her diary she wrote, 'Well if the time does ever come when they think me a burden it will be very very bitter for me and I shall almost regret that I did not continue teaching and so make a calling for myself where I could be independent'[37]. In every section of the nation, even in the South by the 1880s, teaching permitted hordes of young women to gain independence through self-support, to fill the years between childhood and marriage, to put off a little the act of losing their precious independence through marriage.

Social Power Within and Without Marriage

In noting the higher graduation rates of girls than boys from the high schools of the United States, historian Caroline Bird offers this observation:

> The unheralded result has been that some American women have always had to marry men with less formal schooling than themselves. This education gap set up hostility on both sides, and it may be the reason why American women seem bossier and more demanding of their men than women in countries where men are generally better schooled than their wives[38].

If true, those wives who had been teachers should, in general, be expected to have gained proportionately more power in their marital unions and to have wielded even greater authority over their own children.

Among the female cohort that first made women the majority of teachers in Massachusetts (those born around 1830), nearly a half were still single in their late twenties and over a quarter into their thirties[39]. Mary Jane Mudge was twenty-four years old, in her seventh year of teaching in the industrial city of Lynn, Massachusetts, when she wrote in her diary in 1854 about the proposal from her suitor, Philip C. Bryant: 'I told B, I had thought of his proposal, and had decided, I had rather wait another year . . . I never was so prettily situated in school as I now am, and my salary never was so much. Hope I have made the right decision'[40]. Both psychological, and economic factors entered into that decision. In fact favorable reports of her teaching buoyed her self confidence and improvements in teacher wages prompted her to delay her marriage for another two years. In being able to choose, some of the Mary Jane Mudges of America very likely retained a degree of power, egotism, and individualism within the marital relationship that was inconsistent with conventional expectations of marriage.

Historian Anne Scott finds visible change in the private worlds of Southern women by the late years of the nineteenth century: 'The relationship between men and women was subtly affected by the possibility that a woman could earn her own living'[41]. Some economically independent women put the wedding day off permanently. 'I'd rather be a free spinster and paddle my own canoe', declared the noted novelist, Louisa May Alcott[42]. Nearly one half of the 1470 women featured in *A Woman of the Century* authored by prominent feminists Frances Willard and Mary Livermore, lived most of their adult lives as single women[43]. Under the common law inherited from England, the single women possessed independence and property rights denied to her married counterpart, where 'husband and wife are as one, and that one is the husband'[44]. Unwilling to surrender the control over their lives that economic independence and childlessness conferred, many well-educated professional women created surrogate families, or 'Boston marriages' as they were called, especially after 1880 when the rates of non-marriage were especially high. In the words of one such woman, Jesse Taft, women turned to other women, 'finding in them the sympathy and understanding, the bond of similar standards and values', the 'aesthetic and intellectual interests' for which business-oriented American men had no time[45].

Not all women could, in fact, choose the single life freely. Because of the un-balanced local sex ratios — caused by wars, immigration, and the speculative westward movement of men to farms or mines — forty percent of native-born young women who were between ages twenty-six and thirty during or following the Civil War (1860–1880) were single[46]. Yet, married or single, women who had gained some sense of self through employment as teachers were carriers of potentially dangerous feminist tendencies or sympathies. They were also empowered by the competencies gained in teaching, at least in theory.

Qualifying Women for New Roles

The oftentimes subtle but significant alterations in male-female relationships between prospective spouses and within the family or origin had their counterparts in school. In insidious ways the coming of women as teachers into most primary and ungraded schools and into half or more of the secondary classrooms affected the power relations of the sexes. School district reports, references in the cor-respondence of parents, and teachers' and students' own diary comments clearly indicate that many young women proved themselves in the ultimate test of the nineteenth-century school: establishing their authority over the 'large scholars', especially the older boys who had made life so difficult for so many male teachers, often successfully barring them even from entering the schoolhouse. It was these boys whose presence had earlier argued against and delayed women's takeover of the nation's schoolrooms.

While female teachers were gaining new possibilities of control over men as students, males 'found their repertoire diminished when women stepped into the classroom', as Deborah Fitts has noted:

> No longer were they able to express rebellion violently, nor was the barring-out ritual appropriate with a woman teacher. The classroom was (and is) a stage upon which new social identities are forged from old, a platform for experiments in which the experimenters participate. The schoolroom is not only an analog of society, it is that society in action[47].

In the words of the author of *The Five Talents of Woman* (1888), the teacher was *supposed* 'to teach and improve those who came within reach of her influence'. To do less, was to evade her duty[48]. In imposing their will upon schoolboys women teachers arguably had a broader mandate than they would have in their role as the mother of sons, where boys might look to fathers for relief.

There was ample contemporary recognition of the strains being visited on female-male relationships by the fact of women teachers. The 'feminization' of teaching was reported as a problem, in national magazines, from the 1890s to World War I. In 1911 the superintendent of schools of Elizabeth, New Jersey wrote,

> I am strongly in the opinion that the presence of women as teachers of boys in the upper grammar grades, and even in the first and second year of the high school, causes thousands of boys to become disgusted with and to leave the schools. Of my own knowledge, many young men have been driven from school because of their intense dislike to being (using their own words) 'bossed by women'[49].

However, as secondary and higher education began their slow but steady expansion in the late nineteenth century and the economy had less need of adolescent boys, it was becoming progressively less possible for them to escape the school in order to evade the new authority of the woman boss. The best that the male fraternity was able to accomplish was to erect informal but effective barriers preventing women from controlling school administration as they dominated teaching numbers[50].

The new power of the individual woman teacher was also being joined with that of other women. What Nancy Cott calls the 'bonds of womanhood' were highly significant to women in the nineteenth century[51]. The radicals and conservatives each had their bosom woman friends; but the former also had, and probably made more use of, their 'networks'. Through teaching many women made friendships apart from their families and neighborhoods of origin, linking their conciousness with that of other teachers. These were new relationships, peer relationships. Sometimes these associations were begun in school, especially in the female seminaries and normal schools which were important to women in the middle and late years of the nineteenth century.

But networks of teachers were also built through teachers' institutes ('retreats' held periodically for teachers, under county or state auspices), in boarding places, even by the common practice of visiting the schools in neighboring districts on one's own half-holidays. Friendships with other teachers provided moral support, the security of knowing that other teachers also let the 'Monday Morning Blues' ruin their Sunday afternoons; they shared their guilty secret that they did not love all of their students equally well — as they were told they should. Their sense of association as women was strengthened by their common bond as teachers. Fellow teachers were also sources of job information and references. This was always important, but never so important as in those times when the wish of too many young women to teach caused a glut on the market for teachers; then, the informal and casual mechanisms of hiring made personally communicated knowledge especially crucial.

Once women left teaching they were arguably motivated to continue to associate with other like-minded women. They were certainly better equipped to put to use, in any kind of organization, the managerial abilities they had acquired and polished in running a nineteenth-century schoolroom. The rural school, especially, was largely left to the teacher to organize and discipline. Preparing students for the popular public exhibitions which routinely closed the school term called on abilities to plan and execute, as well as to perform in public. Even in the towns, teachers were often left to their own devices, as Irene Hardy, not yet twenty years old, discovered in Eaton, Ohio around 1860. 'There was very little oversight by the principal and the school board', she reported. 'I was absolute mistress in my own room and taught, in whatever way seemed best to me . . .'[52].

Many teachers and former teachers found this experience helpful in assuming leadership of organizations like the Boston Female Anti-Slavery Society, the Women's National Loyal League, the National American Woman Suffrage Association, the Woman's Christian Temperance Union — and, later, the American Association of University Women and the League of Women Voters whose first president, Maud Wood Park, was a teacher. Consider, for example, Jane Cunningham Croly (1829–1901). Born in England, she was brought to the United States in 1841 and taught in district schools for a time. Seeking her fortune she settled in New York City, became a journalist and was, in 1857, the first woman to have a syndicated column. Her son, Herbert David Croly, was the editor of the liberal journal, *The New Republic*. But her influence was also extended beyond the family when she founded Sorosis in 1869, often identified as the first woman's club in the United States.

Such were the organizations which served as training schools where still more women 'learned how to organize and conduct projects, developed skill in public speaking, and articulated a body of interests which women shared'[53]. Teacher Frances Willard, long-time head of the WCTU, spoke expansively of women's powers: 'Alike by endowment, by heredity and environment, she is set forth as nature's supreme specimen for organizing power. Wherever you deposit her she begins to combine, to contrive, to find out how a little may be made to a great way'[54]. The hyperbole aside, later studies of political women — including judges and state legislators — find that women in public life have much higher than average affiliations of an active sort than their male counterparts[55].

Women's experiences as teachers both caused them to seek out such opportunities and to be selected by other women for active roles. Teaching had given young, usually unsophisticated women a 'public existence'. In some cases the tensions of managing and drilling an unruly or too-disparate group of pupils, the failure to meet their own or the community's expectations, drove them into looking for some quiet retreat, a retired domesticity. But in many other cases women surely had their capabilities and self-confidence enhanced by teaching and sought no haven from the storm. Thus, many teachers and former teachers became active in other arenas — and that activism was important to organized feminism.

In sum, women went into teaching in massive numbers because they had the requisite energy and skills to perform a task which society wanted performed. They had the opportunity to use these skills because public opinion was sufficiently ready to accept teaching as modest, respectable work for women, work appropriate to their sex. As an extension of the domestic sphere it proved to have within it sufficient slack or elasticity to accommodate greater potentialities for women than was commonly understood or desired. For some women of growing ambition and talent for leadership teaching was often too small a stage; they left it to take up other work, often related causes, and were probably better equipped to succeed by virtue of having kept school[56]. Other women discovered *themselves* in the schoolroom. Roused by what they observed of injustice and male arrogance they, like Ohio's Irene Hardy, might often keep silent though 'I had some thoughts and 'my heart waxed hot within me''[57]. Such women are, I believe, a large part of the forgotten women of feminist history in the United States — the readied soil to catch the seeds of feminism.

The 'Gentler Sex' and the Political Process

Education was closely linked to the feminist movement in the United States. By the mid-nineteenth century such leaders as Lucretia Mott, a Quaker teacher and abolitionist, and Elizabeth Cady Stanton had decided that extending women's educational opportunities was a crucial step in mounting the political campaign necessary to secure women's rights. Although it was a social and economic movement as well, political goals and political processes suffused organized feminism. Organizational and strategical skills were required. Persons possessing these competencies were recruited and promoted; where necessary, they were acquired by on-the-job experience. Demonstration, petitioning, lobbying, and cutting bargains were evident on either side of virtually every policy clash. Victories were occasionally won. Achieving the franchise was one, and one which had the potential of exploiting the political skills gained by feminist activists, to turn women into legislative and administrative officeholders. As government officials they could speed the course of change and achieve the rest of the feminist agenda.

It was not enough to overturn laws prohibiting women from standing for public office. To be elected women officeholders needed women voters. Well before individual states gave women the vote in state elections and they won female suffrage in federal elections with ratification of the Nineteenth Amendment to the United States Constitution in 1920, women had secured the right to run for and vote for school offices. Kansas gave women the franchise in school elections in 1859 and twenty-three other states had done so by 1910[58]. They did so as a grudging concession to the principle that women both cared about and were competent in matters of education. The fact of women's heavy participation in education as teachers was clearly important in winning these first concessions.

Two Pioneer Teacher-Politicians

One of the earliest states to give women the opportunity to stand before an electorate that included women was Minnesota. When Mrs. Stevens (the former Sarah Jane Christie) stood for the third time for the office of Superintendent of Schools of Blue Earth County in 1894, she appealed to women voters on the ground that she and they were women: they owed it to themselves as women and to the underpaid women teachers of the county to support her candidacy. Like countless other office-seekers, her election was not, she claimed, a matter of politics but of principle — less the principle of equality, however, than that of woman's specialness. Of her candidacy she exhorted that

> It involves a *principle* — a principle much more important than my individual ambitions and interests — the principle of *justice to women* ... Although women's sphere is primarily and chiefly the home, yet in the new order of things, from which we cannot escape, millions and millions of women and girls all over the civilized world are earning their bread and bread for their loved ones .... It is only when they ambitiously and nobly strive to attain to positions of greater responsibility, less drudgery, and higher pay that certain classes of men suddenly discover that there is something unnatural about it, something very unwomanly

and revolting to good taste, and we hear a howl of disapproval, a wail of anguish over the impending destruction of the feminine nature. One would almost infer that money has sex — that big money is masculine and small money feminine .... But the principle has already been proclaimed and has been assented to by conscience everywhere and hence will finally prevail, that since woman by her nature is excluded from most of the professions and trades, it is only just that she *should be given the preference in those few vocations to which she is adapted and restricted to by her nature, capacity, and attainments* .... This principle is involved in my candidacy. Where there are ten offices for men to share among themselves, and a competent woman is a candidate for the eleventh office, which is not political and to which she is eligible by law, no man should be a candidate against her. (The women of this county are entitled to some recognition, and they should insist that they have it.).... Is it anything but right, after having taught at low wages for many years, having spent their earnings in acquiring higher education and qualified themselves for just such a position of higher responsibility and higher pay, that they should receive their reward. I take my stand firmly and fearlessly upon the principle that in right and justice the office of superintendent should go to one of the lady teachers of this county as long as the county has one capable of filling the place; and I ask the women of this county to ratify that principle at the polls[59].

Except for a brief, unsuccessful effort to earn her living as a dressmaker, Sarah Jane Christie (1844–1919) had alternated between being a teacher and a student from about 1862 until her marriage to a widowered farmer in 1879. Born in Ireland of Scottish parents, her large, midwestern family was connected to New England relations and, through a brother, to the foreign mission field in Turkey. She had four stepchildren and bore two daughters of her own. Successfully elected as Superintendent of Schools of Blue Earth County in 1890 on the Peoples (Populist) and Prohibition Parties' ticket, she was twice defeated for reelection, reportedly by the desertion of the women living in town[60]. She retired from teaching and politics to practise homeopathic medicine and buy and sell real estate. Had she been younger, Sarah Christie Stevens would probably have considered standing for offices other than that of school superintendent. Active in the temperance and suffrage movements, her behaviour belied her words; it is very doubtful that she really believed very much in the limitations of women's nature.

Years before, when her father had described algebra as a 'masculine attainment', it vexed her greatly and she wrote him that

I cannot see it as any more *that* than a 'feminine attainment' .... It is the education which a woman gets and the false Ideas that are crammed into them that keeps women where they are .... But let each have a fair

trial and those who are not able let them fall back to their old places . . . .
If the women were rightly educated, as they should be, we would not
read so much about that hackneyed phrase, 'Woman's Mission', nor hear
it *gassed* about either[61].

She went on to tell him about two women of her acquaintance at school: 'real,
true, strong, independent' women of the kind one seldom sees. Sarah was making
herself one of that breed.

Sarah Stevens died in 1919, the year that Mary Elizabeth ('Margie') Neal of
Carthage, Texas was made a member of the State Democratic Executive Committee.
Margie Neal was born in 1875, reared in a small family by parents who migrated
west from Georgia. She never married. Unlike Father Christie who demurred
when Sarah Jane studied algebra, Father Neal objected to Margie's playing with
dolls when she could be reading books. She and her brother and sister were always
excused from farm chores if they had school lessons to study, and Mr. Neal finally
moved the family to town to give them a better schooling. Sarah Christie's
education included a female seminary in Wisconsin and some terms at Carleton
College. Margie Neal received a county scholarship to San Houston Normal
Institute in Huntsville, Texas, courtesy of their representative in Austin, Mr. J. Ras
Jones, the 'sockless legislator'. Yet Sarah Jane Christie of Blue Earth County,
Minnesota and Mary Elizabeth Neal of Panola County, Texas have a great deal in
common.

Margie Neal stayed only one year at Huntsville; that was sufficient to get a
teacher's license but not a degree. She taught in various places in Texas and
Florida, where she went briefly for her health. As a teacher she made friends who
later became her political supporters. She attended a proprietary 'business college', made speeches for the Texas State Suffrage Committee for Women, led the
Legislative Committee of the Texas Federation of Women's Clubs, and ran a
weekly newspaper, *The Texas Mule*. In 1921 she was appointed by the Governor
to the Board of Regents of the State Teachers' Colleges and served until she was
elected to the Texas State Senate in 1927. She recalled how the idea of elective
office first occurred to her, while on Board business in the Capitol:

> It was in connection with legislation affecting not only teachers colleges,
> but public school legislation in which teachers colleges were interested
> . . . . The Board always sent me . . . . I was sitting in the gallery with two
> or three of the teacher college presidents, waiting anxiously on a piece of
> legislation to pass . . . . I said to them, 'If I had a vote down there, I think
> I could do more for education than I am doing sitting up here'. That
> thought kept returning to my mind . . . . I had a good platform — educa-
> tion, good roads, welfare, progress[62].

Margie Neal acquired a new sphere; it was politics. She carried four of the five counties in Senatorial District Number Two. Politics carried her to Washington, DC. During the 1930s she was chief of the Women's Division of the National Recovery Administration and appointed to the Social Security Board. 'I have tried ever since women got the vote to be active in politics', she recorded in autobiographical notes. On the basis of her own experience she sought to interest other women in precinct work — 'where presidents, governors, senators were made'.

Texas politics, like that of other western states, showed some early signs of progressivism on the woman question. In 1868 its constitutional convention debated a female suffrage resolution and it was reintroduced in 1875 with greater support. One reconstruction-era governor even recommended equal pay for women teachers. And, in Annie Webb Blanton, state school superintendent from 1919 to 1923, Texas had another early teacher office holder and feminist.

Women Teachers in Electoral Politics

Despite women's growing participation in electoral campaigns, they won relatively few elected or appointed positions in public life apart from county school super-intendencies in the western states. Not all women appointed or elected to office were either feminists or teachers, of course. Oklahoma's Mary Alice Robertson, a teacher and the first woman elected to Congress, was an anti-suffragist, repre-senting the sometimes vocal segment of women who have periodically joined with those men who would preserve the old social order. As part of her study, *Women in the Twentieth Century* (1933), Sophonisba Breckinridge solicited personal information from all women she could find who had served in state legislatures. She discovered, from the 124 who replied, considerable variability on matters of age, previous experience, motivations, and perspectives on feminism:

> To some their legislative service was a surprise innovation. Others entered the competition with a definite intention to accomplish some objective. Many of them championed measures of special interest to women. Others made a concious effort to avoid adherence to the feminist tradition[63].

Half of this group had advocated suffrage actively, however, as far back as the 1880s. Forty-eight mentioned having had relevant occupational experience. As to occupation, twenty-six had been teachers and six of the teachers had additional experience; the second largest group, attorneys, numbered nine. Twenty-five women had held previous political office, notably but not exclusively as members of local boards of education and, like Sarah Christie Stevens, county school superintendents. One legislator wrote to Breckinridge, 'My first personal contact with politics was when as a high school teacher in Portland, Oregon, I went with a group of instructors to the state capitol to lobby for the Teacher's Tenure Act'[64].

The first woman candidate to be nominated by a major party to the United States Senate was Minnesota's Annie Dickie Olesen. She taught country schools near Waterville and left teaching in 1905 to marry. Activity in the Cloquet Schools' Mothers Club, the Women's Club — where she volunteered to teach English to immigrants — and Minnesota's Federation of Women's Clubs led to suffragist work where she gained a national reputation. Olesen was defeated in the 1922 election but her state sent four women to the legislature that year. Two of the four, and the two who served more than one term, were former teachers; Mable Hurd Paige served twenty-two years and Hannah Kempfer, eighteen[65]. Kempfer's story hardly fits any stereotype of a woman office holder. She was an illegitimate child and inmate of an orphan asylum in Norway, worked as a hired girl, taught school for ten years, beginning before the legal age of eighteen, and again after her childless marriage to a struggling farmer. Her legislative record representing Otter Tail County reflected these experiences.

Minnesota elected other former teachers to state legislative offices. One was Coya Gjesdal Knutson, elected to the legislature and later, in 1954, to Congress. Another was Laura Emilia Johnson Naplin, first appointed in 1927 to fill her dead husband's unexpired State Senate term and incumbent until 1935[66]. Other states had women teachers in their legislatures in this century, including Oregon, California, South Dakota, New York, Georgia, Utah, Massachusetts, and Mississippi. Data from the Center for the American Woman in Politics show that teaching continues to appear more commonly than any other paid occupation among the women more recently elected to state-house offices[67].

Women teachers have been, and remain, similarly well represented among federal office holders and in sub-cabinet positions. The first Congress-woman, Jeanette Rankin — elected in 1916 and 1940, each time casting her vote against the entry of the United States in a war in Europe and each time defeated for reelection — was a former teacher, social worker, and president of the Montana branch of the National American Woman Suffrage Association. Florence Prag Kahn, a high school teacher, whose mother was a teacher and member of the San Francisco Board of Education, was first elected to Congress in 1928. Other teachers in Congress in the period covered in this chapter were Katherine Langley (first elected from Kentucky in 1926) and Effegene Wingo (Arkansas, 1930).

Of the ten women who served in the United States Senate who were studied by Martin Gruberg, the first was appointed in 1922, at age eighty-eight, to fill the two days of her dead husband's term. Senator Rebecca L. Felton of Georgia had, however, a long and distinguished political career before she was so honored[68]. A teacher, writer, and lecturer, Felton was active in women's suffrage, prohibition, compulsory school attendance legislation, campaigns for maternal health, and other causes. These were all matters of intense interest to women in the United States for the better part of a century.

Creating and Expanding a Followership

It is a relatively straightforward, if often frustrating matter, to determine the fact
— if not the meaning — of teaching experience in the lives of political women,
even for those teachers among the second or third tier of leaders. It is a much more
arduous but perhaps more significant accomplishment to establish that women
teachers and one-time teachers were indispensable to the women's political movement as followers. It was followers who persuaded fathers, brothers, and husbands
to vote for female suffrage, to encourage other female causes, and to support the
educational or occupational ambitions of individual women. These were no small
accomplishments given persisting anxieties about the effects these changes would
have on morality, marriageability, fertility, health, and even the survival of 'The
American Way of Life'. Such fears only increased in the forty-five years after 1880
when the United States experienced, for the first time, heavy immigration from
southern and eastern Europe. Nevertheless, it is my contention that unremarkable
and historically unremembered women teachers, most of whom eventually married and settled into relatively conventional domestic lives, were a large, receptive
and influential constituency for feminism.

The entrance of women into teaching was both individually and organiza-
tionally initiated. The Ladies' Society for the Promotion of Education at the West
was one group which assisted single women of the Northeast — commonly known
in the middle and late years of the nineteenth century as 'redundant' or
'superfluous women' — to go to the states of the middle border or farther west
to educate children and extend civilization. It was frequently commented,
however, that many soon married, exchanging their many pupils for that 'single
scholar for life' — a husband.

In 1858, the Board of National Popular Education found that seventy-five of
the 481 teacher sent west by the Board had married. Rather than wastage, it was
reported as a 'source of no little satisfaction, that we have been instrumental in
furnishing seventy-five good wives to as many gentlemen of the West'. A more
extended commentary was printed in the *New York Evangelist* in 1846:

> In regard to forsaking the teacher's office for domestic alliances, which is
> predicted as a serious embarrassment, no evil or disappointment is an-
> ticipated; for it is believed, that in all cases, the school room is the truest
> avenue to domestic happiness. Every such departure can be made good
> by new recruits, who will find their best friends and firmest supporters
> in their predecessors, settled around them as the wives and mothers of
> the most influential members of society[69].

There is an important clue here for historians of feminism. Who were the
wives of male supporters of women's rights, men like Josephus Daniels and Desha
Breckenridge? Were they former teachers? They could well have been. However

much she was ill-paid and treated with condescension because of her youth, public employment, work with children, and femaleness, the schoolma'am was also a local personage. Teachers' diaries and correspondence commonly report the flattering attention they received as newcomers to town. Even in her home community, the teacher acquired something of an edge on the rest of the female population. Gaining, by virtue of her position, a certain *éclat*, it was sufficiently manageable and modest distinction *so as not to frighten off precisely the kind of potential husband who was likely to be or to emerge in the local elite*[70]. It seems probable that one-time teachers were disproportionately to be found as the wives of community leaders: newspaper and shop owners, solid businessmen, the clergy, professionals, prosperous or, at least, respectable farmers, and ambitious young men making the upward move in the professions, business, and politics[71]. For this historical period the most likely exceptions would be found among teachers in declining communities, as in certain parts of the Northeast and South, where for personal reasons women were unable or unwilling to quit their situations for more promising fields. Even there, however, they had intimate access to the men who could vote, if not to the lawmakers themselves.

Polly Kaufman's painstaking retracing of the lives of pioneer women teachers sent west concludes that the women teachers sponsored by the National Board of Popular Education and teaching in Oregon Territory in 1851 all married men who were or became prominent: as successful farmers, governors, judges, or politicians[72]. Their later age of marriage and small numbers of children leads Kaufman to think that they enjoyed greater personal independence in their marriages than did their contemporaries. Some of these teachers also married professional men, especially ministers, or were the second wives of men well-established in their communities.

Of the twentieth-century rural teachers she knew at first hand, Della Lutes wrote,

> Most country schoolma'ams married some well-to-do farmer's son before running any danger of suffering from the opprobrious stigma of 'old maid'. A certain inspector used to sigh and say, after visiting some wretchedly inefficient teacher, 'Well she'll make some good man a wife'. He did not say she would make some man a good wife![73].

While Kate Donnelly's husband turned out 'bigger' if not better than she might have expected, her role as the wife of Ignatius Donnelly suggests what may have been a not-uncommon experience when former teachers, liberated women to varying degrees, 'settled down' into domesticity. Kate McCaffrey, a Philadelphia native, began teaching in 1833; she was sixteen years old. At the time of her marriage to lawyer Donnelly in 1855 she was a school principal. Of their marriage, Gretchen Kreuter concluded, 'The rhetoric of their correspondence was flavoured far more by the Battle of the Sexes than by the conventions of the Cult of True Womanhood':

> In her whole life she repudiated some common stereotypes about what women were or should be. She had no independent reputation except as the wife of a public man, but in her letters she left a record of an articulate, witty and irrepressible personality who defied ordinary categories of description[74].

At the least Ignatius Donnelly was made acutely concious of the woman's rights movement.

Since many women after the mid-nineteenth century were longer schooled than their husbands, and school teachers more so, we may reasonably conclude that such wives probably possessed more influence over their husbands than the image of the domestic prison might suggest. Moreover, teachers could know better how to use that influence since their ability to dominate in the schoolroom often depended on persuasion and moral authority, not the exercise of force which, while still widely used, was increasingly considered by the profession to be the means of disciplining employed only by the weak teacher.

David Allmendinger has used some of the more intimate papers of students at Mount Holyoke Female Seminary in its first decade, as well as institutional records, to try to determine women's motives for education and their physiological change. He notes how much romance and speculation about marriage entered even into the pious atmosphere and regimented lives of these students. Although eighty-two per cent of the graduates became teachers, most taught five or fewer years, and 'marriage returned these women to traditional life careers'. Yet, Allmendinger also concludes of Mount Holyoke and its students that 'its mere existence as an institution would alter their experience, their associations, their life chances, and their mentality'[75]. If it is probable that attendance at a female seminary, normal school, or a college would alter young women, is it not still more probable that adding the weighty responsibilities of the teacher upon female shoulders was sure to change them? And, perhaps, to lift them in some defiance?

If so, then women office holders like Senator Margie Neal in Texas and teacher trade union leaders like San Francisco's Kate Kennedy, Chicago's Margaret Haley, and New York City's Grace Strachan spoke a language of protest and articulated an agenda of change readily understandable to hundreds of thousands of receptive wives and mothers. The 'sensible mothers and keen-eyed schoolmarms' who formed an alliance on the issue of equal pay for women teachers in Memphis in the 1870s raised a conciousness of gender inequity that percolated slowly through the community and eventually caused Tennessee to ratify the federal woman suffrage amendment in 1920[76]. They surely had their counterparts elsewhere.

Conclusion

The teacher has finally been discovered; the signs are everywhere. At this juncture the task for social history and critical sociology is now to rid themselves of simplistic, male-confined conceptions of career, professionalism, and politics. Educational historians have already begun to work with gender as a fundamental category for historical analysis, at least equal to social class and ethnicity in its explanatory power. The presence of women as students, teachers, administrators, researchers, teacher organizers, school board members, parents, and community activists will not only 'fill in the gaps', but promises to reorient much of the historiography — as this essay has tried to illustrate. It is also important to recognize that, even in the absence of women, gender consciousness helps to account for individual and collective behaviour. In educational history this is exemplified in institutional responses to popular American perceptions of all-male colleges as effeminizing places[77].

Additionally, the use by social scientists of personal history documents does more than add human interest and texture to the story being retold. It does more than confirm or challenge existing conclusions, drawn from macro-social perspectives. New lines of inquiry are constantly being uncovered, to keep researchers occupied. More importantly, however, they promise to generate a more useful and meaningful historical reconstruction for a profession that is now *discovering itself*: teachers.

Notes

1 Frances Merritt Quick, diary entry for 7 May 1855. Quick Papers, Schlesinger Library, Radcliffe College, Cambridge, Massachusetts. By permission.

2 One of the earliest and most influential of these was the female academy at Troy, New York, opened in 1821 by Mrs. Emma Willard. See Scott, A. F. (1979) 'The Ever Widening Circle: The Diffusion of Feminist Values from the Troy Female Seminary, 1822–1872.' in *History of Education Quarterly*, 19, 1, pp 3–25.

3 The importance of teaching is suggested by the fact that, in 1973 — after the modern women's movement was well launched and women were being encouraged to pursue 'non-traditional' professions — teachers were fifty-nine per cent of all employed women university graduates. In 1896, when very small proportions of women graduates married, teachers were reportedly ninety per cent of those who took employment. Claghorn, K. H. (1897) 'The Problem of Occupation for College Women', in *Association of Collegiate Alumnae Publications*, Series II, No. 21.

4 A 1918 study of 12,000 employed women graduates of nine eastern colleges showed that 83.5 per cent were or had been teachers. In Robinson, M. L. (1918) *The Curriculum of the Women's College*, Bureau of Education Bulletin, 1918, No. 6, Washington, D.C., United States Bureau of Education.

5 Schools racially segregated by law were effectively unchallenged until 1954 when the United States Supreme Court declared them unconstitutional and the judicial proceedings against *de facto* segregation also began.

6 Diner, H. R. (1983) *Erin's Daughters in America: Irish Immigrant Women in the Nineteenth Century*, Baltimore, Johns Hopkins University Press, pp. 73, 96.

7 Coffman, L. D. (1911) *The Social Composition of the Teaching Population*, New York, Teachers College, Columbia University, p. 55.

8 Buck, P. (1941) *Of Men and Women*, New York: John Day, p. 86.

9 For a detailed discussion of the 'push' and 'pull' factors that led women into teaching in the nineteenth-century United States, see Clifford, G. J. (1983) 'Daughters into Teachers: Educational and Demographic influences on the Transformation of Teaching into Women's Work', in *History of Education Review*, 12, 1, pp. 15–28.

10 After the Civil War, the defeated Confederate States of America saw many women of the middling classes enter the labor force. Among the teachers of Memphis, Tennessee, for example, nearly one-quarter of the women were married; while their persistence rates were not as high as those for single women, as many remained five years or longer as left the field after one year. In Berkeley, K. C. (1984) ''The Ladies Want to Bring About Reform in the Public Schools''. Public Education and Womens Rights in the Post-Civil War South', in *History of Education Quarterly*, 24, 1, p. 50.

11 Wolfe, A.R. (1976) 'Letters of a Lowell Mill Girl and Friends, 1845–1846', in *Labor History*, 17, 1, p. 97

12 Mary Bartlett to Ellen Bartlett, 9 October 1870. Ellen (Helen L.) Bartlett MSS. Manuscript Department, William R. Perkins Library, Duke University, Durham, North Carolina. By permission.

   Manufacturing jobs steadily lost importance for American women. In 1850 women were twenty-four per cent of all manufacturing employees, in 1900 only nineteen per cent.

13 This was true even though, in any given year, teachers represented only two per cent of all white women ages 15 to 60, the majority of women being employed only at home. In Bernard, R. M. and Vinovskis, M. A. (1977) 'The Female School Teacher in Ante-Bellum Massachusetts', *Journal of Social History*, 10, p. 333.

14 Hewes, F. W. (1895) 'The Public Schools of the United States: Teachers', in *Harper's Weekly*, 49 (26 October 1895), pp. 1017, 1020.

15 Wells, C. (1976) 'Kind and Gentle Admonitions: The Education of a Louisiana Teacher', in *Louisiana History*, 17, p. 130.

16 This is an average for twenty-six nations. In *Annuaire International de l'Education et de l'Enseignment* (1936). International Bureau of Education, Geneva, Switzerland.

17 Boone, R. G. (1889) *A History of Education in the United States*, New York, D. Appleton, pp. 381–82; United States Office of Education, (1889–1900) *Report of the Commissioner of Education*, 1, p. lxxii; San Francisco Board of Education, (June 1898), *Annual Report* p. 66; Los Angeles Board of Education, (1899–1900) *Annual Report of the Board of Education*, pp. 48–50. For figures on cities of 8000 inhabitants and over in the first decade of the new century, see *Report of the United States Commissioner of Education for 1907–1908*.

18 Heidenheimer, A. J. (1973) 'The Politics of Public Education, Health and Welfare in

the USA and Western Europe: How Growth and Reform Potentials Have Differed', in *British Journal of Political Science*, 3, p. 320.

19 Clark, B. R. (1985) 'The High School and the University: What Went Wrong in America, Part I', in *Phi Delta Kappan*, 66, 6, pp. 391–7.

20 'As organizations interested in their own maintenance and enhancement, schools sought to extend their services to the children of the middle class'. This meant 'making public schooling sufficiently attractive so that middle-class parents would choose these schools over private forms of education'. In Peterson, P. E. (1985). *The Politics of School Reform. 1870–1940*. Chicago, University of Chicago Press, p. 11.

21 Diner (1983) *op. cit.*, p. 97.

22 *Ibid.*, p. 97.

23 Troen, S. K. (1975) *The Public and The Schools: Shaping the St. Louis System, 1838–1920*, Columbia, University of Missouri Press, esp. p. 94.

24 F. A. Knox to Sarah Stevens, 30 June 1882. In James Christie and Family Papers, Minnesota Historical Society, Minneapolis. By permission.

25 Clifford, G. J. (Ed.) *Lone Voyagers: Academic Women in American Coeducational Universities, 1869–1937*. New York, Feminist Press, forthcoming.

26 Quoted in Berg, B. J. (1978) *The Remembered Gate: Origins of American Feminism: The Women and the City, 1800–1860*, New York, Oxford University Press, p. 86.

27 There were five boys and nine girls in the graduating class. Hamilton, H. and Thornbrough, G. (Eds.) (1964) *Indianapolis in the 'Gay Nineties': High School Diaries of Claude B. Bowers*, Indianapolis, p. 115.

28 A study of the living conditions of women teachers in lightly-settled Michigan in 1860 found two-thirds living with their own families. The situation would have probably been otherwise in the more urban Northeast and even in the rural South, where many teachers and governesses were 'strangers' in the region. See Weingarten, A. (1976) 'Women Common School Teachers in Michigan, 1836–1869: A Study of Their Economic, Social, and Occupational Characteristics'. Senior honors thesis (University of Michigan), p. 87, Michigan Historical Collections, Bentley Library, University of Michigan, Ann Arbor.

29 Jones, J. (1979) 'Women Who Were More Than Men: Sex and Status in Freedmen's Teaching'. in *History of Education Quarterly*, 19, 1, p. 56.

30 This research was generously supported by the Spencer Foundation and a Rockefeller Humanities Fellowship. The results will form the basis of my forthcoming book, *Those Good Gertrudes: Women Teachers in America*.

31 In Kaufman, (1984) *op. cit.*, p. xxii.

32 Tuttle, E. M. (1914) 'Vocational Education for Girls', in *Education*, 34, 7, p. 454.

33 Ryan, M. P. (1975) *Womanhood in America, From Colonial Times to the Present*, New York, New Viewpoints/Franklin Watts, 1975, p. 94.

34 Calverton, V. F. (1929) 'Careers for Women', in *Current History*, 29, pp. 633–38.

35 Lutes, D. T. (1941) *Country Schoolma'am*, Boston, Little Brown, p. 125.

36 Sarah Jane Christie to James Christie, 11 November, 1862. Christie Family Papers, *op. cit.*

37 Carrie White Papers, diary for 1884. University of Washington Library, Seattle, Washington. By permission.

38 Bird, C. (1968) *Born Female*, Rev ed., New York, Pocket Books, pp. 26–7.

39 Uhlenberg, P. R. (1969) 'A Study of Cohort Life Cycles: Cohorts of Native Born Massachusetts Women, 1830–1920', in *Population Studies*, 23, 3, p. 409.

40 Mary Jane Mudge, Diary entry for 11 October 1854. Mudge Papers, Schlesinger Library, Radcliffe College, Cambridge, Massachusetts. Confirmation of her marriage date and the name of her future husband was obtained from the Lynn Historical Society, Lynn, Massachusetts.

41 Scott, A. F. (1970) *The Southern Lady: From Pedestal to Politics 1830-1930*. Chicago, University of Chicago Press, p. 214.

42 Quoted in Sinclair, A. (1965) *The Emancipation of the American Woman*, New York, Harper and Row, p. 81.

43 Willard, F. E. and Livermore, M. (1893) *A Woman of the Century: Fourteen hundred-seventy biographical sketches accompanied by portraits of leading American women of all walks of life*, New York, C. W. Moulton.

44. William Blackstone's *Commentaries on the Laws of England* (1765), II, 433. In Pole, J. R. (1978) 'Sex: Where Equality is Not Identity', in *The Pursuit of Equality in American History*, Berkeley, University of California Press, p. 299.

45 Taft, J. (1916) *The Woman Movement from the Point of View of Social Consciousness*. Chicago, University of Chicago Press, pp. 10–11.

46 Ryan (1975) *op cit.* p. 94.

47 Fitts, D. (1979) 'Una and the Lion: The Feminization of District School-Teaching and Its Effects on the Roles of Students and Teachers in Nineteenth-Century Massachusetts', in Finkelstein, B. (Ed.), *Regulated Children/Liberated Children: Education in Psychohistorical Perspective*, New York, Psychohistory Press, p. 154.

48 Anonymous (1888) *The Five Talents of Woman: A Book for Girls and Women*, New York, Charles Scribner's Sons, p. 135.

49 Quoted in Ayres, L. P. (1911) 'What Educators Think About the Need for Employing Men Teachers in Our Public Schools', in *Journal of Education Psychology*, 2, pp. 89–93. The 'woman peril' was frequently commented on in the years before World War I.

50 The means used are suggested in Tyack, D. and Hansot, Elisabeth (1982) *Managers of Virtue: Public School Leadership in America, 1820–1980*. New York, Basic Books, esp. pp. 187–193.

51 Cott, N. F. (1977) *The Bonds of Womanhood: 'Women's Sphere' in New England, 1790–1835*, New Haven, Conn., Yale University Press.

52 Filler, L. (Ed.) (1980) *An Ohio Schoolmistress: The Memoirs of Irene Hardy*, Kent, Ohio, Kent State University Press, p. 164.

53 Scott, A. F., and Scott, A. M. (1982) *One Half the People: The Fight for Woman Suffrage*, Urbana, University of Illinois Press, p. 21.

54 Willard, F. (1886) 'Power of Organization', in *Lend-a-Hand*, 1, 3, pp. 168–71.

55 Unpublished data from the Center for the American Woman in Politics, Eagleton Institute, Rutgers University, Rutgers, New Jersey.

56 In Clifford, G, J. (1981) *Teaching as a Seedbed of Feminism*. Paper presented at the Fifth Berkshire Conference on Women's History, Vassar College, Poughkeepsie, New York, 16 June 1981 and *Those Good Gertrudes* (forthcoming).

57 Filler (1980) *op. cit.*, p. 165.

58 Gribskov, M. (1980) 'Feminism and the Woman School Administrator, in Biklin, S. K. and Brannigan, M. B. *Women and Educational Leadership*, Lexington, Mass., D. C. Heath, p. 83.

59 Manuscript in James Christie Family. *op. cit.* There are some extracts from Sarah Christie Stephens' diary and correspondence printed in Lerner, G. (1977) *The Female Experience: An American Documentary*, Indianapolis, Bobbs-Merrill.

60 One hint of Mrs. Stevens' political difficulties is the charge that, as county superintendent, she failed to visit the people and schools in some districts. These may have been the districts that were 'republican strongholds', Buell Stevens to Sarah Christie Stevens, 21 October 189? and Helen Barish to Sarah Christie Stevens, nd, Christie Papers, *op. cit.*

61 Sarah Jane Christie to James Christie, 11 November 1862. In Christie Papers, *op. cit.*

62 Transcribed interview in September 1953 and Autobiographical Notes. Margie E. Neal Papers, Barker Texas History Center Archives, University of Texas, Austin.

63 Breckinridge, S. (1933) *Women in the Twentieth Century, A Study of Their Political, Social and Economic Activities.* New York, McGraw-Hill, p. 326.

64 *Ibid*, p. 329.

65 Stuhler, B. and Kreuter, G. (Eds.) (1977) *Women of Minnesota: Selected Biographical Essays*, St. Paul, Minnesota Historical Society Press, pp. 226–46 (On Olesen), 247–83.

66 Such women established a precedent: six of the sixteen Minnesota women elected during the 1970s were teachers.

67 In the period 1970–1975, for example, elementary and secondary school teachers were sixteen per cent and thirteen per cent respectively of women senate and assembly members; the corresponding figures for attorneys were ten per cent and eleven per cent, and for college instructors, nine per cent and six per cent.

68 An attempt at a comprehensive inventory of political women, including participants in party organizations, women's organizations, and governmental service is Gruberg, M. (1968) *Women in American Politics, An Assessment and Sourcebook*, Oshkosh, Wisconsin, Academia Press.

69 Quoted in Morton, Z. S. (1947) 'Harriet Bishop, Frontier Teacher', in *Minnesota History*, 28, pp. 134, 139.

70 Anne Firor Scott makes a complementary point in her discussion of the continuum of values, from traditional to feminist, and the potential for social change that comes from movement in the middle of the social and political spectrum. See Scott (1979) *op. cit.*, esp. pp. 3–5.

71 One is reminded here of a more recent example, Thelma Patricia Ryan. She was a high school teacher of business subjects when she met and married an ambitious California lawyer, Richard Milhous Nixon.

72 Reminiscence of Mary Gray McLench, in Kaufman (1984) *op. cit.*, p. 224. See, also, pp. 43–45.

73 Lutes, *op. cit.*, p. 9.

74 In Stuhler and Kreuter, *op. cit.*, pp. 20–23, esp. pp. 31, 33. Ignatius Donnelly was an orator, served in the United States House of Representatives and the Minnesota Senate, and made and lost several fortunes.

75 Allmendinger, D. F. (1979) 'Mount Holyoke Students Encounter the Need for Life-Planning. 1837–1850', in *History of Education Quarterly*, 19, 1. pp. 40, 41.
76 Kennedy, *op. cit.*, p. 51.
77 Clifford, G. J. (1983) ''Shaking Dangerous Questions from the Crease'. Gender and American Higher Education', in *Feminist Issues*, 3, 2, pp. 3–62.

2
Feminists in Teaching: The National Union of Women Teachers, 1920–1945

Sarah King

In 1919, the year after the vote had at last been granted to some women, the President of the National Federation of Women Teachers wrote of the 'all conquering women's movement'[1]:

> The NFWT is proud to have taken and be taking its very definite part in such a movement. Its existence has been ignored and its members have been maligned but its influence spreads and its powers grow[2].

Yet Miss Dawson reminded members of her union that the fight was far from over. She called upon them:

> For the sake of the girl who is with us now and the women of England that is to be, let us take our trowel and build[3].

Those members, women teachers in elementary schools, responded to the appeal. Throughout the interwar years they campaigned with immense vigour and dedication as part of an extensive feminist movement to challenge the oppression imposed upon women and the educational policies which perpetuated that subordination.

Yet their efforts have been forgotten, their ideals, outlooks and achievements ignored in historical and educational analyses. The feminist movement in which members of the NUWT participated so energetically has been written off as 'organisationally enfeebled, theoretically confused and disastrously fragmented'[4], a feminism lacking glory and power. Although women have been numerically dominant among the staff of state schools throughout the twentieth century, their own perceptions of their role and the relationship of their world outlook to their employment has been disregarded. The NUWT has been particularly hidden, largely because the records of the organisation were lost for many years[5]. It has been assumed that during the twenties and thirties women teachers remained quiescent, worthy of analysis only in terms of their 'numerical dominance' and 'professional passivity'.

This paper will focus on the forgotten feminist teachers in the NUWT and their role within the women's movement during the interwar years. The important part which women teachers played in the vigorous, optimistic feminist network will be explored to suggest the strength of a movement which has been overlooked in most historical accounts. It will then be argued that the members of the NUWT perceived themselves above all as feminist educationalists and saw their work in and outside schools as very important in the struggle to achieve emancipation. Their definition and ideology of feminism shaped both their notion of the role of a teachers' trade union and their perception of the potential and objectives of girls' education. The beliefs of these feminists about the nature of women's subordination and the way in which institutionalised schooling contributed to that oppression will be examined to suggest the way in which they consciously connected their political outlook to the practice of teaching. They rejected the existing assumptions and practices of the education system and challenged other teachers' associations to do the same. These women teachers battled relentlessly in and outside the classroom to achieve a radical new vision of the role in society for which education should prepare girls.

When, in 1918, the much sought-after vote was finally granted to certain women, the suffragists who had campaigned so hard were well aware that much remained to be done. One leading feminist wrote that no women believed that,

the freedom of women in society is either achieved or really stable[6].

Yet this contemporary recognition that the sphere of feminist activity had to be extended has not been generally recognised by historians. The small amount of research which has been conducted into interwar feminism has presented it in disarray, fragmenting into single issue campaigns and critically divided between the 'old style' egalitarian feminists who sought 'liberal and absolute equality' and the 'new' welfare feminists who stressed reforms such as protective legislation which took account of the different nature of women's lives[7]. Although it has been argued that welfare feminism had the potential to become a new radical ideology if it had not diverted energy into general social reform, there have been virtually no positive assessments of egalitarian feminism or suggestions that this had a strong, potentially radical theoretical base[8].

There was certainly an amazing multiplication of women's organisations during this period. Yet in spite of the fragmentation a vibrant *network* existed which, although operating in a very hostile social and political climate, remained theoretically strong and very active[9]. Feminism is an extremely difficult concept to analyse, particularly from the vantage point of secondwave, late twentieth century feminism[10]. The concerns of feminism have always been historically specific, marked by contradictory ideas and this is particularly true of the interwar era. While recognising the continuities in women's lives, it is vital in any historical interpretation to accept the contemporary perceptions of the women involved and in the subsequent analysis the self definitions of individuals and organisations will be used to define feminism. The women of the NUWT constantly and consciously defined their ideals and actions as 'feminist' and this criterion must be recognised in any assessment of their philosophy and work.

The context in which these feminists operated was extremely hostile. The interwar years were not years of social and economic advance for women but a period of reactionary backlash against the perceived emancipation of women. As soon as war ended great efforts were made to ensure that females returned to traditional occupations, marked by inferior conditions and payment. This was certainly so for women teachers, for during this period their employment disadvantages were formally codified; the marriage bar was widely introduced, the payment of female to male teachers was fixed at a ratio of 4 : 5 and the sexual division of labour within the profession hardened. Vera Brittain summed up the atmosphere of conflict about gender roles when she wrote, 'The feminist movement of the present day is not very popular', but she went on adamantly;

> Feminism still lives in England today because the incompleteness of the English franchise represents but one symbol among many others of the incomplete recognition of women as human beings' [11].

Feminism did indeed still live. The great number of women's organisations which existed consciously united in 'the cause', the 'women's movement'. There was a strong sense of hope, of optimism that feminists could, 'at this most critical time for all women', alter women's lives in a radical way. Societies united in demonstrations and deputations, lobbying and public statements while most, like the NUWT, belonged to one or more of the 'umbrella' organisations. Feminists seem to have been very conscious of the need to present a consolidated front and they demonstrated unity regularly as in, for example, the 1929 deputation on Equal Rights to the Prime Minister and the 1933 Right of Married Women to Earn Meeting. At the latter the hall was packed with women of all groups, even those disagreeing with each other on other issues. The strong sense of shared women's culture was demonstrated as usual by community singing. However, after a protest from the NUWT, the 'inappropriate' Land of Hope and Glory was replaced by the more suitable 'Blow the Man Down' [12].

It was as part of this organised and vibrant network that the NUWT existed, seen by contemporaries as

> a true feminist body which is always to be found in the thick of the fight for equality [13].

The Union defined itself as

> a separate women's organisation ... to provide an avenue by which the women of the teaching profession may give clear and unmistakable expression to their opinion[14].

The organisation had started in 1904 as an Equal Pay League formed within the NUT and aiming to secure the principle of equal pay as official NUT policy[15]. In 1909 the League changed its name to the National Federation of Women Teachers and began to work as a separate body although officially still as part of the NUT. Its efforts to secure the adoption of support for women's suffrage and for equal pay continued to fail and relationships became increasingly strained. Miss Phipps was to comment that the 1913 Annual Union Conference demonstrated clearly that

> the men in that Union, like most men, really at times forgot that women existed[16].

Support grew and in 1920 the Federation became the National Union of Women Teachers. Although dual membership of the NUT and NUWT was formally banned only in 1932, the women's organisation became totally independent long before that. Hostility escalated with the formation of the National Association of Schoolmasters, a separate male elementary teachers' union formed to protect men's interests against the 'selfish women' motivated by 'sex hatred'[17].

It is extremely difficult to discover the backgrounds of the women who joined the NUWT for records reveal very little of members' personal history. Although recent research has established that, in the pre-1914 period, elementary teaching increasingly became an occupation for the lower-middle-class girl[18], uncertainty surrounds the class composition of women elementary teachers in the interwar years. It seems likely that it continued to be lower-middle-class females entering the profession while skilled working-class families provided the majority of male entrants. Evidence suggests that these women saw teaching as a relatively secure, long term career, not as a temporary job before marriage. Such expectations and backgrounds obviously affected the attitude of these women brought to their employment and their demands of a trade union or professional association.

It is equally problematic to establish why certain women teachers chose to join the NUWT while the majority, suffering the same disadvantages in employment, remained in the NUT[19]. These were strongly condemned by NUWT members:

> They must be ... women who will play the men's game, who will acknowledge the inherent superiority of man and be his abject follower[20].

Recent research has shown that, in its efforts to achieve recognition as a professional association, the NUT offered no model for the role of its female members[21].

The Ladies Committee was not very active during the inter-war years and for a long time the Union had no paid female officials. The NUWT was very aware that within the rival union,

> we may be quite sure that every effort will be put forward to intimidate the women, to bring them to heel, to stifle any independent act of expression[22].

The women who turned to the new organisation sought an alternative trade union to one whose role had been defined by men. They wanted an association which would reflect their political and educational outlooks and help them challenge the inequalities they perceived in society. Like the rest of the feminist movement, the NUWT was very aware of the minor part women were permitted to play in trade union affairs[23] and of the ambiguous policy of the TUC towards its women members. These teachers sought an alternative association which would

> really concentrate on women ... put us first and make us feel we mattered[24].

Although the Union did perform the 'normal' functions of a trade union, the outlook of its members meant that they sought more from a professional association. The NUWT was to be a support network to help women teachers in their everyday struggle for freedom and equality. It would operate as a

> pioneer among teachers' unions not only in questions particularly affecting the professional interests of women but also in social and educational affairs[25]

If recognition of the NUWT members' perception of its role as a union is important in any analysis of its educational work, so too is an understanding of the group's definition of 'feminism as we know it'[26]. The feminist ideology of these women formed a strong theoretical base not only for all educational policies but also for their teaching within the classroom. This ideology was rooted in the demand for total equality on exactly the same terms as men, above all for economic equality. They believed that women's lack of economic self-determination and men's control of financial resources were the roots of subordination. This idea shaped the attitude of these feminists to marriage, motherhood, men and the role of education in women's lives. In this, 'economic phase of the feminist struggle'[27], it was vital for women to work in paid employment and to achieve,

> a right to work and be paid for the work done[28].

This view fuelled their immense opposition to the marriage bar which not only affected members personally but was perceived as a concrete example of male power operating through an overt restriction on women's economic activities.

A corollary of the need to fight for economic liberation was the idea that male prejudice in refusing to 'allow' women equality in the home and in paid employment was the basic cause of oppression. Virtually every NUWT analysis of women's position made the point that

> we are still fighting feeling ... It is *feeling* which refuses us equal pay ... the feeling that men are superior to women[29].

The constant argument was that men sought to control women's lives, believing it to be in their interests;

> men claim the right to approve or disapprove any enlargement of women's sphere[30].

This concentration on patriarchal power relations is only explicable in the context of interwar Britain and the countless examples of men's patriarchal attitudes and behaviour collected by the NUWT. The contentious issue of protective legislation based on the sex of the worker was also seen as an example of male scheming confining women to certain jobs. Although restrictive legislation might make the lives of some women a little easier, to the NUWT women equality *per se* had to be the overriding priority. They agreed social reforms for all were desirable, but these teachers were realistic, recognising that women had to have equality with men *before* they could make a more radical challenge to the structure of society[31].

The belief that economic self-determination would lead the way to ending men's domination of women was very apparent in the attitude of the NUWT towards marriage and motherhood. Although these women tactically could not and indeed probably did not want to appear to be challenging the family unit, they did want to challenge the division of labour within the home and the financial dependence on men of many wives. In 1937 an Editorial in *The Woman Teacher*, weekly journal of the Union, stated:

> Inequality between the sexes has its roots in the marriage relationship ...
> (men know) the power of the purse is the most real kind of power[32].

The 'solution' was not a rejection of marriage as such but the rejection of marriage as a trade and the constant advocation of continued paid employment after marriage. As will be examined, both these ideas featured strongly in the educational policies of the Union as did the notion that marriage should be a partnership in which there was an equal division of household work. The employed wife should not have to fulfil a dual role:

> The old adage that women's work is never done should not be tolerated for the women of the future[33].

Unlike the 'new' welfare feminists who assumed mothers should stay at home but be paid family allowances, the egalitarian feminists of the NUWT argued adamantly that a mother too should work outside the home for her own independence and for the good of her sex:

> There is something neurotic in the woman who is 'wife' and 'mother' and nothing else whatever ... The notion that motherhood totally incapacitates a woman for any work but tending a baby is untruthful[34].

If motherhood was seen as simply precluding a woman from paid employment the sexual division of labour would continue and harden. The question of how practically a working mother could cope was not entirely ignored although it did not receive great attention. In years of great criticism of working-class mothers, these teachers who daily came into contact with the mothers' offspring do seem to have recognised the horrendous hardships many women suffered. Although, probably for tactical reasons, the Union never advocated nursery schools simply so that women could continue in paid employment, they did plead for nurseries, especially in working class districts,

> where mothers toil hard to make homes happy for husband and children and where they did marvellously but at the expense of health and leisure[35].

Organised feminists have long been berated for being middle-class and unaware of the realities of the lives of working-class women. Whatever their own backgrounds, the women of the NUWT did perceive society as being divided on social class lines as well as by gender. Moreover, they tended to assume that the much praised professional woman, employed as part of her quest for self-determination, was the norm rather than the industrial woman who worked to eat. Thus frequently in *The Woman Teacher* the view was expressed that a professional woman would not be a bad homemaker because she would never have to face housework:

> plenty of woman like doing these things, some do not[36]

and thus the latter group could employ someone else to do their chores. This ambivalence was part of these women's own experiences in a hostile society. However, recognition of the confusion and class-based outlook should not detract from their positive attitude towards *all* women and particularly the mainly working-class girls they taught. Many of the NUWT members were well aware of economic hardship and were supporting dependents. It may be argued that their beliefs about paid employment as a means to liberation also ignored the fact that there is nothing innately rewarding or emancipating in being given the opportunity to work within a capitalist economy[37]. Yet these feminists knew that woman always worked, the relevant point was whether it was paid or unpaid work, low-status jobs or more skilled, secure employment. Above all, this group of teachers wanted all women to be able to shape their own lives:

> let us help ourselves and decide for ourselves what work is best for us[38].

It was this ideology which pervaded their critique of girls' schooling, their radical ideals for change and their educational work. Armed with these beliefs the Union fought ceaselessly to achieve their aims, always conscious of being,

of fullest possible service to the women's movement[39].

Thus any differences within the feminist network had to be put aside in order to achieve a successful fight. As the NUWT motto proclaimed:

she who would be free herself must strike the blow.

These teachers struck their blow by a great barrage of propaganda and constant public visibility — frequently in yellow and green dresses. *The Woman Teacher* was foremost in the education of public opinion. It was

a women's paper written by women, controlled by women and above all read by women in order that the women's point of view shall no longer be submerged or distorted[40].

The first issue made clear that there would be no fashion, cookery or advice on how to make bedroom suites out of packing cases — there would be 'too much propaganda for that'[41]. There was a strong sense of involvement and commitment within the Union, as one member recalled:

We were always kept informed ... you knew what to do[42].

Young members were encouraged to speak in public and learn lobbying while an endless flow of correspondence between Headquarters and local branches intensified the solidarity. A set of instructions sent in 1931 to all units stated:

Are there mixed organisations in the district in which the women's point of view needs putting? ... every real branch of the NUWT should be prominent in everything but obsessed by nothing that does not lead directly to the goal of equality[43].

The many social and cultural events added to the immensely important part of the Union in its members' lives.

The activities of the NUWT within the feminist network are too extensive to recount in detail but a sample suggests the inordinate activity. This began immediately in November 1918 when the Union mounted an election campaign in three weeks, financed and run entirely by members. Miss Phipps stood as an Independent in Chelsea and managed to retain her deposit. Political work continued with deputations, lobbying, questionnaires to MPs and the financial support of Agnes Dawson on the London County Council (LCC). Wherever possible, active support was given to bills such as the 1927 Married Women (Employment) Bill. The sheer volume of feminist events attended was enormous. In the late twenties there were frequently three or four open air meetings a week in

London. In 1928, during celebrations of Equal Political Rights, *The Woman Teacher* commented that right until the end of the campaign,

> the NUWT continued the work, open air speaking every Saturday in Hyde Park and Wandsworth Common, lobbying, deputations, processions and mass meetings[44].

In all publicity it was stressed that feminist teachers were operating as a part of a united movement

> cooperating with other feminist organisations ... with the object of spreading the doctrine and practice of equality[45].

Yet although the NUWT was thus involved in challenging every aspect of women's subordination it saw itself as 'pre-eminently an educational body', the organisation for women who wished to 'combine feminist activity with inspired work in their profession'[46]. They sought, as the Editorial of the first *Woman Teacher* stated:

> to proclaim from the housetops our judgement on things that matter vitally to the work of education[47].

The women teachers of the NUWT recognised that in a society where the domestic ideology located women within the home, the opportunities of girls within institutionalised educational provision were likely to be restricted. Their resistance to this and efforts to combat discrimination were an integral part of their feminist outlook, for they saw education as another example of the platforms of male power which shaped women's lives. They had to guard the educational opportunities of women won by feminists in the past and ensure

> that all the remaining barriers be flung down[48].

This paper will now examine the feminist critique of the structure and curriculum of the state schools.

Actual interwar educational policy certainly presented these women teachers with much to criticise, for the majority of elementary school girls continued to be perceived as headed for domesticity, only temporarily workers in unskilled, low paid employment[49]. Policies throughout the Twenties and Thirties stressed a 'feminine' curriculum and assumed that the educational requirements of boys and girls were not identical. Reports repeatedly stressed that the ultimate social role of the girl as a homemaker must determine schooling. The 1923 Report on the Differentiation of the Curriculum for Boys and Girls in Secondary Schools lamented that,

> old and delicate graces had been lost and individuality of womanhood has been sacrificed upon the austere altar of sex equality[50].

During years of increasing awareness of the importance of vocational skills in future life, the influential Spens Report of 1938 virtually ignored girls. While it defined boys by aptitude for certain types of schooling, girls were defined only by gender, a homogenous grouping which should be taught how to use the many books published in the interest of the home.

It is important to recognise such trends in official policy both in order to understand the accepted educational ideology of the time and to comprehend how radical the views of the NUWT feminists were. They stood virtually alone in the educational world in renouncing underlying assumptions about girls in policy[51]. Their position was made more difficult and indeed more significant by the extraordinary hostility they faced in their arguments about girls' schooling. Attacks from other teachers' unions and society in general were extremely vicious. One incident in 1913, at the NUT Annual Conference, was typical of the opposition of the post-war years. Miss Cutten, a leading member of the NFWT, was listening to a speech by a Board of Education official:

> Lord Haldane was outlining the education of the future. *Boys* should have this, boys must have that but not one word about girls did he say. ... At last, when it appeared that the education of the future generation of girls was to be overlooked altogether, Miss Cutten ventured to put the pertinent question, 'What about the education of girls?' Pandemonium followed. Men rose in the hall with their backs to the platform and shouted wildly: the organised stewards rushed upon Miss Cutten, seized her by the legs and dragged her from the chair on which she was standing.[52]

Attacks continued: these women teachers would feminise the nation, they were Bolshevists, they were jaundiced spinsters 'for whom a cold douche is the best treatment'[53]. One Willesden headmaster commented authoritatively that 'women's minds are always intent on sexual matters'[54] while another man worried about the effect of these teachers' 'damned up sexual urge' on pupils.[55].

Undaunted, the NUWT women remained convinced that education was women's strongest weapon and that their own sex must control the provision made for girls.

> This gives to the women opportunity for working out the kind of education which they consider most suitable ... it is up to them to see that such schemes fit the girl for the place in life which must be taken by the women of the future[56].

They argued that unless the overwhelmingly male composition of policy-making bodies was changed, the needs of girls would continue to be,

> entirely overlooked or treated as of quite secondary importance[57].

Thus the union fought fiercely against the increasing amalgamation of single-sex schools into mixed establishments. They demanded that wherever possible, girls should be taught by women in separate schools for,

> under a headmaster the boys are likely to get more attention both in the curriculum and in the provision of sport[58].

In arguing for women teachers for girls, professional concerns about members' increasing displacement from the higher-status jobs were, of course, considered, but it is clear that policy also reflected deeply-held feminist beliefs about the need of girls to be taught by females. Union records chronicle countless examples of the disadvantages to girls of a male-dominated structure of authority in schools, an aspect of the hidden curriculum which so concerns the feminist educationalists today. The Union stressed that the continual subjection of women teachers to younger, often inexperienced male headteachers affected both girls and boys adversely:

> For a man to be at the head of a mixed school engendered in a boy a false idea that nature had destined him, the Lord of Creation, for positions of authority and it developed in the girl a cramping lack of confidence and ambition[59].

A corollary of this was the argument that women teachers themselves were critically important as role models to teach girls to 'believe in themselves'[60] and to fight against the humility society imposed.

Such a feminist outlook shaped the organisation's stand on coeducation. Although it was seen as theoretically a progressive development, worthy of support by the most 'advanced feminists'[61], the NUWT argued that mixed schools did not provide true coeducation since girls were subject to a gender-differentiated curriculum within them. No official pronouncements in favour of coeducation were ever made for the difficulty that 'feminists feared' was that the girl would be overshadowed in such schools[62]. The NUWT repeatedly contended that the whole matter of coeducation was closely bound to that of equal opportunities in society in general. Before it would earn feminist approval, coeducation had to offer,

> facilities for boys and girls alike and any differentiation in education should be based on the child's needs or aptitudes and not upon sex[63].

Until this occurred, the NUWT continued, with limited success, to fight against mixed schools, their feminist educationalist concerns as central to their arguments as fears about their own promotion.

The critique of these women teachers of how the structure of schooling transmitted patriarchal power relationships and accepted gender roles extended to the curriculum, to the 'knowledge' transmitted within the classroom. They believed that in their daily work they were being required to impart a gender differentiated curriculum which vehemently reinforced traditional attitudes about and towards women. The challenge of the NUWT to this curriculum reflected two basic corner-stones of their feminism — the belief that women must be given exactly the same opportunities and be judged on the same terms as men, and the notion that women had to be prepared for paid employment to become economically inde-pendent and free. Schooling thus had to not assume all girls would become wives and mothers but equip them to forge their own destiny.

The overriding principle that these true 'egalitarian' feminists fought for within their individual schools and on a national level was to ensure that girls received identical lessons and opportunities to those of boys; so called 'equal but different' provision was dangerous as a 1928 article pointed out:

> The education given to the boy is designed and calculated to be that which will give him the best all round training of soul, mind and body. We claim for the girl an education which will equally give her the best all round training[64].

The NUWT thus relentlessly protested against the countless 'insidious forms of sex favouritism' apparent in the education system. These included the allocation of Local Education Authority scholarships to secondary schools to far fewer girls than boys and the fact that girls' schools taught botany as it required less expen-sive resources than physics. The syllabi of examination subjects also received heavy criticism for perpetuating detrimental stereotypes of women or ignoring them altogether. *The Women Teacher* pointed out in 1923 that,

> unwise examples in arithmetic occur as of a man earning more than a woman and there are books like John Halifax where the man is infallible and the woman weak and clinging[65].

In answer to girls' supposed innate lack of mathematical ability, it was pointed out:

> if girls spend so many hours on needlework and domestic work while boys are studying maths the girls cannot possibly attain the standard in this subject achieved by the boys[66].

The Union did not confine its concern entirely to one sex. These women teachers saw themselves as educationalists fighting for a 'progressive' policy for all. They were well aware that they worked within a system divided on social class as well as on gender lines. The NUWT argued for the right of all to free secondary education and for the Raising of the School Leaving Age (ROSLA). Yet even on this latter general question the Union was made only too aware of the need for their battle specifically on behalf of girls, a battle which these women teachers believed had to take priority over general reform. When it was proposed that

ROSLA should take place in 1939, special provisions were made for some children to be exempt from remaining at school for an extra year. The terms made it easy for girls to be excused if they were 'needed' at home. Miss Dawson wrote angrily:

> How easy it would be under some Authorities for girls to get this exemption, earning nothing, adding nothing to their own status or dignity but just being the home drudge[67].

The greatest energies of the Union were therefore directed at changing the domestic education which perpetuated the sexual division of labour and which denied girls other technical training for a variety of skilled work. Their attack on existing assumptions was radical, threatening both the accepted patterns of work and power within the home and the strict occupational segregation of the interwar economy. Throughout this period domestic subjects continued to take up a very large proportion of an elementary schoolgirl's hours at school. Official policy insisted on its national importance, on girls being 'trained to guard the home life and home keeping of the nation'[68]. There was also the consideration, despite frequent official denials, of directing girls towards domestic service, deemed suitably feminine work, particularly in years of servant shortage. Thus girls spent many hours on practical lessons in dusting, laundry and cooking.

The NUWT argued vehemently against such policy, above all against making domestic lessons compulsory for all girls from an early age.

> We protest against, we quarrel eternally with the view that girls in an elementary school are necessarily doomed to become household drudges and that they should be sidetracked into this position while they are still at school[69].

Their quarrel was not with domestic subjects *per se* but with the facts that the lessons did not form part of a broad general education and that they took so many hours in girls' short school lives. The Union accepted that limited domestic economy lessons did have some value — for both sexes. It was quite obvious, these feminists argued, that there should be,

> equal preparation for home life as between boys and girls by the giving of instruction to boys in the simple elements of domestic subjects such as needlework and cookery[70].

Similarly girls should learn about woodcraft, electricity and engines. The suggestion that boys should be given domestic lessons in exactly the same form as girls was official NUWT policy throughout the interwar years and was consciously a challenge to the traditional sexual division of labour and the

> assumption that the male worker is always to have someone to do such work for him but that the female is always expected to do two jobs, the one at lower pay than the male worker and the other for no pay at all[71].

Although these women did want domestic labour to receive higher social and economic reward within society, they recognised that the existing status of housework placed,

> an unfair handicap on girls' education as compared with a boy for future wage earning employment[72].

The corollary of this was that schooling should give girls the potential to enter a wide range of employment and to achieve economic independence and stability.

> Woman are so handicapped now; they are *not* free to choose their own work for unless they adopt a career supposedly suitable for women they have no chance of acquiring skill[73].

The interwar years were a time of great debate about the links of education to industry and the economy. However, while facilities for boys were greatly extended, the provision for girls in Junior Technical, Central and Elementary Schools perpetuated their disadvantages in the Labour Market by directing them towards stereotypically women's work, such as laundry work or dressmaking, characterised by low status and insecurity. The NUWT predicted that, in a time of economic depression, this would accentuate women's problems in the job market and create,

> an artificially large supply of half skilled or unskilled women's labour with a corresponding fall in wages[74].

These feminist teachers adopted a number of strategies to combat this. The London Unit was particularly active in securing equality of treatment in LCC technical scholarships and training schemes, seeing this work as part of the,

> educational, egalitarian and feminist aims of the NUWT[75].

The Union was one of the few dissenting voices to speak out against the much-heralded Spens Report of 1938 which advocated technical schools for the less academic, more practically-minded secondary pupils but did not even mention girls in its discussion of the merits of such schools. Mrs McMillan, then President of the NUWT, tiraded that since these schools were

> based on the view that they provide the best type of education for pupils of certain abilities ... there can be no good reason for debarring girls from participating. Failure to provide girls with facilities equal to those of boys handicaps the girl at the outset[76].

The concern of the women teachers was accentuated by the widely acknowledged juvenile unemployment problem of the 1930s. The Junior Instruction Centres (JIC) set up to help alleviate this, worked to disadvantage girls by providing less grant per head to unemployed female adolescents[77]. Miss Fisher inquired of a Ministry of Labour official sent to placate the Central Council[78], why the girls' centres received such meagre resources when they were supposed to function to maintain employability? Miss Fisher deplored

> the tendency to regard the needs of employment of girls less seriously than that of boys. Unemployed girls, she said, were as great a menace to the nation as unemployed boys and there was no reason to suppose that the home could ever provide every girl with adequate employment[79].

Moreover, the curricula of JIC limited girls to hygiene and domestic science lessons. As Miss Coleman wrote to Miss Froud, having just read the Ministry's 1934 Publication, 'Junior Instruction Centres and Their Future':

> It seems that boys are the juveniles that matter — it looks like 78 Centres for boys and 25 for girls. It was ever thus![80]

The NUWT's concerns about and policies for girls' vocational education thus reflected their feminist beliefs about economic emancipation and the right of women to shape their own lives. Their analysis of why girls were confined to training in only low-status employment also reflected their theoretical perspective on the roots of women's oppression, their belief that male prejudice and patriarchy contributed greatly to women's subordination. Their archives contain many examples of men, both employers and employees, forcing women out of certain jobs or refusing to allow them to train for skilled work. The Union united with allies in the feminist network to fight this and to change technical education. In 1928 the NUWT participated in a deputation against women being forced to train for domestic service and in 1930 joined a conference on female unemployment. It worked most closely with the Open Door Council, particularly in 1937–8 when they together drew up a memorandum to send to the International Labour Office reaffirming the conviction that,

> without full technical education women can never take their rightful place in industry[81].

Thus the feminist teachers of the NUWT recognised how the models of knowledge presented within schools, the subjects taught to girls and the lessons of which they were deprived, all operated to eventually disadvantage women as employees, citizens and in the home. Their feminist outlook and demand for change were inextricably related to the notion of the role for which education *could* prepare girls in an equal society. They perceived their fight for equality in schooling as part of the overall struggle for women's emancipation in all areas of life:

> the attitude towards the education of girls is merely a reflection of the attitude taken in the world in general to women's value as a person, to women's work and to women's remuneration[82].

The inability of the NUWT members to win changes in official policy is hardly surprising given the enormous weight of opposition in a society torn by confusion about appropriate gender roles. Yet lack of success does not diminish the importance of these women. Their achievement rests in their unrelenting feminist critique of the way in which institutionalised schooling was perpetuating gender inequalities. They knew that the struggle to achieve their alternative vision for girls' schooling would be hard but they believed that ultimately equality could be reached in state schooling. They could help bring about a 'different conception of woman'. As *The Woman Teacher* commented in 1930:

> To secure that end the members of the NUWT will devote their many talents, their wonderful energy and their great courage[83].

Notes

Throughout the footnotes the place of publication is London unless otherwise stated.

1   The National Federation of Women Teachers changed its name in 1920 to the National Union of Women Teachers. It will hereafter be abbreviated to NFWT and NUWT in this work.

2   *The Woman Teacher*, 26.9.19, p 2.

3   *ibid*, 31.10.19, p 45.

4   D. Doughan, *Lobbying for Liberation*, LLRS Publications, 1980, p 8.

5   The NUWT was wound up as an independent organisation in 1961 and an embargo placed on its records for twenty years. When the archives became available to historians their whereabouts remained unknown for some years. They were finally located in the London Institute of Education but remain uncatalogued.

6   R. Strachey (Ed.), *Our Freedom and its Results*, Hogarth Press, 1936, p 9.

7   Until recently, with the exception of Jane Lewis, very few historians had conducted research into interwar feminism. See O. Banks, (1981) *Faces of Feminism, a study of Feminism as a Social Movement*, Martin Robertson; D. Doughan, *Lobbying for Liberation, op.cit*; J. Lewis, 'In search of a real equality — women between the wars' in F. Gloversmith, (Ed.), (1980) *Class, Culture and Social Change, a new view of the 1930s*, Brighton, Harvester, pp. 208–39.

8   See Lewis, *In search of a real equality, op. cit.* for a full account of the 'new' feminist ideology.

9   For a much fuller account of the activities and interconnections of the interwar feminist network see S. King, (1986) *'Our Strongest Weapon: An Examination of the Attitude of the NUWT towards the Education of Girls, 1918–39'*, M. A. University of Sussex.

10   Oram has made this point. A. Oram, (1983) *'Sex Antagonism in the Teaching Profession, Employment Issues and the Woman Teacher in Elementary Education 1910–30'*, Bristol University, PhD.

11   NUWT Archives Box 123, Why Feminism Lives - V. Brittain, 6 Point Group, n.d., p 1.

12   NUWT Archives Box 60, Miss Pierotti to Miss Whateley, 13.11.33.

13 The Catholic Citizen, 15.2.27 reported in *The Woman Teacher*, 4.3.27, p 172.

14 *The Woman Teacher*, 16.9.29, Call to the Young Teacher.

15 The National Union of Teachers was the trade union of the vast majority of elementary teachers at this time. See P. H. J. H. Gosden, (1972) *The Evolution of a Profession*, Oxford, Blackwell.

16 E. Phipps, (1928) *The History of the NUWT*, NUWT, p 22.

17 Very little has been written about the relationship of the NAS to other teachers' groups but see M. Littlewood, (1985) Makers of Men, *Trouble and Strife*, 5, pp. 23–29.

18 F. Widdowson, (1980) *Going Up Into the Next Class: Women and Elementary Teacher Training 1840–1914*, WRRC.

19 It must be remembered that the majority of women elementary teachers remained in the NUT. The NUWT never published membership figures but estimates suggest a total of 7,000–10,000 members during the interwar years.

20 *The Woman Teacher*, 28.11.19, pp. 76–78.

21 D. Copelman, '*Women in the Classroom Struggle: Elementary Schoolteachers in London 1870–1940*', Ph.D., Princeton University, 1985; B. Walker, '*Women and the NUT*', Bristol University, M.Ed, 1981.

22 *The Woman Teacher*, 14.1.21, p 114.

23 See S. Boston, (1983) *Women Workers and the Trade Union Movement*, Davis-Poynter, pp. 132–185 and S. Lewenhak, (1977) *Women and Trade Unions*, Benn.

24 Mrs.Anderson, Interview with the author, 16.7.86. Mrs. Anderson joined the NUWT in 1922.

25 *The Woman Teacher*, 21.9.28, p 336.

26 NUWT Archives Box 73, Report of a Meeting of the National Council of Women, 9.11.29.

27 *ibid*, 20.12.35, p 91.

28 NUWT Archives Box 255, Report of the 1933 Conference, Presidential Speech.

29 *The Woman Teacher*, 11.4.24, p 220.

30 *ibid*, 20.12.35, p 91.

31 Although it is clear that a number of NUWT Members were active socialists more research is needed into how they perceived the relationship of feminism to socialism.

32 *The Woman Teacher*, 12.3.37, p 203.

33 *ibid*, 13.1.28, pp 113–4.

34 *The Woman Teacher*, 12.3.37, p 203.

35 NUWT Archives Box 255, Speech of Miss Dawson recorded in press clipping, 14.6.19.

36 *The Woman Teacher*, 12.5.22, p 244.

37 Braybon makes this point. Braybon, *Women Workers, op. cit.*, Introduction.

38 *The Woman Teacher*, 16.1.20, p 130.

39 NUWT Archives Box 144, Miss Pierotti to Miss Wharram, 21.11.31.

40 *The Woman Teacher*, 7.11.19, p 50

41 *ibid*, 26.9.19, p 2.

42 Mrs Anderson, Interview with the author, 16.7.86.

43 Suggestions for the Conducting of Local Associations, NUWT, 1931, p 15.

44 *The Woman Teacher*, 13.7.28.

45 *ibid*, 21.9.28, p 336.
46 *ibid*, 15.5.36, p 269.
47 *ibid*, 26.9.19, p 1.
48 *ibid*, 28.5.37, p 283.
49 There does seem to have been some recognition in educational policies of the fact that some girls would never marry and acknowledgement of the careers 'opportunities' of secondary school girls. However, recent research, currently being undertaken by Felicity Hunt and Penny Summerfield, has suggested ambivalence in the minds of policy makers about the extent to which girls should be prepared at all for paid employment.
50 *Report of the Consultative Committee on the Differentiation of the Curriculum for Boys and Girls Respectively in Secondary Schools*, HMSO, (1923) p.xiii. This Report was concerned with secondary schools but the ideas that it expressed were held to be applicable to girls' education in general given the official tendency to define girls as a homogenous group.
51 The Association of Headmistresses and The Association of Assistant Mistresses were concerned with the education of girls but confined their work to secondary schools.
52 Phipps, *The History op. cit.*, p 11.
53 *The Woman Teacher*, 30.1.20, p 150.
54 NUWT Archives, Box 123, The Policy of the Woman Teacher, n.d.
55 Alec Craig quoted in S. Jeffreys, (1985) *The Spinster and Her Enemies: Feminism and Sexuality 1880–1930*, Pandora, p 180.
56 *The Woman Teacher*, 6.5.27, p 241.
57 NUWT Archives Box 256, The 1927 Annual Report.
58 NUWT Archives Box 129, Note written by Miss Froud, nd.
59 *ibid*, cutting from The *Daily Herald*, 3.1.35. Report of the Presidential Address at the NUWT Conference.
60 *The Woman Teacher*, 14.1.21, p 114.
61 *ibid*, 30.1.20, pp 148–9.
62 Significantly, in the evidence to the previously mentioned 1923 Differentiation of the Curriculum Committee, only women witnesses spoke against coeducation.
63 NUWT Archives Box 129, letter from Miss Pierotti to Miss Orton, 13.12.43.
64 *The Woman Teacher*, 20.4.28, p 217.
65 *ibid*, 14.9.23, p 349.
66 *ibid*, 14.2.36, p 177.
67 *ibid*, 26.11.37, p 72.
68 *Report to the Ministry of Labour of the Committee appointed to enquire into the present conditions as to the supply of Female Domestic Servants*, HMSO, (1923) para 13.
69 *The Woman Teacher*, 20.4.28, p 216.
70 *ibid*, 19.1.34, p 374.
71 NUWT Archives Box 144, statement sent to Open Door International, Jan. 1939.
72 *The Woman Teacher*, 19.1.23, p 122.
73 *ibid*, 14.9.23, p 349.
74 *ibid*, 27.2.20, p 181.
75 NUWT Archives box 306, London Unit Minute Book of Education Committee.
76 NUWT Archives Box 121, Speech by Mrs. McMillan, 1938.

77 All boys centres were granted 5/10 per head, mixed centres 5/6½ and all girls centres 5/3.

78 The Ministry of Labour rather than the Board of Education controlled the Centres, much to the NUWT's disgust.

79 NUWT Archives Box 121, Report of Miss Evans' visit, nid.

80 *ibid*, Miss Coleman to Miss Froud, 2.11.34.

81 NUWT Archives Box 144.

82 *The Education of Girls*, NUWT, 1950, p 7.

83 *ibid*.

3
What is the Teacher's Job? Work and Welfare in Elementary Teaching, 1940–1945

Martin Lawn

> Upon the teacher, as guide, counsellor and instructor of the young, devolves the greatest responsibility in this hour of Britain's crisis ... how magnificently the teacher of England upheld that responsibility in 1940 and 1941'[1].

The definition and practice of teachers' work changes according to local demand, national priorities, the historical period and not least, the teacher's own view, made in response to these factors. Every change leaves a residue of practice or ideas in the work of teachers and the contradictions between new and old demands accumulate in their biographies.

During the Second World War changes were made in the management of schooling which shaped teachers' work for the next few decades and remains with us still. It is possible to list the new duties in which teachers were involved: collecting savings and salvage; distributing clothes, milk and meals; working in lunch-hours, evenings and holidays; taking responsibility for emergency centres and fire-watching in schools; developing curricula around new wartime aims for weapons or allies. It is also possible to try to describe the particular conditions prevailing in schools disrupted by evacuation, bombing and the steady erosion of health and morale[2]. Yet many of these practices and conditions were temporary and left no obvious changes except in the way older teachers saw their work and purpose, yet in significant ways teachers' work *was* altered. Their relation to their local or national employers altered for they were used to new requests or demands for changes in school practices. They had become quasi-civil servants and part of a social welfare administration, a key element in the developing welfare state. Their work time was difficult to distinguish from non-work time as lunch-hours, evenings and holidays became expected duty periods. But a further significant way in which their work was altered was in their inclusion into not only government planning but the national interest and purpose as it was articulated in the late war and early post-war period. Elementary teachers felt that their sector of education had come in from the cold and that the revolution of ideas and politics had swept them into centre stage and finished their old private school educated employers and the reactionary, patronising local cliques of councillors who had intimidated them and held a strong financial hold over their schools. For the moment they felt freedom, responsibility and autonomy — no longer in a poor local service but teachers in a national public service.

After 1941, the responsibility in wartime schools for education fell mainly upon women teachers, who were augmented by the return of specially sanctioned married women teachers and by retired teachers. The Board of Education appealed to them in January 1942, saying

> '... it is essential in the national interest that women teachers should remain in the schools. No woman teacher should feel any doubt where her duty lies'[3].

Drawing material from the wartime diary of a woman teacher it is possible to observe this process of increasing duties and extended working hours upon a teacher[4]. The diary, of course, tells us much more about the teacher, 'May', and her view of the world and her daily life than is possible to use in relation to the main focus of this essay. But May's diary is not used just to illustrate a theme derived from other research, it reveals, week by week, the new tasks asked of teachers and May's response to them. The diary contains the story of a teacher who continually relates daily staffroom conversations with feelings about teaching under an emergency and with her views upon the social, educational and political tasks needed to reconstruct the society. The diary links together in one whole, however fragmentary or contradictory, a teacher's life in a classroom and in the wider society. Indeed these two areas cannot be divorced or distinguished readily; each is a necessity in understanding the teacher[5]. This is also the diary, not just of an observer, but an analyst and an actor — she copes with new demands, worries, and goes to political and educational meetings which offer hope of change. The general argument of the paper is about the changing nature of teachers' labour process in wartime and with the advent of the welfare state, but the texture, the detail and the contradictions of this teacher's life, acted upon and acting against, in support of the general argument, go beyond it and establish the right for teachers' work to be seen as rooted in the personal, the political, and the classroom life.

In her early thirties at the beginning of the war, May had been a teacher for eleven years, most of them in the same elementary school in Thornaby, Yorkshire. She worked in the Junior Department (there were two others, an Infant and a Secondary department) and lived at home with her parents. Her mother was a housewife and local bowling champion, her father worked as an inspector on the railway.

May had reasonably good relations with her Headteacher, Miss B. Like May,

Miss B. was an active member of the National Union of Teachers and they often talked about union policy and local developments. Also, like May, Miss B. was a Labour sympathiser (a New Statesman reader) and supported equal rights for women (she was not a supporter of the feminist teachers union, the NUWT, believing that the NUT could be dominated by the women members if they so desired. *May 1, 1942*). This sharing of political and social ideas led to a fairly harmonious relation between May and her Head and differences, if they occurred, were reported without comment and so a conflict can only be surmised. May's own interest in education appears to be more practical than her Head's. She was very interested in the new spirit of education and the plans for reconstruction, but she reveals (in numerous asides) a common tension in teaching: that she worked in the *Head's School*. Change could only occur after delicate negotiations. Class sizes were large and there was no hope of temporary supply teacher cover. When, for six weeks in 1943, another teacher, Miss W. is absent from school; this leads to class sizes shooting up — May's class was already 50 in number.

The school was built in 1913 and, judging from comments made, could have been built around a central hall. The school was poorly ventilated, classes were large, and the washing facilities and lavatories for the children were inadequate. Materials from its use as a Rest Centre and Emergency Feeding Centre must have been packed in every available space, and when an evacuation class was started with London school children, May taught her class in the hall. These conditions of work began to demoralise even teachers used to improvising and 'make do and mend'.

> *Feb. 8, 1944* Someone has burnt a piano key with a cigarette end. Firewatchers are suspect.
>
> *Feb. 10,* All who desire are to be permitted to have dinner, i.e. 150 in school hall where there is also a class. 2 sittings down if necessary. Cloakroom accommodation is so bad that pegs are to be put in the corridor.
>
> *Feb. 11,* Move from hall into classroom. Am I glad!
>
> *Feb. 14,* Boys *will* come filthy in afternoon. Conditions most unsuitable for washing[6].

Rumours of the school being painted in a vacation or, in 1945, the return of a window cleaner, can lift spirits straightaway. Generally, because of the pressure of work on the caretaker, the children and the teacher cleaned their own rooms. Quite late in the war, the water supply could be interrupted for a day and sometimes there was no fuel.

> '*April 26, 1944* I take a carrier bag full of coal so that we can have a fire on a cold day'.

In the early years of the war, May worried a lot about the decline of standards in her work. In an answer to a Directive in November 1942, May writes:

> Lower standard of efficiency in work. Daily struggle to accomplish many extra tasks which are not productive of any educational good has resulted in my frequently losing sight of the true aims of teaching which I have endeavoured to follow before the war. At the same time I am conscious that there is a greater need than ever for positive ideas and constructive thought and action and I am feverishly trying to twist the happenings of today into some form which will bespeak good. I excuse actions in the children which before the war I would not have condoned.

Again in May 1943:

> I work much harder than I have ever done before but results are very unsatisfactory. Frequently I have doubts as to the reasons — is it lack of concentration on the part of the children [is this due to physical conditions — air raids, lack of the right food, insufficient sleep, less parental control?] or my own depreciation in patience, stability, etc. due to similar causes, or outside influences such as constant interruption, change of timetable, evacuation, extra jobs to be done in the same time?

It is apparent in these extracts that May needed a sense of purpose to her teaching and without it she felt she wasn't teaching effectively. Yet it is clear from the diary that May is a conscientious teacher — she is rarely absent, she takes responsibility for school activities, she is confided in by the Head. She is constantly on the lookout for classroom resources and buys them with her own money; at one point her dedication is remarked upon, to her surprise, by another teacher. Her conscientiousness did not come from working to the prescription of a Head, a local authority or the Board of Education (nor, paradoxically, by ignoring them) but from her own sense of the purpose of teaching. May has her own goals and standards. Sometimes these are undeniably personal, such as the determination to drive herself harder on a poor diet and feeling 'shabby' (April 1943), but gradually, in her war diary, there is a sense in which she feels part of a new beginning in education, and this builds up, from conversations with friends and staffroom talk of 'afterwards' to a shared programme of necessities and purposes.

One of the unproductive extra tasks to which she refers was the regular collection of children's savings for National Savings Certificates. Each day savings are collected:

> *Jan. 6th, 1942* 'Return to school — large amounts of money for war savings and many children bringing money for the first time for themselves and relatives — children's Christmas presents, postal orders, etc.'.

Teachers were acting as quasi-civil servants and May's diary reflects her new work for the state and how it soon began to reflect her view of what was 'right'; for instance, that not enough children were regularly saving small amounts of money (August. 25 1942). By September 1942, forty out of forty-seven children in her class were contributing; again she notes that seven boys were not contributing (there is a hint here of her concern that boys were getting out of control). At the same time, children in the school collected farthings for the Red Cross scheme to send parcels to prisoners of war — by 1943, they had supported one prisoner for two-and-a-half years. Then there were special collections relating to national priorities, such as 'Wings for Victory' week.

> '*March 19, 1943*, Miss B. asks us to state our class targets for Victory week. One class suggests £100, another £75 and a third £50'.

War priorities soon turned at school level into new tasks for the teacher, who in turn, might try and make sense of them by using them as focus for the curriculum. An 'Aid to Russia' week, chosen by the school, was turned into a major school effort.

> '*Jan. 12, 1943*, Explain to children who are keen and plan out school of activities. Room is filled with maps, headlines, cuttings and books about Russia'.

(That this would be a popular choice with the local Director of Education can be judged from May's observation that he took the chair at a local meeting of the Anglo-Soviet Council for the area on 'Soviet education' for which it had leafletted all the schools, Feb. 27, 1943). In July of the previous year, the school had decided to have an Aid to China week.

> '*July 14, 1942* ... class contributions of Chinese articles, geography lessons and pictures, setting up of small libraries, reading stories, using local library etc. leading to individual activities taking place out of school in which children earn money for the China fund'.

The school also collected salvage, under the auspices of the Ministry of Supply;

> '*Jan. 28, 1942* ... we have had to tell the children not to bring any more as it is overflowing down the corridors and causing much inconvenience'.

For the Board of Trade they were involved in the issue of additional children's clothing coupons —

> '*Nov. 18, 1942* weighing and measuring of children for extra clothing coupons takes place'.

The new school became designated as a Rest Centre; these were typically schools, and teachers and others were expected to help the homeless in a blitz emergency.

In this school, the teachers were indignant that the cook and her helpers who prepared the daily meals for some of the children would not be in charge but would be under the orders of others (themselves, perhaps?). The school was already designated an Emergency Feeding Centre after the blitz. In a rehearsal on May 12, 1942, 'teachers from other schools act realistically as homeless and members of the Educational Staff, including the Director, (act) as umpires at the different sections. Beds are made, tables are laid, injuries are attended to, enquiries answered, babies are bathed and people are supplied with clothing . . .'.

The teachers and their friends (including some mothers of the school children) seemed to have been pleased by their showing at the rehearsal, considering that they were learning new skills and duties in difficult circumstances. The limited space within the school, used for mattresses, blankets, food, cookery, etc. for the Rest Centre work, must have been jammed, and May mentions in September, 1944, when the material was removed, that the teachers made plans to use the cupboards again.

The length of the school day was determined by the Regional Transport Commissioners who had asked the local authority to begin the school day at 9.30 a.m., not 9 a.m., so as to reduce the demand from pupils during the rush hour. This was one more burden on the teachers. Both the Director of Education and the Board Inspectors repeatedly said that the children couldn't afford to lose two and a half hours per week. May commented at one point:

> *'Jan. 19, 1943* . . . for another month we continue arriving at 9.30 a.m. . . . we are dismayed as it is exhausting trying to do the same amount of work with $2\frac{1}{2}$ hours a week less and so many extraneous duties'.

Holidays, too, were no longer their own. In the Summer of 1942, May's local NUT branch had a meeting to discuss the proposals for holiday work —

> *'July 15, 1942.* It was obvious from the beginning that there was nothing to do but accept. Only 25 per cent staff was to be scheduled for duty each week but everything rested on numbers of children likely to attend, which was unknown . . . all were unanimous in saying that without compulsion (of the children) the scheme would be a failure'.

In her record of the debate, May shows that teachers felt conscripted into these duties and that they were also worried at the trend they felt was revealed that 'parents are throwing off more and more responsibility on to teachers'.

This comment is echoed in other parts of May's diary. Teachers resented a decline in the quality of parental care that they felt was happening locally.

> *'July 6, 1942.* At school we notice again and again how children whose mothers are working look daily more grubby and neglected'.

Yet the school is in what would today be called an inner city priority area; the staff refer to it as a 'slum school'. It has its own clothing collection for the children and the children are in poor health (Jan. 1942); one out of three hundred children had teeth perfect in every respect, (formation, etc). The resentment they felt may be due to the growing prosperity in the area due to full employment and the increasing numbers of married women working. May, working in the holidays with just a few children, talks about the wasted food in the school canteen (as numbers fluctuate) and the difficulty of entertaining the children:

> '*Aug. 17, 1942* This small group of children have been at school practically every day in the holidays, fifty per cent of mothers being out at work'.

Perhaps this is less a social resentment, in which the charitable teachers feel spurned by their erstwhile clients, than a resentment against doing vacation work with little purpose. There is also a question about the ambiguity towards married women working which is expressed in staffroom conversations with regard to married women teachers. This is of interest to May who often appears to be arguing a more progressive line than other staffroom teachers . . . a close friend of hers had tried to avoid returning to teaching because 'she will hate breaking away from it again' (Jan. 27, 1943) after the war. May reported the arrival of a supply teacher with a baby who explains that she will work certain days of the week and morning or afternoon on Friday but not both 'I thought it was better to tell you', she said (Nov. 10, 1943). May argues for equality in teaching, including nurseries for women teachers with young children, but in her own life she felt that she would not have been able to leave her children for others to bring up (March 1944). The teachers, in varying degrees, wanted to help the poor children in the school but resented demands made upon them by people who should not be working, that is, other women who unlike them were married *and* working. This attitude also illuminates their view of themselves — they were teachers of children and of subjects but not yet part of a social service.

It is this contradiction which the arrival and steady growth of the dining service in the school revealed. The school moved from a situation where they were still recommending deserving poor children to receive free milk (Feb. 24 1942) to one where seventy-five per cent of the children were coming to a school dinner, many for free (Dec. 1st 1944). In those two years, the school moved from being an ad hoc agency for social welfare to an essential part of the war economy and with a considered role in the welfare provision of the post-war state.

Progressive teachers had for many years been in the forefront of the demand for better health care provisions for children and in schools there had been teacher-promoted schemes for hot meals or milk provision. May practically starts her diary with 'I wished we would start to take dinners at school' (Jan. 27 1942), but May was talking about necessitous children, not about a school-wide service.

As the months go on, May becomes confused about the issue; it begins to have consequences for the way the school is run and what is to constitute teacher's work. By May 1942, a school dinner service is about to start in Thornaby, free for poor children and for those whose mothers are working (who will pay 2/- per week). The Headteacher and the Senior Assistant visited a local school to see how it would work —

> '*May 22, 1942* . . . They find the dinner good. The only help with laying, serving, etc. is that which the Headteacher herself obtains and at this school the teachers have done nothing at all about table manners, etc. as they have not solved the problem of rapid serving and everything else'.

In the holidays, teachers were now expected to be on dinner duty rota for these children and as the holiday entertainment scheme was finished with, dinner duty was now *the* holiday work for teachers. By November school duties have moved up from sixteen (in May) to seventy-five, as more mothers went out to work.

The Union was divided over this policy. Mander, the General Secretary, had been threatened by the Board of Education that if teachers did not undertake this vacation duty their holidays would be compulsorily reduced and brought into line with the fortnight's holiday given for clerical workers in industry[7]. Gould, the President, had declared that 'if meals were to be provided in schools then teachers must accept some responsibility for them'[8]. Yet May quotes another executive member as saying that 'teachers should refuse to serve school dinners — the job has been thrust upon them and is outside their capacity as teachers' (November 20, 1942). Very soon the 'helper' or canteen assistant, who serves the meals, alongside the teachers, then washes up the crockery, asks if she can eat with the children and not by herself in the kitchen. The Head refuses — conscious perhaps of this symbolic crossing into the teacher's territory of the school and their role, as they appeared to see it, of social mentors at the table. It would also mean that an assistant would be eating with the teachers, themselves forbidden to eat in the staffroom by the Director of Education (Nov. 20, 1942).

On May 3 1942, May writes

> 'still on holiday but went to serve school dinner. Blackout only half drawn — school cold, dark and cheerless. Feel sorry for children who seemed lonely and depressed. The same faces are always there in holiday time . . .'.

Ten days later, ovens with hot plates arrive which starts another discussion about the money spent on this new service. Some of the teachers feel it will encourage parental irresponsibility but May argues for communality 'I am for it and think that it is education that fails - I stress the values of communal living' (May 13, 1942). May has begun to transform the new duty into a positive act according to her values — the social duty of the teacher she sees as less individualistic and moralistic and more as communal.

In a discussion with Miss B., the Head, (in February 1944), May's view is again developed. Miss B. said that teachers should supervise school meals, that no one else could do it as successfully and that they would become the social side of school life. May argued that

> '. . . the scope of education should be broadened and that children and adults should be made to feel that it is part of life. Many people besides teachers should take part in the education of children, the more the better, but they should have a very clear purpose'.

The Head is arguing an extension of an older professional argument about teachers and their duty, and incorporating the meal service into their domain on their terms, May uses the discussion to argue for a new kind of education in which the barriers between life and schooling are broken down. Two versions of teacher's work and definitions of 'being a teacher' are produced in opposition.

The previous Christmas vacation local authorities had allowed 'helpers' to operate the meal service without teachers. By Easter (1944) May mentions that the children had been unruly on Ascension Day and is concerned about this, yet a London teacher, evacuated to their school, said that teachers should refuse to do dinner duties under the present conditions, and then that dinners should not be served in school buildings. The London teacher does not have May's respect (a sense of Southerner superiority is present in other comments) but her comment must also have made sense to May. May is Union-minded. She says, at one time, that notwithstanding a sort of patriotic duty, 'doing one's share', among teachers, there was a new mood among them for reform in education and in the short term, against extraneous duties. At the Union meetings, there is more unanimity of purpose and co-operation among teachers about these duties (March 1944) and this contrasts with her obsession a year earlier (in another directive) that morale is low but more are hoping to find a collective solution to their duties.

The extraneous duties place teachers in a contradictory position. Some are just onerous or tediously clerical but several ministries, not just the Board, regarded the teacher as a positive worker for them. At the same time, teachers recognised the importance of the new effort and the generally good social provisions that were being made, with which they were helping. This was clear on the issue of dinner duties. Teachers rejected compulsion yet valiantly undertook the dinner duties; they believed in free dinners following their traditional interest in poor children but resented school dinners as a social right for others, or at least, if it then became an additional labour for them. May represents these contradictions and social reasons but is dismayed by what is happening to children using them and by the extra work she is involved in, but cannot see who else but teachers should be involved in them without a thoroughgoing restructuring of the nature of schooling.

The school curriculum was changed by the necessities of wartime so, for instance, a school garden was dug to produce vegetables, but the change went beyond a reflection of new circumstances. The topic work on Russia or China or the curriculum involvement in a Weapons Week saw the school teachers use their new freedom in organisation and pedagogy to politicise the school curriculum. Paradoxically, the new curriculum changes were tied to wartime demands and through them to a national purpose, something which the elementary schools had never been fully involved with before. This was a qualitatively different situation for the teachers in their relations to work than existed earlier in the century when the children had to display themselves for Empire Day. This time the government and elementary schools were at one, equal partners in a shared purpose. In themselves the projects, for say a Warship Week, were unremarkable (in fact, the national project outlines were more educationally conservative than their own projects) but the effect of them was to tie-in classroom work to the extraneous duties which the teachers were involved with and to transform their work, in practice and purpose.

May had a strong interest in physical training which corresponds with a major government interest during the war. A Physical Training organiser visited her school early in 1944 and persuades her to give a class demonstration to training college students later in the year. The school curriculum begins to widen as the war continued.

> '*Nov. 26, 1943* Librarian is at school checking library books which
> we get from the Public Library and issued to children through the school.
> *Sept. 30, 1943* New woman Assistant Director (of Education) comes
> from the Education Office to discuss the installation of a relay of a wireless
> into a classroom'.

A swimming lesson is arranged weekly, health films and a projector arrive, and (in Sept. 26, 1944) 'we are to have the services of a pianist one morning each week to play for dancing'. Sustaining the curriculum began to mean extra work for teachers, using their own time.

> '*July 16, 1942* P.T. apparatus is very scarce. Practising after school
> is becoming too frequent and is establishing a precedent (e.g. swimming,
> sports, concerts, etc.)'.

Towards the end of the war, May talks often about the new reconstruction of the education service and attends the inaugural meetings of the Nursery school and Junior school associations. She was determined that the new schools should have a new curriculum.

> '*May 30, 1945* Go to a meeting to consider the formation of a Junior
> school allocation under the auspices of the NUT .. There has been a

strong feeling for a while that the Junior school was being forgotten and neglected, and that now is the time to put it on the map, by deciding while we have our new freedom, what sort of school it is to be. Experiments on activity lines are to take place in different schools and then the teachers will report the results to the Association. Thus a common policy may be arrived at'.

May herself struggled to prepare a talk on 'Activity teaching' for their discussion, the only time in the diary when she needs to write a speech. It is interesting to note that in the previous July, May had taken her class out to the park for Nature Study and felt obliged to add 'in school time' (July 6, 1944). There is a sense in which the loosening of wartime restrictions and the need to continue their new curriculum takes place simultaneously; the teachers had been given some freedom during the war and intended, in peacetime, to continue positive strategies for change. May saw herself as working for a new national purpose in society, the new order vanquishing the old, even though she was still nervous at her own temerity in taking the children in the park in school time.

The school itself was no longer the teacher's domain. True, the Board Inspectors and Director of Education were always able to make inspections, but the school was the teacher's work place, nobody else's. By the war's end, there was a cook and meal 'helpers' working in the school and causing problems for the Head. A clerical assistant was now to be given to the Head, either part-time or full-time, depending on the size of the school. A new innovation, a PT organiser, has quite an effect on the school. Other new school workers include the dentist, regular visits from the nurse, special lectures (introducing a new subject, sex education, to teachers and later to parents) and a psychologist.

'*Feb. 1, 1944*. A newly appointed psychologist pays a visit. Wants a list of children who are unstable or delinquent'.

Throughout the war, the school had firewatchers in it every night. The teachers were on a rota but the local authority also provided local workers (who had to firewatch or be sent to other duties). Mattresses and bunks were provided for these people at night. In passing, the discussions, while firewatching, which May had with other teachers or with steelworkers, etc., were important to her in developing her views on the Beveridge plan for the new Welfare State and the post war reconstruction *and* for confirming her social views on class and change. These outsiders were temporary, but they helped in the transformation of May and perhaps other teachers.

The Teacher in Wartime

The nature of teachers' work changed in wartime. They acted as quasi-civil servants for the different ministries and they responded more quickly to the new, interventionist demands of their own Board of Education. They were loaded down with new civilian duties, such as firewatching, and the duties which coalesced around teachers — in the Rest Centres, Emergency Feeding Centres and earlier, in the evacuation. The school day was often indeterminate in length and holidays become another kind of work, entertaining and minding children. School activities were based on national priorities, such as the collection of savings or salvage, and the curriculum became an extension of these priorities in War Weapons week, Salute the Soldier week, Wings for Victory week or later in Health weeks. The distinction between the voluntary activities of teachers and their duties became blurred.

A general thesis which can be derived from May's diary is that the extraneous duties and the heavy workload of teachers was tiring and demoralising, yet as the war developed, a sense of national importance, derived from their wartime service, new duties and talk of a new education system was reached by teachers. It was not the duties themselves necessarily which brought importance, but the new place of the school in the developing welfare state, built out of wartime needs and priorities. The neglected elementary schools and their teachers were to be reborn in their nursery, infant, junior and secondary stages in partnership with their employers, locally and nationally. They were a full part of the new society, not an agency for the neglected majority.

There was a further contradiction, seen inside May's diary, and remarked upon by observers at the time. The welfare side of schooling, generally supported by elementary teachers, pre-war, against neglectful education authorities, was gradually provided in the school milk and meals service but at the expense of their own quality of working life. Teachers valued this development yet felt exploited by it. Kenneth Richmond described it so: '(the elementary teacher) gained some insight into the meaning of social service; he was becoming a welfare officer in the best sense of the word. True he detested this metamorphosis; protested that 'he didn't know what things were coming to'; felt that his status was being degraded to that of an odd-job man, forever at the beck and call of pestering officials; but there was no gainsaying his broadened outlook'[9].

A development of schooling supported by teachers turned into a new source of exploitation. Of course, the idea of welfare had changed — it was supported by teachers in progressive municipalities or as acts of charity, but now it had turned them into civil servants in a state system of welfare provision. Many teachers thought, at the time, it should be a distinct service, others argued that they should be financially compensated. Their achilles heel, their determination to see their role in the meals service as a form of social training, was turned against them and they lost their lunchtime break to the employer.

Harold Dent could ask, quite rightly: '(All these developments) have combined with other war time developments in the educational situation to present the teachers with a pretty — and embarrassing — problem: what is the teacher's job? Is it to teach or to do a multitude of other jobs as well?'[10].

May asked this question of herself many times, one way or another but her answer, unlike Dent's own, was contradictory. He saw it as a move 'towards the school as a society, a community of human beings learning and living co-operatively'. So did May, yet she was also a worker in the system and a unionist. It wasn't a community of people, the school, but had all the signs of being an organisation of individuals, deeply fragmented in their work and in their own view of themselves as workers.

Dent argued that new curriculum approaches, more practical and realistic, 'were developing out of the war situation and the teachers' new responsibility within it'. From May's diary, one can recognise some truth in this view, though clouded with ambiguities as the teachers tentatively move into new ways of learning and in new places, yet not quite certain what 'activity' learning means. This view of the elementary school is premature, as the school is restructured; these ideas, such as they are, reside in the new primary school and are lost to the secondary. There are clues in May's observations which suggest there is a gender division among teachers and their schools here. Her conversations in the staffroom are with other women teachers, so is her correspondence and meetings with friends; rarely do men teachers appear in the pages. They were fewer in number anyway, but the kind of extension of the curriculum, the new pedagogy or even May's communitarian view of teaching don't seem to involve men teachers. When they appear, as in this extract, their talk is very different.

> '*Sept. 5, 1942*. Firewatching from 6.30 p.m. Talk to two men teachers. They advocate much more Reading, Writing and Arithmetic in schools as opposed to Art, P.E., etc. One favours good grounding in Maths, as basis for teaching children to face life "two and two make four, not five"'.

These two are fairly left wing (describing the post-war Education policy of the Conservatives as 'undiluted Fascism') yet their view is very unlike her own. When Edward Blishen visited London elementary schools in the late '40s during his emergency training, the pedagogical and disciplinary framework of the schools, boys' schools, appear very unlike May's own school[11]. The elementary teacher described by Richmond might really have felt 'degraded to (the status) of an odd-job man', an argument not present in the Thornaby school.

The wartime teacher can be seen as the forerunner of the present-day teacher. A new definition of the teacher was created in which teaching time was expanded and controlled by the employer, yet the teacher felt herself to be valued and having a major role in the schools of a new education system, indeed a valuable place in the reconstruction of a new society. Not until the welfare system was in the process of being dismantled and the ideology which sustained it eroded, did the definition of teachers' work become fundamentally revised once again.

May's diary allows us to see this process in closely focused detail. It also shows us that teachers were themselves divided, perhaps by gender or politics, but that the conflicts between them were minor compared to their need to respond to changes imposed upon them. The diary also shows us a teacher with her own definition of what teaching is; willing to take on new responsibilities but questioning them; acting in a social and political sphere to determine a new kind of school and society, in a period when there appeared to be a relative freedom for teachers. May's diary allows us to avoid a Braverman-like approach to the changing labour process by connecting it to the needs of the state *and* of the teacher and seeing both in fluid encounters[12]. But since this is May's life, a real life of a contradictory person trying to manage forceful alternatives, she should have the last word, almost the last one of her wartime account and one in which a deeply felt and perceptive point is made about the life of the teacher —

> '*Sept. 44* My personal anxieties are not great (for the future) — I expect to keep my job but am wondering what sort it will be. Will we have to go on 'making do' spending half of our school life doing clerical work, supplying dinners and having no personal dinner hour, teaching huge classes in inadequate buildings and trying to 'educate' in impossible conditions?'.

Notes

1 Times Educational Supplement 14 Sept. 1940 quoted in Dent, H. C. (1944) '*Education in Transition - A Sociological Study of the impact of war on English Education 1939–1943*', Kegan Paul; London.

2 Gosden, P. H. J. H. (1976) '*Education in the Second World War*' Methuen; London. Dent, H. C. (1944) *op.cit.*
Richmond, W. K. (1945) '*Education in England*', Pelican.

3 Gosden, P. H. J. H. (1976) *op.cit* p. 98.

4 This wartime diary was selected from the collection at the Mass Observation Archive at the University of Sussex and is used by permission of its Trustees. It was collected as part of an Open University funded research project.
Mass Observation (MO), was a social survey movement, beginning in the late 30s, and continuing into the early 50s. Its intention was to create an 'anthropology of ourselves', begun by photographer poets and artists and continued by many ordinary observers in their diaries in response to central directives. 'May' is a pseudonym. Her diary began in 1941 and continued into the early 50s. She also responded to MO Directives or specific requests for information on contemporary issues.

5 I have argued for this approach in other places — (with J. T. Ozga) 'The Educational Worker — a reassessment of teachers' in Barton, L. and Walker, S. (Eds.) (1981)

Schools, Teachers and Teaching' Falmer Press — and in 'Teachers in Dispute — The Portsmouth and West Ham Strikes' in *History of Education* 1985, vol. 14, no. 1, pp. 35–47.

This approach has recently been most clearly argued for in Danylewycz, M. and Prentice, A., 'Teachers' Work: Changing Patterns and Perceptions in the Emerging School Systems of 19th and early 20th Century Central Canada' in *Labour/Le Travail* No. 17, 1986, where particular emphasis is placed on the changing nature of women's work in teaching and the importance of investigating it.

May's political life is not the focus for this essay but it is a part of it. May was a Labour Party member for the war years, though, early in the war, in disgust at the lack of a Second Front, she joined the Communist Party for six months. She was a regular attender at meetings of the local Literary and Philosophical Society; speakers included Ernest Bevin and Harold Laski and the subject of the meetings was invariably some aspect of post-war reconstruction. May was a socialist, based on moral and communitarian arguments, and today, would be called a utopian socialist.

6   The diary is organised according to date and year. When placed in this text, it is inset and the entry date given.

7   Gosden, P. H. J. H. (1976) *op.cit.* p. 203. Gosden quotes, from Board of Education files, a comment by Mander that there had been more widespread and bitter trouble over the subject of meals and milk than any other subject in the union's history.

8   *'Bournville Junior School - the first eighty years 1906–1986'* Bournville p. 110.

9   Richmond, W. K. (1945) *op.cit.* p. 134.

10   Dent, H. G. (1944) *op.cit.* p. 161.

11   Blishen, E. (1980) *A Nest of Teachers.* Hamish Hamilton.

12   Braverman, H. (1974) *Labor and Monopoly Capital.* Monthly Review Press.
Braverman argued a case in which capital was capable of strongly determining the labour process and the worker unable to resist its control.

Part Two
Working in Contemporary Schools

4
Being a Feminist Teacher

Marilyn Joyce

Who Are They?

In this chapter I shall be exploring and describing some of the problems, contradictions and pressures of being a feminist teacher in Britain today. However, it would be quite wrong to imply that 'feminist teachers' are some kind of new breed; research in recent years has reclaimed some of our past, though much remains to be said about a profession in which women have always been in the majority. Sheer weight of numbers, then as now, was no guarantee of either status or financial reward for women teachers. Frances Widdowson (*Going up into the Next Class*) points out that although by 1908 women elementary teachers outnumbered men by three to one, the ratio of women to men in the lowest teaching grades as Uncertified Assistants and Supplementary Teachers was ten to one. Their rate of pay was approximately two-thirds that of a man.

The fight for equal pay began in 1904 with the formation of the Equal Pay League within the NUT and the extent of male teachers' opposition to this proposal quickly became apparent. The renamed National Federation of Women Teachers began to table motions on equal pay at NUT conferences after 1908, but these were resoundingly rejected amidst scenes of disorder where women delegates were howled down and insulted. The thirty-five-member executive of the NUT in 1909 included only two women. From this time until 1914 the broader question of women's suffrage became the focus for activists within the NFWT, but NUT Conferences consistently and overwhelmingly rejected any proposal to back women's right to vote. The result of the 1914 Conference was apparently met with laughter by the predominantly male audience[1].

Despite the change in attitude to women's work following the First World War, women teachers faced new difficulties with the gradual imposition of a marriage bar to female teachers in the 1920s[2]. LEAs implemented this policy with regard to women new to the profession, primarily as a means of cutting salary costs. Supply teachers were often exempted to provide an emergency pool who could be paid even less than their permanent counterparts.

Full equal pay for women teachers took over fifty years to achieve and was finally attained in 1961. Other goals remain: women are still disproportionately clustered on the lowest teaching scales, and those of us striving for real equality of opportunity for staff and pupils still face outright hostility. Contemporary accounts of the experiences of feminist teachers are now being written (Spender and Sarah; Weiner; Howe, amongst others) but there is still plenty we need to know.

Mine is a modest contribution[3]. The women I talked to work in a variety of educational establishments, mostly in Inner London. They comprise four infant teachers, three junior teachers, three secondary teachers and a lecturer in a College of Education, all of whom currently teach. It is clear, therefore, that they are teachers, but what about the label 'feminist'? I decline to give a definition of 'feminist' here since we are in the business of helping and supporting other women, not amassing our credentials as feminists. When I asked the question, 'Are you happy to be referred to as a feminist?' sometimes the answer was 'Of course', but more usually it was, 'Yes, whatever that means'. This obviously has no sociological/scientific objectivity but women did and still do suffer so frequently from male descriptions and definitions of them which are grossly inadequate that we now relish any opportunity to be self-defining. 'Feminist — whatever that means' is a term which suits both the women I talked to and me (though I have subsequently abbrieved it to simply 'feminist'). Those who object to such a vague terminology have the same freedom to define themselves as readers or non-readers of this paper.

Although the biographies of these feminist teachers are not of relevance here, two points require elaboration. Firstly, teachers as a body belong in everything but their salary to the professional class and consequently have been traditionally designated as middle-class. Several of the teachers in my sample are of working-class origin and maintain a close identification with working-class values and lifestyles.

Secondly, I must point out that all these women, like me, are white. Institutionalised racism in education and elsewhere has seen to it that only a few Black women become teachers, yet Black parents and teachers have together demonstrated that despite being scarcely represented in the teaching force, let alone in the bureaucracy of LEAs, they will take on the establishment and fight both for their children's right to fair treatment under the present system and to alter that system to take account of their specific needs (Coard, 1971; Thomas, 1985; Benjamin, 1985; Bryan, Dadzie and Scafe, 1985). Bryan, Dadzie and Scafe explain why it has often been Black mothers who have confronted the schools' racism, organised community campaigns to establish Saturday and Supplementary

Schools, and challenged the widespread placement of Black children in disruptive units.

Although the teachers I interviewed all spoke of their commitment to an anti-racist, as well as an anti-sexist perspective, they acknowledge with me that we cannot and would not want to speak for Black women or women of colour. Consequently, this paper will provide only a partial evaluation of the experiences of feminist teachers.

It is impossible to estimate how many feminist teachers there are working in the ILEA, or anywhere else. Some Divisions within the ILEA have support groups which meet at the local Teacher's Centre, but these tend to have a fluctuating membership. Groups like the Anti-Sexist Working Party in Hackney are well established, having produced resources for use in schools, published articles (Chapter 11, Weiner 1985), offered support to other teachers wanting to set up their own group, and for the last two years have run a Girls' Fun Day in July. With its published statements of Equal Opportunities for all children regardless of sex, race or class, an Inspector and a team of Advisory Teachers for Equal Opportunities (Gender) and its requirement that every school devise its own anti-sexist and anti-racist policies, the ILEA has apparently put anti-sexism firmly centre stage. Yet even in London, staff who want to work on this issue have to battle, often single-handed, against massive resistance and refusal even to consider the arguments[4].

What They Teach and How

Two of the questions I asked were 'How does being a feminist teacher affect what you teach?' and 'How does it affect your teaching style?' The right wing pillory feminists amongst others as part of the 'loony left', deliberately and blatantly feeding children with propaganda about politics, religion, sex, CND and so on. It is hardly surprising that some members of society should feel vulnerable; a teaching system which openly and explicitly attacked racism, sexism, and class prejudice would be bound to threaten a structure serving the interests of white middle-class men. It is clear that these feminist teachers do see their activities in the classroom as part of a whole philosophy:

> 'I try to carry out what I believe in the classroom as well as outside the school. It's really part of a whole philosophy of encouraging children to work together cooperatively and to question everything intelligently'.
> (*Infant teacher*)

Presumably the vast majority of teachers would argue that their job is to help children to learn to question intelligently. For feminists, though, the key word is 'everything' since this includes stereotypical assumptions about men and women, boys and girls.

Of fundamental importance is the use of materials, and all the primary teachers remarked on the considerable problems posed by the lack of resources:

'You have to make nearly everything. The lack of good anti-sexist materials demands that a lot of what you use in the classroom has to be stuff you or the children have actually made and that is directly relevant to them. I think often teachers tend to fit their work in with what happens to be available rather than the other way around. My view is that you fit your resources to match your work so that every time you do something new, you create a new set of resources'. (*Infant teacher*)

This is obviously exceedingly time-consuming, yet it is seen as an indispensable requirement of good anti-sexist teaching.

'One example was when we were doing a topic on South Africa, the emphasis was on women, on Winnie rather than Nelson Mandela. The problem is lack of information, and you end up spending ages looking for materials or rewriting adult literature as almost nothing serious and anti-oppressive is produced for young kids of junior age'. (*Junior teacher*).

One woman had chosen a theme of 'People at work', but found it extraordinarily difficult to find books and pictures that accurately reflected the wide range of jobs women actually do these days, let alone those that have traditionally been a male preserve but where increasing numbers of women are present, such as carpentry or bus driving. Most books featured women, if at all, as nurses, hairdressers and waitresses, a parallel to the research finding that the illustrations in children's reading schemes depict women in an even more circumscribed range of activities than is true in real life (Lobban 1977). Partly as a consequence, this teacher and a friend successfully applied for a grant from the ILEA Sex Equality Education Fund and have worked for a year to produce a series of four books for general classroom use which illustrate with photographs 'People at Work' from an anti-sexist, anti-racist perspective. This has involved immense personal effort, but is only a drop in the ocean of mostly stereotyped information books produced by mainstream publishers.

For many children, much of what school presents to them as 'facts' does not match up to their own experience of reality; for example at least one fifth of all working women in Britain are the sole wage earners (Byrne 1978) yet there is little or no recognition of this in primary materials. What is alarming is the extent to which small children will deny the reality they know and have experienced in favour of a stereotyped image presented to them by school or television. One peripatetic teacher said:

'I had a hospital in the home corner in one reception class. The children had an argument, some claiming that girls couldn't be doctors even though the school doctor they'd all been examined by and the local G.P. were both women. It's the same with mums doing repairs and dads cooking — most of them had seen their parents swap traditional roles, if only minimally, but their public perceptions and private knowledge are two distinct things. (*Infant teacher*).

It is not really surprising that lots of children, especially Black and working-class ones, should assume that their reality is not acceptable in school. A common admonishment is 'We don't do/say/behave like that in school' ('Whatever you might do at home' being the unstated implication)[5].

Since so much of the primary, and increasingly, the secondary curriculum is topic-based, the choice of topic is crucially important and it requires thoughtful planning and considerable expertise to incorporate anti-sexist, anti-racist strategies:

'I look at my yearly programme and I make sure that at least one and quite often all the topics I'm going to consider have an area that I can develop from an equal opportunities perspective, and I also try to create a play area to fit into it. With the 'Time and Change' topic we made a time machine in place of the home corner, which allowed for a lot of imaginative play as astronauts, explorers and scientists. There's still a time when you need a home corner, particularly for boys who don't have the opportunity for a lot of experiences of caring. They need encouragement to do that, so sometimes I direct the play, give them a task or create a situation where they've got to wash the baby or whatever. From time to time I put one of the more aggressive boys in with the more sensitive ones and maybe some girls who want to play and that can allow that boy to open up and play in a totally new way. Role-play is so useful for starting the children off. With the time-machine I directed a situation where it had broken down and they were stranded so they had to work together on how they'd survive, mend the machine, what tools they'd need ... this was with six girls'. (*Infant teacher*).

This kind of interventionist technique appears to be at odds with the progressive mode of 'discovery through freeplay' but feminist teachers believe that without it and other strategies, children will often 'choose freely' to follow a stereotypical activity or pattern of behaviour, and in so doing effectively limit their own opportunities for new experiences. It is essential to learn to use situations that arise in the classroom to heighten pupil awareness through genuine discussion. A teacher of seven year olds:

'I proposed to start reading 'The Wrestling Princess' but the boys protested and claimed that we were "always reading stories about girls". So as a class we did an analysis of stories we'd read that year and discovered of course that far more had been about boys than girls. For me, this highlighted the fact that as soon as you start to compensate for the girls, the boys are very aware of it and complain even though you're not even approaching an equal distribution of male/female leads. They're so used to being the heroes all the time. And it's no good just telling them: somehow you've got to find a way of proving it to them. Any teacher could ask their class to take a sample of fifty library books and note the numbers of male and female characters and make a block graph. Do it a few times — it's a valuable pupil activity because it involves reading, examining books closely, group cooperation, recording numeracy work and extending the investigative approach — this is simply good practice'. (*Infant teacher*).

Complaints about compensating the girls aren't restricted to small boys. A primary Head who was leaving ILEA remarked bitterly to me that a man we were discussing who'd thought of applying for an ILEA headship 'should have a sex-change operation. They only give headships to women now'. The most recent figures show that in ILEA, 80 per cent of primary school teachers are women, 90 percent of Scale one teachers are women and yet only 54 per cent of headteachers are women (ASWP, 1985).

All the teachers commented on the huge discrepancy between their contact time with boys and with girls, and try to compensate with time for girls. They perceive boys to be more demanding both in terms of their problematic behaviour and because of their learning difficulties:

'I'm very aware of trying all the time to make time for the girls, to correct the balance. I find drama is one of the greatest sources of being able to develop different characterisations and different qualities in children. You can use it to give the girls the chance to be more vocal and assertive, and the boys to experience not being in control all the time'[6]. (*Junior teacher*).

'I've taped myself in the classroom and now I try to fight the boys' domination of the lesson and give the girls a more positive reinforcement'. (*Secondary teacher*).

Some teachers were aware of the research by Dale Spender and others into boys' domination of teachers' time in secondary mixed-sex classrooms. Spender tape-recorded lessons in some of which:

'the explicit aim has been to spend an equal amount of time with both sexes ... Out of ten taped lessons ... the maximum time I spent interacting with girls was 42 per cent and an average of 38 per cent, and the minimum time with boys 58 per cent ... Other teachers have also been reasonably confident that they have achieved their aim of allocating their time equally between the sexes only to find when the tapes have been analysed, that spending approximately 38 per cent of their time with girls feels like *compensating* the girls, feels like artificially constructed equality'. (Spender 1982).

The same pattern emerges in adult mixed-sex discussion groups (Spender 1980) and readers may well be able to supply examples from their own experience. Finding the means to combat this particular form of domination is difficult and wearing, demanding as it does constant attention, a high level of awareness of dynamics within the classroom, and multiple decisions about intervention. One strategy adopted by teachers at all levels is that of single-sex grouping. In primary classrooms it can be used to suit a variety of purposes:

'I sometimes use single-sex groupings for girls to use the construction toys. Or I might work with a group of boys trying to develop a more cooperative approach to listening and talking, to get them to give opportunities for other people in the group to talk and to listen rather than always jumping in front of other people'. (*Junior teacher*).
'I became increasingly aware that girls' stories are often very domestically centered . Even when giving them something quite exciting like a dragon or a space story, most girls tended to pitch stories within a domestic framework, and their characters didn't go out into the world and have adventures. So I worked on that, both by the stories I read and discussed with them and through shared writing with a group where I could take the story in different directions and help them experiment with characterisation. I saw a big improvement and a researcher who came into my room found it difficult to tell whether stories were by a boy or a girl'. (*Infant teacher*).

Several teachers were extremely concerned to give girls equal access to activities they saw as crucially important to mathematical development:

'I sometimes ban boys from using the construction sets for a session because otherwise the boys' spatial awareness is so much better by six years old that girls become discouraged if they're beside the boys. Girls need a boost to their confidence before children can work alongside each other. It's the same with the computer — you must monitor who's had a turn and who hasn't. Some girls at six are already convinced that they 'can't do' certain things and the computer tends to be one of them. It's really important for women to become proficient with computers to provide a role model for them'. (*Infant teacher*).
'When it comes to construction toys I sometimes put a lot more structure on what they have to do rather than always letting them play freely. For instance with Lego, I get them to copy models, make games, follow diagrams ... using the catalogue pictures is a great stimulus for girls

whose experience may have been minimal. Making 3-D models is the beginning of Craft Design and Technology in their later schooling'. (*Infant teacher*).

Rosie Walden and Valerie Walkerdine's recent research suggests that there is no evidence to suggest that girls of three to four have a less-well developed spatial awareness than boys. In an experiment where the use of Lego by a group of children was compared:

> 'There was no perceptible difference in the structures made by boys and girls. Nor was there any difference in their ability to manipulate the materials. What was most interesting — and also acknowledged by the teachers — was that despite the fact that the teachers themselves thought the girls would not play with Lego, when this was suggested the girls could do so effectively. We would suggest (with writers such as Byrne 1978) that it is lack of opportunity and encouragement which leads to the situation in which girls do not play with construction toys. Further, on the occasions when this does happen, teacher expectations are such that the activity may well go unnoticed'. (Walden and Walkerdine, 1982).

Girls are unlikely to be given that opportunity and encouragement in classes where staff hold stereotyped views about the supposed 'natural' interests and abilities of boys and girls.

Mixed secondary schools in various parts of the country have run single-sex groupings with encouraging results (Cornbleet and Sanders, 1982, Smith, 1984). A recent attempt to do this in a London Comprehensive involved a Head of Third Year suggesting the formation of one class of girls and two of boys for fourth year Physics to avoid the girls being numerically swamped. The female Head of Science and male Physics teacher were enthusiastic but the girls themselves rejected the idea. They were concerned it would look as if they needed 'special treatment' and weren't good enough to compete with boys on an equal footing: the proposal was dropped. This is especially depressing, remembering the enormous unchallenged input of time, resources and energy into compensating boys right through the school system, from the remedial reading groups and disruptive pupils units where they predominate, to those parts of the country which retained a selection at eleven plus and where girls had to score significantly higher marks to pass. By the age of fourteen these London girls had learnt that they must expect to be judged by male standards and their ability to be 'as good as the boys'.

For feminist secondary teachers, resources are a major concern:

> 'It means hours spent evaluating the materials, checking the books for racism and sexism and deciding which ones we've got to keep ... we can't afford to replace them all, and anyway, what with?'.

Marion Scott, in an analysis of text books used with the upper secondary age range found that they 'present a biased, distorted and sometimes explicitly sexist view of the world' (Scott 1981) and when Anna Walters noted the sex of authors of the prescribed A-level texts in English literature of three Examining Boards in 1978, she found that only two women were represented as opposed to fifty-one men. (Walters, 1978). Some secondary school departments have developed their own Mode III CSE courses to include an anti-racist and anti-sexist perspective and further opportunities exist with the introduction of GCSE. The vast majority of this work will continue to be done by teachers in their own time as funding and preparation time for GCSE are hopelessly inadequate. It goes without saying that any teacher who wants to see a syllabus free from sex, race and class bias will first have to convince the other staff before she can even begin to find appropriate materials.

The college lecturer had the least direct control over curriculum content of anyone I interviewed, being one of the twelve who jointly construct the course. However, it is interesting to note the similarities between her description of teaching style (I) as a lecturer in Higher Education, and those of an infant teacher, (II) and junior teacher (III).

I   'Whatever we're doing, I try to include in it a feminist perspective, and I've moved further and further away from didactic methods. I used to do most of the talking but now I get them to do group work or make a personal input. I make it clear that I think it's important to be able to talk from your personal experience and that's quite definitely a feminist position. Also trying to get them to listen to each other, take each other seriously, and work in a cooperative way. I don't put them across as specifically feminist ways of working, but I do present them as alternatives, to help them decide how *they* are going to teach'.

II 'I want the children to be autonomous, self-reliant and to value what they do. I allow them to take as much responsibility as possible for their own learning, and my expectations are very high. The emphasis is on cooperation and consideration as opposed to competition, and I create situations where work can only be done if children work together. I'm not in favour of Reading Schemes and workbooks where there is obvious standardisation and children can compare themselves. Inevitably children are aware that one is better at reading than another but I use that to positive advantage by putting them to work together so each will offer something to the other'.

III 'You have to challenge the status quo i.e. the domination of boys. I don't know if this is possible if you teach in a formal way. I teach children as individuals, and I want to increase their self-esteem, especially the girls. The girl/boy ratio affects how you can do this, but the way you teach is affected by your beliefs. You have to teach in a 'free' way to be able to address issues as they arise, to challenge things, and to resolve conflict you must be prepared to take things up and resolve them then and there. This can't be done if you teach in a rigid, inflexible way'.

The twin problems of resources and the level of awareness required to implement equality of opportunity which have absorbed these teachers for years are now beginning to be addressed by those outside the classroom. This is an inversion of the traditional pattern in which research evidence and theories of learning and teaching filter down through the academic system from the 'experts' to the classroom teacher: feminist teachers, often in Scale one posts, have generated knowledge that demands a response. In 1984 the ILEA published an 'Anti-Sexist Resources Guide' (compiled by Sue Adler and Annie Cornbleet) because of the work of feminist teachers in London, and in 1986 produced 'Everyone Counts — looking for bias and insensitivity in primary mathematics materials' which covers all aspects of discrimination in its examination.

Single-sex groupings are a relatively recent development in the old question of single-sex versus coeducational schools. Current and past debates on this complex issue have been concentrated at secondary level, but I would argue that the primary setting is by no means unproblematic for girls. In addition to their experiences in the classroom, they must contend with life in the playground (where young children may spend up to a quarter of each day). In my interviews I repeatedly heard allegations that sexual harassment of infant and junior girls is rife, but tolerated as 'normal' i.e. boys will be boys. I can confirm these accusations from my own observations as a teacher and from the experiences of my daughters. It is beyond the scope of this paper to consider this issue in any detail, but I have been unable to find any published reference to what may constitute another barrier to girls' self-esteem and consequently to their achievement.

Relationships

All the teachers were asked to comment on their relationships with other people at work, whether teaching staff, ancillary workers, parents or students. Every one of them had problems in their working lives, from being treated as a joke because of their views, to being openly criticised or deviously undermined:

'Some teachers see me as the lunatic fringe. Joking is the main response I get from parents and staff. One particularly sexist male on the senior staff is a constant thorn in my side. The usual stuff — calling a boy in my class a 'pouff' — refusing to call me Ms — patronising me — commenting on my appearance etc.' (*Secondary teacher*).

'There's no outright hostility but I know I've been labelled and written off by most staff'. (*Junior teacher*).

'Schools have ways of defusing you. At one I was laughed at openly every day for my clothes — that was their way of coping with my views'. (*Infant teacher*).

'Because I'm peripatetic I go into a lot of schools and the Staff Room is the hardest part. I find I'm at odds with the way lots of people think and I constantly have to justify myself. I insist on being called Ms. but in one school I was told 'We don't have that here'. That's important because it's my definition of who I am. Also people feel they can write off what I say because they've pigeonholed me, and often have stunning preconceptions about what I will think'. (*Infant teacher*).

'You have to either respond to or ignore the maddening comments in the Staff Room and elsewhere. Generally you end up more angry, tense and upset than if you could just shut your eyes to it and pretend it wasn't happening'. (*Junior teacher*).

'People are always looking for ways to fault me. I'm very careful about doing my job properly. A friend made a small mistake and the hierarchy were down on her like a ton of bricks'. (*College lecturer*).

This is just a selection from the negative responses feminists in schools can encounter every working day. It became apparent from the universality of the experience that educational establishments frequently individualise and personalise conflicts in order to devalue both feminists teachers' pedagogic innovation and their criticisms of those in positions of power. This technique has been noted by Grace in respect of urban teachers:

'. . . .it would seem, that teachers associated with overt conflict over school policies *might well become characterized in derogatory personality terms*'. (Grace, 1978).

Yet another strain is the pressure on them not to react as they would wish to actions or statements which are downright offensive:

'I spend much of my time preparing myself for a non-threatening non-emotional front. I really resent not being allowed an emotional response when I see the horror of what's happening in front of me, and the complacency of so-called educationalists'. (*Secondary teacher*).

'There's a superficial liberal veneer of tolerance in my department that we're all professionals and will take everyone's position seriously. As soon as you're being challenging about your feminism then the battlelines are drawn. There's a very strong ethos of 'professionalism' and to challenge someone in a 'professional' way you must be very polite, mustn't get angry or show your feelings in any way. You're supposed to wrap it all up in professional language and invite them to a dialogue. So if someone says something offensive to me from a feminist point of view, the onus is on me to invite them to a dialogue. When I do get angry and insist on the right to say how they've made me feel then accusations of un-professionalism are thrown about'. (*College lecturer*).

When it comes to relationships with staff other than teachers, the feminists were unanimous in their concern to treat them as equals in institutions which make definite distinctions, with secretaries, ancillary workers and cleaners well down in the hierarchy. The women in my sample appear to have made every effort to work with them cooperatively and to be considerate about the repetitive work such staff often have to do, although often encountering suspicion:

> 'When I first started this job I was known as the Women's Libber by the helpers. But now we've had time to get to know each other I find I can raise issues with them'. (*Junior teacher*).

The artificial barriers erected by capitalism and patriarchy which undermine the solidarity of women were recognised, as was the difficulty of breaking them down:

> 'A lot of people treat the secretaries as a lower form of life and are very patronising . . . I want them to feel that I'm on their side despite our dif-ferences. I'm on very friendly terms with some of them but there's a lot of suspicion of feminism. There's a culture of feminity amongst them which I'm opposed to . . . but I would never voice any criticisms. They assume I'll be critical but I never am'. (*College lecturer*).

Teachers have long been the scapegoats for a range of society's ills, and schools are frequently blamed for alleged falling standards of literacy and numeracy, lack of discipline amongst young people and all the other bogeys the media and right-wing elements enjoy conjuring up. By 'schools' of course is meant 'teachers, especially trendy lefty ones'. For primary teachers, this can be particularly stressful when they are expected not only to have expertise in all areas of the curriculum but are often struggling to implement new and progressive practices in mathematics and approaches to literacy and/or cope with increased numbers of pupils in the classroom and reduced allowances for materials. On top of this they are on the spot to explain and, if necessary, defend their practice if it is queried by parents. (Secondary teachers, though accountable, at least generally have the benefit of a warning that a parent wants to see them). I was interested to find out how feminist teachers presented anti-sexism and anti-racism to parents. A by-now familiar pattern emerged of commitment translated into action and a willingness to go on elaborating their position:

> 'Parents can of course try to use your anti-sexist work as a weapon against you if they have *any* grievance. You need to put far more time and effort

into establishing relationships with parents than other teachers do, to explain what you're doing and why. You have to be prepared to go over the issues many times to lots of people'. (*Junior teacher*).

'You have a duty to discuss issues with parents if you feel as strongly as I do about anti-sexism and anti-racism ... Most parents don't have a perception that the gender of their child makes any difference at the infant stage, while they're busy conditioning them at home. I don't ever wade in unless it's appropriate; for instance, I had a seven year old boy who was so contemptuous of girls and women that I couldn't take it any more. He even claimed that boys' footprints in the snow were better than girls'. I had to talk to his mother about his attitude'. (*Infant teacher*).

Sometimes parents respond positively; for example, the mother who sought out and congratulated a teacher for an assembly she had organised highlighting the part played by women in the Second World War. Pupils, too, give positive feed-back. It seems from my inquiries that pupils of both sexes who realise a teacher's position on stereotyping will often seek them out for discussion, advice and con-firmation of their own thoughts.

Parents and children are not a consideration for college of education lec-turers, but the one I interviewed experiences great difficulty in her relations with many of the schools where her students are placed for their Teaching Practice. She has to make forty to fifty visits to schools each year and on every occassion:

'I have to be very careful, and soft-pedal on my feminism. The determin-ing factor is the effect on the student. If the school doesn't like the super-visor, or finds her politically unacceptable, then that will rebound on the student — that's been my experience'.

She then gave an account of how a school had victimised one of her students who was a single parent and a feminist:

'On one occasion she was late because her child was ill and she didn't have any one to look after the child. Yet they held that against her for the rest of the year and kept referring to her 'domestic difficulties'. Well, she didn't have any 'domestic difficulties'. . . apart from that one occa-sion she was never absent or late. In fact she was always there early and did all sorts of extra activities she didn't have to do as a student on teaching practice. Yet in her final T.P. report there were all these references to her 'domestic difficulties', implying she'd have done much better without them. I couldn't make them see what they were doing so in the end I asked my Head of Department to intervene because it was important enough for us to take a stand on. This student was good — and a maths teacher. Women maths teachers aren't exactly thick on the ground. She decided because of her experience she wasn't going into teaching in school ... she just couldn't put up with that attitude. The whole experience was very draining'.

What little has been written about feminist teachers' experiences in the workplace appears to confirm my respondents' claims. The DASI Project (Designing Anti-Sexist Initiatives, 1984) emphasised the importance of establishing relationships with support staff in schools, and Carol Jones has exposed the hostility women, feminist or not, can face when they confront male violence in schools (Weiner 1985). As Pat Mahony has pointed out:

'Feminists continue to carry a triple load. They must possess male knowledge otherwise they are not regarded as competent. They must possess female knowledge otherwise nothing changes and thus they must spend hours reconstructing knowledge of themselves in the past which men have written out. And they must do all this in the context of resisting the offensive comments and abuse unleashed by such engagement'. (Mahony 1982).

Isolation

Conflict is inevitable when the workplace is patriarchal, capitalist, racist, sexist and saturated with hierarchies, and the worker is a feminist. Of all the pressures under which feminist teachers find themselves, isolation seems to be the most universal and debilitating in its effects. Every single woman had experienced it in her work and all had tried to develop methods of breaking out of it:

'You can *never* be entirely sure of getting support and so you have to know your arguments inside out and be prepared to battle alone'. (*Junior teacher*).
'The pressure (before the new Head came) was in always feeling that I was having to stick up for things on my own all the time, that I was having to be the crusader, to take a stance that nobody else sympathised with. You begin to feel there's something wrong with *you*'. (*Infant teacher*).
'I definitely have to be even better at my job to prevent them writing me off for my opinions ... I've needed an awful lot of support outside school, and wouldn't have been able to work as positively if it hadn't been for friends, groups at the teachers' centre and so on. I'm lucky in mixing socially with lots of people who also consider race, sex and class as serious matters. It must be very hard for women who don't have that back-up'. (*Infant teacher*).

Everyone recognised the need for a support network to counteract this sense of isolation, share ideas and make resources. In London the Women in Education Group (WedG) fulfil this function, as does the Anti-Sexist Working Party, but access and availability are obviously a problem for women scattered over the whole of London with so many demands on their time and energy.

Isolation is particularly acute for those women who are the only one in their workplace challenging stereotypes, but *particularly* so for those who don't conform to another of society's expectations: that they be heterosexual. Being a feminist teacher is hard but if you're a feminist lesbian it's even more so:

> 'I know heterosexual feminists have all sorts of conflicts with the institutions but I don't think they experience quite the vulnerability that I do. I've never been in the closet at work but on the rare occasions when I raise issues of sexuality then I feel scared. I guess gay men feel the same thing. It makes me reluctant to raise these issues yet there are times when I can't not … In college there's a liberal gloss, a veneer of tolerance, but that isn't true of most schools.' (See Teaching London Kids no. 23, 1985 for one woman's account of being a lesbian teacher in a boys' school).

Many lesbian teachers live in dread of being identified as such, fearing the open hostility and abuse they have learnt to expect from the world at large. Some believe they would lose their jobs — or a way would be found of encouraging them to resign — others that work would become intolerable. The vulnerability of being a lesbian or gay teacher in schools is exacerbated by the media hysteria and misinformation about alleged dangers to children. In reality, as recent research demonstrates, the vast majority of cases of sexual abuse are performed by heterosexual males. (Forward and Buck, 1981).

The whole question of heterosexism has begun to be raised, notably by the GLC before its abolition, and some borough councils, but resistance to the change is phenomenal. Heterosexism appears to be seen as very much less significant than racism or sexism. A lesbian teacher said:

> 'I resent that it's always me who's raising the issue, trying to make people aware. A lot of people I work with consider themselves to be politically aware in other respects — class and race for example — yet they seem dense in relation to sexuality. (*Secondary teacher*).

Those who are trying to put heterosexism on the agenda for discussion see some parallels with the Black experience over racism, in that it used to be unusual for people to take up questions of race in educational institutions, and it was left to Black people to demand that they should. Now more whites (since it is still they who are generally in power in those institutions) are willing to do so. Perhaps the status of anti-heterosexist work will improve?

'The people I'm thinking of have been in politics for a very long time.

> They are mostly middle-class and white yet they were very quick to take up the questions of class and race and more recently and reluctantly, gender. But heterosexism seems to threaten them much more ... Sociologists in particular tend to deal with racism and sexism as structural issues not personal ones as well, which makes them safer and easier to handle. But they don't think of heterosexism in a structural way — they just want to see it as sexual orientation without seeing that that attitude denies the politics of it all'. (*College lecturer*)

The Lesbians in Education Group in London provides a setting where lesbians from any branch of education can meet in safety. Although by no means all lesbians define themselves as feminists, the founding and maintenance of such support groups is very much within the feminist tradition of providing help and encouragement for each other in a hostile world. For those ten or twenty per cent of girl pupils who are lesbian (Trenchard and Warren 1984) and even more powerless than adult women, there are a handful of youth projects in London specifically designed to meet their needs.

It must be remembered that women who attempt to participate in supportive networks do so in their own time by their own efforts; there is no provision for this in any anti-sexist programme currently running. 'Burn-out' is not unknown amongst committed feminists who remain classroom teachers, and indeed it is difficult to see how so many keep going for so long at such a level of involvement. When I posed this query to my respondents the usual response was hollow laughter. Most teachers have no other marketable skills and (like everyone else) dread unemployment. Since the bills must be paid, they must carry on teaching, and for feminists that means continuing to question, publicise and act upon their convictions. The development of a feminist consciousness necessarily produces a 'double vision' of reality (Stanley and Wise 1983) which, once attained, cannot be ignored. It is not possible to go back to not noticing sexist language, behaviour and materials. Several respondents said that they found that working around issues of bias can, paradoxically, be enormously energising, but only if a network of support can be created and maintained. This is on top of the extra workload created by being a feminist teacher in the first place. The mutuality of sharing (perceptions, experiences, strategies) is so fundamental to the development of feminist thought and action that such support networks are truly indispensible, yet like much of significance to women down the ages, they are invisible and invalidated.

What Difference Does a Policy Make?

How many LEAs have a policy on gender? The Equal Opportunities Commission does not have this information, and I have been unable to find anyone who does.

Frankly it is anybody's guess how many LEAs, let alone schools, are working on or have developed such a policy. The ILEA produced its Anti-Sexist Statement in March 1984, some eighteen months after its Anti-Racist Statement, in which it explicitly recognises the contribution to anti-sexism of individual teachers, and 'aims to validate this work through the adoption and implementation of official policy'. In theory then, all ILEA teachers have the sanction of their employers for any anti-sexist initiatives they might undertake, and some certainly feel this helps:

> 'At the back of my mind is the knowledge that the Authority is behind me and now I'm allowed to have the views I've held for years'. (*Infant teacher*).

The ILEA has now required that all schools develop an anti-sexist policy for submission (though no deadline has been set) so again in theory, anti-sexism should be a central point of discussion in ILEA schools. Some concerned teachers see this as a golden opportunity while recognising the multitude of difficulties in pursuing it. Several women pointed out that having a policy is one thing: ensuring that staff adhere to it is quite another. A peripatetic teacher remarked:

> 'I've known people in schools where there is ostensibly a policy pay lip service and then go away and do exactly as they want. Primary teachers have enormous autonomy within their rooms'. (*Infant teacher*).

and

> 'I suddenly realised the futility of these policies when I came to work at ... where Equal Opportunities is official policy, and then saw what teachers were doing in their classrooms. If you've got a policy then staff must be made to follow it'. (*Infant teacher*).

Considerable discussion takes place among feminists as to the most effective ways of developing and implementing anti-racist and anti-sexist policies. Obviously it places a further demand on already hard-pressed teachers, and persuading the majority of the validity of the arguments is an uphill task, as a lot of feminists and the Letters page of 'Contact' Magazine[8] will testify. For those who are opposed or even neutral to Equal Opportunities, they have become associated with left-wing politics instead of being seen as part of an educational debate about achievement and expectations. The ILEA's 'piecemeal' approach to Equal Opportunites has been criticised as presenting teachers with a double load to consider — first an anti-racist policy then an anti-sexist one — instead of a fusion of considerations of race, sex, and class into one coherent policy statement. The necessity not to separate these three issues was emphasised time and again in my interviews, as each has a complex relation with the other two[9].

Feminist teachers accept that for such a coherent policy to be properly implemented would involve a great change in the fundamental attitudes of many staff:

> 'There has got to be time and opportunity for thrashing out the issues in an atmosphere of genuine tolerance, for those people who haven't had the chance to do so, particularly if their whole social set-up is one where those kinds of questions aren't dealt with … It's not an excuse to carry on working in the way they've worked but it means they've got to change and for some that's a great threat and a great struggle'. (*Infant teacher*).

In the London Borough of Brent, the Equal Opportunities Advisor, Hazel Taylor, has recogized this:

> 'In Brent I have resisted any pressure that policy should be centrally formulated by me or anyone else in the education department, on the grounds that policy must be produced by the teachers who will implement it if it is to have any meaning for them. If Equal Opportunities is to be taken seriously then it must have implicit in it democratic control of policy making: centralised imposition of policy denies that'.

One woman I interviewed, who has taught in over 14 schools, explained why in her view the potential for extended in-depth discussion on questions of sex and race is limited in the infant sector:

> 'Firstly, infant teachers fear they are being judged on the behaviour of their class, so the prime focus is on control[10]. Secondly, the primary day is so fraught, with no non-teaching time usually, that there's no time to externalize and evaluate — infant teachers must be the only ones who have to move furniture around all the time. Thirdly, there's no framework in most infant schools to bring problems to meetings for discussion. You have to be seen to be coping all the time, like motherhood. Fourthly, it's not safe to express contentious views or have an argument because the staff is so small and you have to get along with each other somehow'. (*Infant teacher*).

To this list may be added two further points: one, the pervasive notion which exists among some educators of the 'innocence' of childhood and the claim that to consider the class, race and gender of young children is inappropriate. In reality, many inner-city children lead lives of extreme material deprivation, poorly housed, sometimes inadequately clothed and fed, and in a setting of continuing urban decay. In a time of unremitting long-term high unemployment their families haven't even the prospect of an improvement in their circumstances. Physical hardship and poverty are not conducive to 'innocence' and to deny this is to deny life as it is experienced by thousands of children. (The Child Poverty Action Group estimates that in 1981, one and three-quarter million children in

Britain were living on or below Supplementary Benefit level). Child-centred education should take account of *all* the factors affecting a child's experiences.

The second additional point is that primary teaching has traditionally been viewed as work which combines well with raising children[11]. Given the widespread lack of adequate childcare provision after school, teachers who are also mothers must rush from their paid job to their unpaid one. It is therefore essential that time be made available during the school day for meetings to be held, perhaps along workshop lines where teachers can focus on specific curriculum areas or even individual children causing concern, as a means of legitimising teachers' having problems and doubts. Such a system would necessitate a massive increase in expenditure by the Authority to provide the necessary supply cover. At present there seems little hope of such an increase and many feminist teachers see the ILEA's current spending on anti-sexist initiatives as paltry, pointing out that one Advisory Teacher is supposed to be available to nearly six hundred schools. One was more explicit:

'The ILEA spends a lot of time and money publicising its Equal Opportunities policies and some women have made a good career out of it. But feminist teachers have no support in the classroom where it's needed. Sexual harassment isn't taken seriously, there's no paid leave for teachers who have sick children, no paternity leave, no crèche provision or care allowance for attendance at meetings'. (*Junior teacher*).

Amongst the schoolteachers I interviewed, opinions on ILEA policies on gender and race ranged from gratitude at the very existence of official statements validating individuals' work to criticisms of the various short-comings of those policies. Clearly there is a need for considerable discussion around the whole question of making, implementing and monitoring policies, and much has been learnt from the initiatives of those LEAs that pioneered Equal Opportunities. WedG (1984) raised three main points of dissatisfaction with the route ILEA have taken:

1 there is a danger that written policies may become an end in themselves instead of working documents to be constantly reappraised. Constraints of time and money can easily make re-evaluation almost impossible
2 policy can be seen to be being imposed from above. This begs the question of how the majority of teachers who show little sign as yet of rampant enthusiasm for anti-sexism are to develop a commitment to anti-sexist practice
3 without real back-up in terms of resources and enough committed staff such policies will be worth little. Developing non-oppressive curricula, resources and teaching styles is time and energy consuming

and must be taken seriously, and any policies need to be carefully monitored both within the institution by teachers and by advisors and the Inspectorate.

Adopting an approach which validates and supports the work already undertaken by feminist teachers, while simultaneously helping all staff to take on board the issue of anti-sexism and change their practice accordingly will obviously be no mean feat. Hazel Taylor has offered some helpful observations:

> . . . if policy is to be useful it must have guidelines as well. Half-baked new practices are worse than old ones if they achieve notoriety and lose ground for the issue — we need space to experiment to find out what will work so we need plenty of time before anything has to be enshrined in policy.
>
> However . . . I am now recommending that secondary schools be required to produce policy statements because a) some schools have made a lot of progress and the Authority can validate their work by requiring policy which they are ready to develop, based on solid preparation and b) other schools are doing little and won't unless it is required of them. We cannot guarantee that making policy will change practice but we can and must be seen not to let schools ignore the issue. Here the concentration must be on providing appropriate support during the policy making to bring about the maximum effectiveness. I would want to see *all* teachers involved in policy making, with enough feminist teachers spread across departments to ensure that the agenda is properly discussed and sensible recommendations are made. I would much prefer to see a plan of action and review for each school than a policy statement.
>
> This leads me on to . . . monitoring. To be committed to equality, a school must have a series of short and long term aims and actually have conceptualised what a school that does not reproduce patriarchy would look like. It is then essential to decide on time scales for the achievement of aims and to monitor progress. . . . In my view, the school should be responsible for monitoring its policy implementation and the Authority should monitor by requiring information on a regular basis about what has been achieved.

In focusing in detail on feminist teachers' own accounts of their struggles within educational institutions to develop and legitimate anti-sexist practices, I hope I have highlighted their quite phenomenal level of commitment, energy and persistence. Much of their work is ignored or even derided, and although all of them recounted instances of positive feedback from other staff or pupils, sometimes years later, plainly the personal cost of such dedication is high.

Frankie Ord and Jane Quigley point out that 'Change involves an uneasy balance between conflict and consensus'. (Ord and Quigley 1985). If they are right, then those feminists who are bearing the brunt of the conflict on a daily basis will be the ones to thank for the change when it comes: when an anti-discriminatory perspective is seen as a prerequisite of good educational practice.

Notes

1 Quoted from 'The Schoolmaster' by Pamela Horne in 'Hippolytas and Amazons Times', Education Supplement, 22.8.86.
2 See Alison Oram's 'Serving Two Masters? The Introduction of a Marriage Bar in the 1920s' in London Feminist History Group *The Sexual Dynamics of History* (Pluto Press), 1983.
3 The responses I gathered were either from tape recorded interviews with me or sometimes lengthy answers to a questionnaire where meeting was impossible. In both cases I asked particular questions but encouraged the teachers to develop and expand any issue which they saw as important in the context. It became curiously difficult to locate feminist teachers once I stepped outside my own circle and although I did manage to meet and interview quite a number of new contacts, the isolation of feminist teachers from each other and the ways in which we are prevented from building and maintaining networks emerged as recurrent themes.
4 One example: a Junior School Head recently told me in the course of a discussion on challenging stereotypes in children's books that he was in direct conflict with his employers (the ILEA) over the issue of anti-sexism and had no intention of implementing any initiatives in his school.
5 Valerie Walkerdine observes that it is 'high, middle-class culture which is taken to be 'natural' in child-centredness' in *Investigating Gender in the Primary School*, ILEA 1986.
6 A fascinating account of one teacher's use of drama to stimulate reverse-role experiences is given by Karen Coulthard in 'Exploring Gender through Role Play' in *Primary Matters* ILEA 1986 p. 78–9.
7 See *The Tidy House: little girls writing* by Carolyn Steedman, Virago 1983, for a detailed description of a parallel finding.
8 Until December 1986 'Contact' was the name of the free newspaper produced by ILEA for its teaching staff.
9 See 'An Open Cupboard Policy' by Hazel Taylor for an enlightening dicussion of their relationship, in *The English Curriculum: Gender* ILEA 1984.
10 See Katherine Clarricoates 'Dinosaurs in the Classroom: A re-examination of Some Aspect of the Hidden Curriculum in Primary Schools' in *Women's Studies International Quarterly*, Vol I, No 4.
11 See 'All in a Day's Work' by Katherine Clarricoates in *Learning to Lose* D. Spender and E. Sarah, (Ed.), The Women's Press, 1980.

References

Anti-Sexist Working Party (1985) '"Look, Jane, Look": Anti-Sexist initiatives in primary schools' in Weiner G. (Ed.), *Just a Bunch of Girls*, Open University Press.

BENJAMIN, M. (1985) 'Who Feels It, Knows It' in Hemmings S. (Ed.), *A Wealth of Experience*, Pandora Press.

BRYAN, B., DADZIE, S. and SCARFE, S. (1985) *The Heart of the Race*, Virago.

COARD, B. (1971) *How the West Indian Child is Made Educationally Sub-Normal by the British School System*, New Beacon Books.

CORNBLEET, A. and SANDERS, S. (1982) *Designing Anti-Sexist Initiatives*, ILEA/EOC publications.

FORWARD, S. and BUCK, C. (1981) 'Betrayal of Innocence: Incest and its devastation', quoted in Nelson S. (1982) *Incest: Fact and Myth*, Stramullion Press.

GRACE, G. R. (1978) *Teachers, Ideology and Control*, Routledge and Kegan Paul.

HOWE, F. (1984) *Myths of Coeducation*, Indiana University Press.

JONES, C. (1985) 'Sexual tyranny: male violence in a mixed secondary school', in Weiner, G., *Just a Bunch of Girls*, Open University Press.

Lesbians in Education, c/o A Woman's Place, Hungerford House, Victoria Embankment, London WC2.

LOBBAN, G (1977) 'Sexist Bias in Reading Schemes', in Hoyles, M. (Ed.) *The Politics of Lieracy*, Writers and Readers Publishing Cooperative.

London Feminist History Group (1983). *The Sexual Dynamics of History*, Pluto Press

MAHONY, P. (1982) 'Silence is a Woman's glory: the sexist content of education' *Women's Studies International Forum*, Vol 5 No 5.

MAHONY, P. (1986) *Schools for the Boys? Co-education Reassessed*, Hutchinson in association with the Explorations in Feminism Collective.

ORAM A. (1983) 'Serving Two Masters? The Introduction of A Marriage Bar in the 1920s' in *The Sexual Dynamics of History, op. cit.*

ORD, F. and QUIGLEY, J. (1985) 'Anti-sexism as Good Educational Practice: What can feminists realistically achieve?' in Weiner, G. *Just a Bunch of Girls*, Open University Press.

RUSS, J. (1984) *How to Suppress Women's Writing*, The Women's Press.

SCOTT, M. (1980) 'Teach her a lesson: Sexist Curriculum in Patriarchal Education' in Spender, D. and Sarah, E. (Eds.) *Learning to Lose*, The Women's Press.

SMITH S. (1984) 'Single-Sex Setting' in Deem, R. (Ed.) *Coeducation Reconsidered*, Open University Press.

SPENDER D. (1980) *Man Made Language*, Routledge and Kegan Paul.

SPENDER D. (1982) *Invisible Women: The Schooling Scandal*, Writers and Readers Publishing Cooprative.

STANLEY, L. and Wise, S. (1983) *Breaking Out: Feminist Consciousness and Feminist Research*, Routledge and Kegan Paul.

TAYLOR, H. (1984) 'Reflection on the role of policy' Unpublished paper, quoted in Mahony, P. (1986) '*Schools for the boys?*'

Teaching London Kids. A quarterly magazine for teachers.

THOMAS, C. (1985) 'Finding the Strong Inner Core' in Hemmings, S. (Ed.) *A Wealth of Experience*, Pandora Press.

TRENCHARD, L. and WARREN, H. (1984) *Something to Tell You*, London Gay Teenage Group.

WALDEN R. and WALKERDINE, V. (1982) *Girls and Mathematics: the Early Years*, Bedford Way Papers.

WALTERS, A. (1978) 'Women writers and prescribed texts', WASTE papers, presented at National Association for the Teaching of English Annual Conference, York.

WEINER, G. (Ed.) (1985) *Just a Bunch of Girls*, Open University Press.

WIDDOWSON, F. (1980) *Going up into the next class. Women and elementary teacher training, 1840–1914*, Women's Research and Resources Centre Publications.

Women in Education Group (WedG, 1984) 'Reflections on policy' Unpublished paper quoted in *Schools for the Boys?* Mahony, P. (1986).

5
Pride and Prejudice: Teachers, Class and an Inner-City Infants School

Jan Lee

'The teachers ... remain in the same essential position in the matrix of class relations as did their Victorian predecessors. They find themselves at the meeting point of classes; at the point where 'official' culture with its understandings, values and world view meets alternative realities; where middle-class prescription meets working-class resistance...' (Grace 1978, p. 53).

Schooling and Class

Education plays a crucial role in legitimating the class structure of society. The majority of teachers covertly collude in this process. An analysis of the class position and class perspectives of teachers is then primordial in any attempt to understand the interrelationships between classroom practice and social context. Research has consistently demonstrated that 'success' in the educational system is principally related to social class, gender and racial origin (e.g. Boudon 1974; Halsey *et al.* 1980; ILEA 1983; Rampton 1981; Swann 1985). Early explanations of the 'failure' of the working-class, women and black children were based on 'scientific' theories of biological, genetic differences and substantiated by intelligence tests. Much educational policy and practice is still predicated upon these assumptions, albeit unconsciously. The 1960s saw the ascendancy of theories of social and cultural deprivation enshrined in the Plowden Report and promulgated through the establishment of Educational Priority Areas. Reasons for 'failure' at school are then attributed to various social factors such as: socialisation, size of family, language, etc. These social theories, whilst allowing for some remedial action, still perceive the origin and cause of educational failure as being due to deficit in the pupils and parents. More recently the acknowledgement of anti-racist theories has explored the relationship between black pupils' educational failure, racism in the wider social context and its manifestations at school and teacher level. Cecile Wright's (1985) case-studies highlight the role that largely unconscious or unintentional racism plays in the widespread disaffection, resistance and educational 'failure' of black pupils, particularly those of Afro-Caribbean heritage. There are many elements of black working-class pupils' responses to schooling that are comparable to those of white working-class pupils (see: Willis 1977; Corrigan 1979; Woods 1980).

Bernstein's early work postulated possible discontinuities between home and school and therefore potential sources of 'mismatch' and conflict.

> 'It is suggested that there may be, for the working-class child in the primary school, two sources of discontinuity; one in the area of skill acquisition and the other in the area of inter-personal relations. If, for example, the school emphasises autonomy in the acquisition of skills but the implicit concept of learning in the home is didactic in relation to skills, this will be a major source of discontinuity. Similarly, if the school is concerned with the development of reflexive relations in the area of inter-personal relations but the implicit concept of social learning in the home operates to reduce reflexiveness in this area, then this will be another source of discontinuity. It may be unreasonable to expect children exposed to such discontinuities to respond initially to forms of control which presuppose a culture and socialisation very different from their own'. (Bernstein and Henderson, 1969, p. 16).

More recently, Janet Holland (1981) has worked within the framework of Bernstein's theory of sociolinguistic codes with particular reference to the class differences in orientation to meaning i.e., 'the selection and organisation of meaning, of what is seen as relevant and taken as the focus of attention in any situation, and the way in which these meanings are organised in practical discourse', (p. 1). A major point being made by both Bernstein and Holland is that 'differences' are not 'deficiencies' in any cognitive sense but that they are *social* incongruencies and therefore *social* judgements which are being made and which crucially disadvantage the working-class:

> 'It is important to point out that . . . we are not referring to a narrowly defined cognitive orientation, but rather are suggesting that children are differentially positioned by the school's re-contextualising principle and practice and that this re-contextualising principle and practice is an unwitting realisation of class relations'. (Holland, 1981, p. 3).

Shirley Brice Heath's work (1983) has, in her detailed and absorbing ethnographic studies, more graphically demonstrated the way in which the implicit assumptions, expectations, and ideology of the schooling process deny, militate against and in many instance denigrate the culture, knowledge, procedural rules and learning processes of the white and black working-class, and thus prevent educational 'success' when measured by narrow, middle-class norms. Shirley Brice Heath's work demonstrates, albeit implicitly, that it is not that the middle-class knowledge, discourse, understanding, meaning, etc. are cognitively and intellectually superior to that of the working-classes but that they have the power to legitimate their versions of the 'stories'.

> 'We have even less information about the variety of ways children from *non-mainstream* homes learn about reading, writing and using oral language to display knowledge in their pre-school environment. The general view has been that whatever it is mainstream school-oriented homes have, these other homes do not have it: thus these children are not from the literate tradition and are not likely to succeed in school'. (Brice Heath , 1983, p. 50).

Teachers and Class

Teachers, therefore, play a crucial if unintentional role in the process of educational failure and legitimation of 'authorised versions of the story'. Both their own class position and class perspectives are powerful if insidious factors in the perpetuation of an inegalitarian society. Analysis of teachers' practice and its often implicit, philosophical/political base can provide a greater understanding of the complex relationship between the wider social context and the policy and practice of schools and individual teachers. There appears to have been an 'upsurge' of interest and research into primary schools in recent years (see: Alexander 1984; Bennett *et al.* 1984; Bell *et al.* 1987; Galton *et al.* 1980a, 1980b, 1983; Hartley 1985; Kirby 1981; Lowe 1987; Marriott 1985; Pollard 1985; Richards 1982, 1984, 1985a, 1985b). It should be noted that this research and exposition of issues in the primary school has been conducted by men (about predominantly female work) and men whose experience of teaching, if indeed they have any, is likely to have been in the secondary sector. Much of the research into primary classrooms appears to either ignore or deliberately deny the social, political and economic context of schooling. In particular, King (1978) and Hartley (1985) are at pains to promote an analysis of status differentiation (*à la* Weber) rather than an analysis of class differentiation. King's work has been critiqued elsewhere (see: Lee 1980). Hartley's work is similar to King's in that he attempts to diminish the importance of a class analysis of schooling by emphasising gender and ethnic 'status' differences *within* a working-class school. Whilst it is doubtful whether anybody would deny the existence of status differences *within* classes, these status differences do not alter the inequality that exists *between* classes. So, for instance, since working-class girls are far less likely to get into higher education than working-class boys, it does not then follow that working-class boys are *as* likely to get into higher education as middle-class girls.

The research details that follow are taken from a study of an inner-city, multi-racial *Infant* school. The research was primarily concerned with developing an understanding of teacher ideology and the ways in which these ideologies were manifest in the pedagogical practice of the teachers (see: Lee 1980). The following is an account of that part of the research which extrapolated the teachers' 'world views' and social class perspectives. The teachers' ideologies were evolved from their statements and discussions during 'in-depth' interviews. Their views on the socio-political nature of the wider society were elicited, as well as those on the nature of their immediate work situation and their perspectives on the classroom as a work place. That is to say, the intention was to construct what could be described as the *'weltanschauung'* of infant teachers in a social milieu where the conflicts and contradictions of this society are in sharp relief i.e., in the inner-city.

The present study found, as have other studies (e.g. King 1978; Sharp and Green 1975; Grace 1978; Pollard 1985; Hartley 1985), that there were many similarities in the teachers' ideologies as regards the wider society. It was apparent that the teachers' views on issues of the socio-political nature of society etc., were derived almost exclusively from the educationist context or some relationship between that and their own socialisation. The teachers' views were remarkable for their naiveté as regards the structural, political and wider relational features of society. This expressed itself in their professed 'classless', 'apolitical', or 'neutral' view of society. Their views tended to the psychological rather than the sociological, and therefore to ignore or evade issues of power, economics and conflict.

Biographical and Professional Background of the Teachers

The biographical and professional backgrounds of the teachers demonstrate many continuities and similarities both historically and within the school. Arguably the most significant historical continuity is the social class background of the teachers. In this study, the teachers, as has been the case historically, originate from the lower middle-class and 'respectable' working-class backgrounds; the lower middle-class appearing to come from a rural background, whilst the two 'respectable' working-class were from the relatively local urban environment. It can be argued that historically the class background of teachers had been a factor related to the social-control function of schooling in the 19th and early 20th centuries. Silver (1974) notes a statement for subscribers published by the Kennington Committee in 1837 which could be seen to support the view that, at a time of social conflict and change, education was becoming accepted as a 'necessary barrier not only, as previously, to crime and pauperism, but increasingly to social and political disorder'. (Silver 1974 p. 64). The statement to subscribers re-affirmed that the system of instruction at the schools and the children's attendance at church meant that:

> '. . . the infant poor are thus trained to habits of obedience and good order, and they acquire that knowledge which is calculated to fit them for the stations of life they may hereafter fill, and to enable them to become good Christians, as well as useful and industrious members of society'. (*ibid.*)

The educational background of the teachers is also very similar (with perhaps the exception of the head) and the differences that do exist are largely a reflection of the changing structure of the national educational system over the past 50 years or so. Hence, *Teacher B* — the deputy head — aged 55 years, had attended a local infant school 'at $6\frac{1}{2}$ years old' and had won a scholarship to a local direct-grant Grammar School. She was evacuated to Brighton during the war, where she completed a two-year teacher training course in nursery/infant/lower junior education. She returned to her present home, a few minutes from the school, in 1947. She has been teaching in Canal School for thirty years and had been deputy head since 1956. She did not stop work when she had a child in 1948, although she constantly referred to the present 'problems' of educating the children attending the school, as being due to parents putting their children with 'child-minders and all sorts of people' and going out to work in order 'to be like the Joneses next door and have what they've got'. She had taught in this same school under three different women heads before the present head took over the school.

Teacher C, aged 36 years, was educated in a village primary school which was 'all age till 15, when I went to a co-ed grammar school, small, in Suffolk'. She also had taught mostly in the inner city, apart from one year in a primary school in Ipswich. She had taught in two other inner city schools, one of which the present head had also taught in. However, their friendship appeared to be the consequence of a similar religious ideology, rather than similar educational ideology. She had been teaching in Canal School for the past four years, having stopped teaching for 5 ½ years when her two children were younger, and her husband — a Church of England clergyman — had moved to a parish on the outskirts of London.

Teacher A, single, aged 28 years, had been to a Church of England junior mixed and infant school in a 'respectable' working-class area in the borough. She had attended a London Comprehensive from 11–18 years and then went to a Technical College for one year 'to get better grades and another A level, because I thought I wanted to go to University'. She then attended a three-year course at a London teacher training college and her first appointment was to Canal School soon after the present head had been appointed, six years previously.

Teacher D, the probationer, aged 24 years, was educated in a small rural primary school (50 children on roll) and then attended a larger girls' Grammar School (500 children). She had trained in London and gained a B.Ed. degree. On leaving college, she had difficulty getting a job, highlighting the particular state of education in the 1970s and in particular the inner city, i.e., falling rolls and teacher unemployment. Initially she had applied for a part-time job in the school, and had been taken on, on a temporary terminal basis, when various teachers left. At the time of the research this teacher was then in her first year as a full time divisional member of staff and was therefore regarded by the ILEA as in her probationary year. She was married and expecting her first child.

The Head, male, aged 34 years, described his class origins as lower middle-class. He had also attended a small rural school and then a 'very small anciently founded County Grammar School' (180 on roll). The head, however, went to Oxford and graduated in Theology. He then taught in a secondary school in Birmingham but that experience decided him on training for the priesthood; but after one year he went back to teaching, this time in a private school in a noted, wealthy area of SE London. He then commenced working for ILEA in the junior department of a J.M. and I. school where he became interested in the infant stage of teaching. He attended a six-week graduate induction course in infant teaching, and after some difficulty over persuading the Head, he was allowed to take the reception class (i.e., rising 5s and 5 year olds). Soon after he became deputy-head of the infant school (the school having separated due to the increase in pupils on roll). Two years later he became head teacher of Canal School where he was then in his seventh year. This rapid promotion is also *partly* a reflection of the changing urban context and its effect on schools. The Head was now finding promotion difficult and, during the time of the research was granted secondment to do the Diploma in Education in order that he could gain a teacher training qualification.

The Head's professional experience and promotion is an example of the sexist practices that operate at a particularly pernicious level within first-school/nursery/infant sectors of the schooling system. Any man entering this sector of education is valued for his rarity. In addition he has the usual advantages of confidence and the facilities to put himself forward for promotion. A double-bind of injustice prevails in that, unlike women going into traditionally male professions, the men entering this traditionally female sector of education do not have to be twice as qualified, experienced, etc. This head's experience would imply that, indeed, they require a good deal less in qualifications, experience, etc.; it is with scepticism then that many view the present trend of some male secondary teachers 'retraining' for the primary sector. Equally misguided is the view held by many teacher educators that male applicants for primary education courses should receive positive discrimination as should (in theory) black people, because both are in short supply! This clearly disregards the wider social context and male positions in the social structure. One of the reasons so few men are in primary education, particularly nursery/infant, is because of its low status which in turn is related to its association with 'female' qualities of nurturing and caring which are systematically debased in society in general. The position and social experience of black people could not be more different. This example emphasises the crucial role of an analysis of power in any discussions on inequality.

From this brief resumé of the teachers' background it is apparent that they had similar class backgrounds and similar educational experiences. In general the teachers did not feel that teacher training college had had any conscious effect on them; although there were variations in the degree to which they felt this to be the case, from outright rejection by Teacher A: 'Absolutely none', to some acknowledgement by Teacher B: 'You've got some ideas even before you go to college and then you get their ideas as well'. Dale (1977) argues that there are at least three different sources of the 'commonsense' that underpins teachers' professional knowledge. These are: (i) the view they gain of the process of teaching as a result of their own educational experience as pupils, (ii) their professional education, and (iii) their ongoing teacher experience. He concentrates on the professional training of teachers and justifies this not as being the most important, but 'because it is where what is required of teachers is made most explicit'. He then examines the impact of teachers' professional education on their consciousness in three areas, (i) their cognitive style, (ii) the impact of the social organisation of their student career, i.e., authority, responsibility, etc., and (iii) the relationship between the direct experience of teacher education, its routines and rituals, and their professional consciousness. However, he feels that it is at the 'broad level' of the impact on cognitive style that teacher-training has the greatest effect on teachers' eventual professional performance, often without the teachers being conscious of this. He analyses the subjects which he sees as dominating teacher education — psychology, philosophy and traditional sociology — to show how each plays a part in inculcating a 'cognitive style' which is called 'liberal individualism'. This style of thought encourages teachers to see educational problems as 'deriving from individuals and the solutions to them as lying in individual treatments...'. It does not encourage them 'either to question the nature and values of the system in which they practise or seek the sources of the problems confronting them in social relations rather than in individuals' (Dale 1977 p. 20).

The present study would certainly seem to re-affirm Dale's conjecture that teacher training has little *conscious* effect on the teachers' cognitive style. Teacher C endorses this view: 'There are certain things at the back of your mind that you don't consciously use, but you absorb them and take them (sic.). The actual business of controlling the class you won't learn until you come out. You learn that from other teachers'. The distinction between the 'theory' of training college and the 'practice' of the school situation, is explicated by all the teachers. Teacher A thought that 'they would teach one thing but mean something quite different.

In theory progressive but they didn't expect that in practice'. The inadequacy of the theory and the passive acceptance of the training is epitomised in the following statements:

> *Teacher C:* 'When we were at college we used to hear the theories and methods put forward by different people, so you must be aware that there is more than one way. At our college there was Montessori, Neill, Froebel, Steiner (is it?)'.
>
> *I:* 'Were their methods encouraged by your college?'
>
> *Teacher C:* 'I don't know, you took them in along with Freud and Piaget, Rousseau, you got the whole spectrum'.

However, as regards the rest of Dale's argument, i.e., the role of teacher training in *promoting* the cult of liberal individualism, this should perhaps be seen more as an indirect consequence of teacher training, rather than a direct one. Whilst the present study would not pretend to offer more substantive evidence on this issue, it would appear possible to imply a notion of false consciousness: the most positive statement that the researcher feels able to make is that of the negative effect of teacher training, i.e., that one of effects of teacher training is *not* to promote a critical, political or social consciousness in the teachers. Moreover, the person in this study who presents perhaps the most ideal typical, liberal, individualist philosophy, is the Head who had not received any formal teacher training. Whilst this one example could not invalidate Dale's argument, the statements, both implicit and explicit, of the teachers in this study would suggest that practical experience plays a much more significant part in effecting teacher consciousness (see also: Fuchs 1973) and that only where there is no disjuncture between training college philosophy and school philosophy can the training colleges be seen to be effective.

Continuities in the teachers' social, educational and professional backgrounds persist despite the disparity in age, and equally appear not to be influenced by the rural/urban dichotomy or by the 'respectable' working-class/lower middle-class distinction. Marsden (1977) demonstrates how, in the 19th century, there appeared to be 'marked discontinuities' in attitudes between the upper and lower middle-class, and equally between the 'respectable' working-class and the 'low poor'. He notes that the aspirations of the 'respectable' working-class and the lower middle-class appeared to converge and grow over time, 'with the late 1880s and 1890s an important take-off period, no doubt made possible by the increased demand for white-collar workers at that time'. He also notes that 'there was a certain harmony of perception between aspiring parents and the promoters of education as to the function of elementary schooling', with the limited aim of mobility into white-collar work. He concludes that 'elementary education as an agency of social mobility was a reality only for the favoured segment of the working class, and probably only for those of that group who made conscious and purposive use of it' (Marsden 1977 pp. 223–224). This could then be regarded as an earlier indication of the similarities in values and attitudes between these two groups. Their emphasis on education as a means of social mobility would help to explain the predominance of teachers from this background.

It is perhaps appropriate at this point to speculate on Bernstein's (1975) argument about the development of conflict between the 'old' and 'new' middle class. The assertion that the progressive pedagogy is the domain of the 'new' middle-class could mean that the development of the former in the 1960s and 1970s was made possible by the changing occupational structure (similar to that which occurred in the 1880s and 1890s). It could also mean that the conflict over this pedagogy, is not so much a manifestation of an 'old' conflict *within* the middle class, but of a changing relationship between the 'new' middle-class and the 'respectable' working class. As regards the educational sphere then, we could postulate a possible new alliance between sectors of the working class and the 'old' middle class; but with the educational sphere decreasing in social importance and with the 'new' middle classes' power, derived from education, also diminishing.

Socio-Political Framework in which the Teachers Operated

The socio-political views of the teachers were remarkable for their insignificance rather than any expressed similarities. The question, 'What views do you hold on the social and political nature of society?', in most cases, caused perplexity. Assuming that this may in part have been attributable to the vague and general nature of the question; further supportive prompting produced replies that implied either that the teacher regarded the nature of society as having universal properties that were 'commonsense' to all, and therefore needed no explanation; or that the 'realm of the political' was far removed from the educational sphere and almost therefore by definition, superior but separate. Again, the educationist context and/or their own social-class background, appears to be the source and the limit of the teachers' views. Consequently, no theory of the organisation, functioning or general nature of society was proffered. Instead, specific problems such as 'vandalism' (Teacher B), 'greed' (Teacher C), 'housing' (Teachers A and D), 'poor education' (Head), are identified as 'problems' of society; but they are in reality the teachers' own experiences, working in a working-class, inner city school. There was no attempt to extend or generalise their understanding of the problem. For example, Teacher B, who expressed considerable sympathy for the 'lot' of the parents, when asked why she thought that areas such as that surrounding the school existed, replied:

> 'It's the housing. If a parent isn't happy then it obviously goes on to his
> children. If his housing is dreadful then he's not going to have much to

laugh about. If his job's dreadful or he's not getting paid a lot, etc. There are so many factors but bad housing is one helluva factor for our kids. No facilities. A dead life, vacuum. There are parents on this estate who don't leave it. They shop here, live here, go to the launderette here; their children go to school here'.

An explication of the problems, but no explanation of why they exist. So, whilst the teachers may differ as to the identification of the 'problems' and their proposed solutions they are all based on 'apolitical' or 'neutral' assumptions about society and in particular education's role in that society. Closer questioning about the home lives and occupations of the children's families revealed scant understanding of those factors in relation to the occupational and economic organisation of society. This is perhaps best exemplified in the Head's reply — bearing in mind that at the time the rapidly rising unemployment figures were hitting the headlines and that unemployment is notoriously higher among black communities.

I: 'Do you know what work the parents do, in this area?'
Head: 'It varies. I do not have any statistics to hand but I mean a lot of fathers are unemployed, and there seems to be quite a pattern where the father is unemployed and mum works'.
I: 'Is this a recent phenomena?'.
Head: Increasingly recent I would say, although there has always been that element and I would probably say it's on the increase though again . . . it would just be an impression. The sort of jobs the fathers do are very mixed really: We have got a couple of taxi drivers; at one stage we seemed to have quite a lot of lorry drivers; that seems to be less now. Bus conductors, railway workers. *Very, very mixed. Difficult to generalise about that, I think*' (My emphasis).

Whilst the actual jobs that the parents do may be 'mixed' the obvious generalisation is that the majority are unskilled, manual jobs. The researcher would also speculatively see a correlation between the movement off the estate, that the teachers so frequently referred to, as being indicated by the decrease in lorry drivers. The changing composition of families on the estate, as regards race, could also be deduced from this; since some occupations such as taxi driving and lorry driving are noticeable by their 'whiteness'; whereas black people regardless of their class origins have historically been employed on public transport.

Political parties are not referred to, neither are political issues — not even those that could be seen to affect education such as cuts in public expenditure or Rhodes Boyson and the Black Papers. The views of the Head on these issues and most others would seem to approximate most closely to what Sharp and Green define as 'romantic radical conservatism' which involves an 'emotional turning away from society and an attempt within the confines of education to bring about that transformation of individual consciousness which is seen to be the key to social regeneration'. Whilst there do appear to be some differences between the teachers as regards their implicit assumptions about society and education's function within it; the general framework within which they work is similar by its absence of any conscious developed notions about the structure, organisation or functioning of society. The Head provides the fullest exposition of this perspective:

> 'I am not really particularly politically minded from a personal point of view, politics is something I can (take or leave) I think I am one of those rather apathetic, and a vast majority are, I suspect, rather apathetic and cynical people about politics. And it does not really seem to me to have very much connection with what actually happens, to real people or to make very much difference which political party is in power'.

Since the interviewer regarded this as a rather narrow definition of the term 'political' she pursued the point in relation to 'class politics'. The Head admitted that he did not feel that he had resolved issues related to class and politics in his own mind. He felt that he 'would have views that tinged on the left-wing about the distribution of wealth and so forth'. On the other hand, he believed in 'rights of property and rights to private ownership and the need for endeavour being rewarded in some way by a society'. He expressed suspicion of 'middle class bleeding-heart liberals'. Morever, he did not believe that there are

> 'social panaceas which are going to right all ills. But I think there are always going to be people who are under-privileged; there are always going to be people who are not getting a fair share of the cake, and I do not see that there is some instant solution you can find to that'.

Acknowledgement of this inequality in society, combined with an acceptance of the 'status quo' is resolved through the 'cult of the individual'. This 'cult of the individual' appears to be a necessary 'coping strategy' evolved, partly, in order to resolve conflicts within the progressive pedagogy both theoretically and at the substantive level. In contrast to the 'bleeding-heart liberals', who merely *'think* they are involved in what is going on in the world', the Head sees his job as being: 'much more to do with individual people and individual families and trying to help support them as best they can, and a large part of that, of course, is helping them to understand and cope with the sort of system they are facing. And it seems to me that *politics are about generalisations and generalisations do not apply'* (my emphasis). Nowhere is there any understanding on the part of the Head or the other teachers, that 'helping them to understand and cope with the sort of system they are facing' implicitly contains certain political assumptions as regards that system. This conservatism further ensures that the response to the system is 'adjustment' by the parents rather than 'adjustment' of the system. Furthermore, the 'classless' view of society that the teachers purportedly hold, militates against notions of social conflict and the root causes of the problems are therefore explained variously in terms of the 'old' notions of moral depravity, or the more liberal notions of 'cultural deprivation'. This notion of 'classlessness' will now be further explicated and analysed.

Class and Status

The most striking similarity in the teachers' attitudes in relation to their world views, is their professed 'classless' view of society. The teachers were unanimous in their denial of the existence or the value of notions of class, and yet they frequently used such terms. Most had refused to or omitted to answer the question on class in the questionnaire and there had been heated discussion in the staff room as to the point of such a question. Teacher B, the deputy head, made the classic response:

> 'We're all working class aren't we? We all work for our living we do have those who have a little more money than us, but generally I would say we're all working class (but some are better than others!)'.

The other teachers responded by emphasising that their criterion for evaluation was based on an assessment of the individual. '. . . People work. There are just different people and their parents are people with different problems' (Teacher A). Teacher D, perhaps presents some rapprochement to the 'embourgeoisement' thesis: 'There are middle class values that some working class hold and working class values that some middle class hold. I prefer to think of the individual'.

It might be interesting to note here the responses of a group of students in the first year of their B.Ed. degree in September 1986. The students made remarkably similar responses to the issue of class-groupings and their own positions within this structure. One student response was: 'All people are working class who do any kind of work . . . . No matter what work people do it is as relevant as any other work'. Another responded 'I do not find any of the criteria used for labelling class groupings acceptable and therefore cannot put myself in a particular group'. Yet another: '. . . I feel class systems are misleading and also pointless, as they only cause social problems'. And another: 'Respectable working class because my family have had to get where they are and have not accepted the position they were placed in. Personally I don't agree with the class system'. This view probably reflects most closely the views of teachers B and C in the research study. This continuity of class perspectives has implications for considerations about the 'self-selection' of students applying for primary teacher education courses; the role of the admissions/selection procedure in colleges; the 'failure' of colleges to tackle these issues in any meaningful way, and it reinforces the points made earlier about the role of teacher education in the development of teacher ideology and practice.

The Head in the present study appears to present a particularly naive view of class, for, whilst acknowledging that education has a socially reproductive function, he denies the relation of this to the stratification process in society:

> 'I don't find it (the term working class) a particularly appropriate or useful term to use. The crucial thing to me is to be successful in education. Parents who themselves have been failures in the education system, seem to produce children who are also failures, often for very similar reasons'.

However, all the teachers do in fact utilise class notions and concepts both explicitly and implicitly. If, however, this view is related to what appears to be the main source of the teachers' world views, i.e., the educationist context, a possible explanation becomes apparent. It would seem that what the teachers are wanting to emphasise in their denial of the existence of class, is that they do not evaluate or accord rigid, static differences, on the basis of a class analysis. This is perhaps expressed in the following statement where Teacher C, who has already demonstrated a fairly forceful opinion on the 'classlessness' of society, and herself in particular, is then asked:

> *I*: 'Would you not say that children around here are working class and that they have certain characteristics . . .?'.
> *Teacher C*: 'Yes, I would say that. Obviously there are different attitudes. But then if you're going to put them in class distinctions, a lot of these working class parents are very concerned about their childrens' educations. They might not have been so well educated themselves that they can develop that enough — whereas a professional or middle class person probably has had a better education. Because it is not necessarily intelligence, you see, it *is* that they've had their outlooks broadened and see the value. But it does mean that in some ways they are deprived'.

Implicit in these statements are a number of distinctions and assumptions, about the difference between working-class and middle-class. The term working-class appears to be associated with some notion of 'less intelligent' and the teacher is therefore at pains to indicate that despite this, some can see the importance of education and that this will presumably affect their childrens' chances in the educational system. So this 'space' allows the crucial notion of the liberal democratic society to operate, i.e., equality of opportunity. The teachers' attitudes would appear to differ from their historical location, in that their *explicit* function is not the 'civilising of the poor'. As Silver (1974) points out: 'the primary school is no longer, however, by *definition* for the infant poor'. So, if the teachers regard themselves as classless, they cannot conceive of their role as teachers and their typification of the children as having any basis in the notion of class. Equally, if they regard the rest of society as classless they must have to attribute differences in educational achievement to concepts of heredity (innate ability) or to a deficit in the home background (social pathology). This analysis could be seen to support the views of those such as Richard Johnson, in explicating a shift from explicit social control to social hegemony (or class/cultural control) (Johnson, 1976). This development is epitomised in a quotation from Silver's book (1974). The following quotation is taken from information given to parents by St Mark's School, Kennington in 1971:

> 'Each child is encouraged to be self-disciplined — to behave, speak, dress and work well, *not because he or she has been told to do so but because these are the natural and reasonable things to do* for the child's own sake and for the sake of others' (my emphasis). (Silver 1974 p. 177).

Universal laws of 'nature' and 'reason', it could be argued, entail that different behaviour will be construed as *deviant* behaviour. Also, implicit in this statement is an assumption that society can be, or is, organised on the principle of Adam's 'invisible hand'. (This assumption is also made by the teachers in this study), i.e., what is good for the individual is good for the whole. This does not allow for the 'social' to have any different properties other than the sum of the individual properties it contains. Hence, the belief that change can and must be brought about on the individual plane, if at all. Furthermore, if different behaviour is construed as deviant, then its 'rational' or 'class' base is denied and so too are notions of conflict or resistance as class manifestations. Instead individualist theories of psychological abnormality etc., are likely to be invoked. In many ways, however, this must militate against the development of class resistance and must seriously limit the possibility of education as a 'site of the class struggle'.

Despite the teachers' world views asserting a classless view of society (but possibly for educational reasons), their work situation exemplifies quite specific class assumptions. Two areas presented themselves as of particular importance: (i) The distinction, albeit implicit, that is made between the 'deserving' and 'non-deserving' poor or the 'respectable' and 'rough' working-class. (ii) The class values that are implicit in the teachers' ideas about how they would like the children prepared for school, and why they fail in the education system.

Firstly, the distinction between the 'deserving' and 'feckless' poor is implied by all the teachers, although for two of the teachers it appears to be the basis of their 'apolitical' world view. Teacher C's reference to her own background and in particular her mother's experience illustrates how she regards society as not rewarding the 'deserving' poor:

> '. . . she (her mother) made sure that four children had a decent educa-

tion and went without herself in lots of different ways and now she's on the breadline. That, to me, is all wrong'.

Her values appear to have been consciously influenced to a very large extent by her socialisation in the home and family. 'But my standards came from my home not my school', and it is apparent that she regards these standards as 'normal' and something that all children should be taught. She constantly makes reference to deserving/undeserving distinctions between families that are based on values and assumptions related to her own socialisation and class position in society. She talks about a parent being 'pathetically grateful' for help received. Those views are perhaps most clearly expressed in the following quotation:

> '. . . I see in this school a lot of problem families where the parents never ask for anything and have that determination to help themselves and keep above water and do the best they can even if it is in poor circumstances. But there are others who think 'why should I bother?'. Able-bodied men and women who don't go out and work and just sit and expect to be provided for'.

Teacher B also held the view that people were depending too much on the state —in particular the Welfare State. She stated sarcastically, that schools could no longer do without involvement in social services; 'not the way things are now. Parents expect it. They come in and ask us for it'. She felt that the response of the schools to the prospect of vast unemployment in the future should be '. . . a course in make-do and mend', because these parents just sit back and wait for somebody to put it in their laps. *They* can do it; *they* can look after my kids; *they* can give me money; *they* can buy shoes. Nobody has ever said to them, 'Have you tried to do anything yourself?'. 'Bad management' is seen as the cause of these parents' problems:

> 'It's not that they haven't enough money coming in, it's just that they can't manage. They have their priorities wrong: mum and dad have their cigarettes and beer, etc., to the cost of the children's clothing'.

This was Teacher B's reply to a question about possible evidence of material poverty amongst the families. So despite their acknowledgement as to the increasing number of single-parent families and unemployed people on the estate, they all laid the blame on mismanagement. Teacher A epitomises this view:

> '. . . I've seen parents give them (their children) 10p to shut up and let them stuff themselves with sweets instead of saving that 10p, even if you're poor, to cook them an egg. It's a strange mentality'.

The kind of criteria that are used to make the distinctions between the 'deserving' and 'feckless' poor, are surprisingly similar — given the differences that exist between the teachers on other issues to do with the families. For example, Teacher A:

> 'You can always tell the parents who are always moaning they have no money, yet smoke and stuff their children with sweets . . . And then you can tell the child whose parents say they're poor and you realise they are because their clothing is well cared for, but it's old and they never have things like sweets and treats; never go out. You know that sort of parent is finding it hard and they're not putting it on. They are trying and they can't'.

There would certainly be evidence enough to suggest a continuity here with the Victorian morality of 'self-help' etc. However, the teachers do not consciously see this as a moral or socialising role of the school, as their replies to that question later indicate. Equally, they are unaware of the class-bias of this notion 'bad management'. A person is only considered a bad manager, if their income is so low that the 'bad management' requires them to seek support of some kind. The term is therefore only applicable to those whose incomes are low in the first place.

The implicit class bias in the teachers' views is particularly apparent in their response to questions about how parents do, and should, prepare their children for school. All the teachers stressed the importance for parental involvement with the children and the need for books etc., in the home. Talking to children, taking them out, doing things with them (like reading stories to them and 'making things' together). Teacher C was very specific:

> 'I'd like every child when they come to school to be able to cope with their own clothing; tie laces; go to the toilet by themselves; be able to hold a knife, fork and spoon and be able to eat properly'.

Teacher B was particularly concerned about the children not knowing nursery rhymes and that they 'haven't played with sand, water, etc., made dough, pastry or helped mum cooking — all the things that my grand-daughter does'. The teachers also feel that television played too great a role in the children's lives. The Head feels that many parents do not want to be bothered with their children after school and so one reaction is that 'they are told to sit quietly and watch TV'. The teachers also felt that parents 'threatened' their children with school before they come. 'You wait till you go to school you have to do as you're told' (Teacher B).

These views of what teachers see the children as lacking when they come to school, appeared to greatly influence their views about the children's homes as well. This, despite the fact that most of the teachers seldom visited (and some had *never* visited) the children's homes. Moreover, they constantly emphasised their feeling of social distance from the environment. 'I would *hate* to have young children and live here' (Teacher C). 'I wouldn't live here, not in a million years' (Teacher D). Teacher B felt that the home life of the children was 'not a very nice one; TV and rough play. Unsupervised'. Others felt that there were no 'shared family activities' or 'pretty dull outside of school'. Teacher B felt that the homes were pretty basic: 'No luxuries, no something special to interest them, very few books'. At other times, the teachers stated that the children had too many toys. The Head in particular emphasised this point on several occasions and further-more, was concerned that the children did not know how to *play* with the toys:

> 'The parents say: 'He's got plenty of toys at home, why does he need toys at school?. To which I usually say: 'What does he do with them at home, does he play with them?'. 'He doesn't seem to': 'that's why we have toys in school. It's to teach them how to play''.

These views reflect the teachers' own class values about the value and form that family life should take. The briefest historical perspective would indicate that this view of the family and the vital importance of the child at the centre of the family is largely a 'new' middle-class phenomenon. The wealthy have continued to pay other people to look after their children whether in the form of nannies or private schools. The poor working-class have been too concerned with earning a living, as are many of these parents, to have, or to want to have, so much time for their children. Often this has meant that these latter children are 'left to their own devices', resulting in independent, capable, often precocious children. The teachers, in particular the Head, felt that children should be encouraged to be as independent as possible before coming to school. That they did not appear to acknowledge these characteristics among the working-class poor, suggests that their definition of 'independent' was class-culturally bound. For example, the Head describes what he regards as 'being encouraged to take on independence': 'As many opportunities being made of making decisions for themselves. Something quite small about what colour sock they are going to wear that day ...'. Whereas, on other occasions, he talks about the children who were allocated to the Nurture Group, as requiring a highly directive approach 'because by and large we feel they are the children who are not yet at the stage where they can cope with the amount of choice and the amount of autonomy which is expected from the rest of the school'. It could be argued that these children were perhaps regarded as having 'behavioural problems' because they exercised *too much* choice and autonomy, or a different manifestation of choice. In doing so, they challenged the boundaries of choice and autonomy that are implicit in any formal situation.

Another notable omission in the teachers' descriptions of the childrens' home background was the cultural differences that one might expect to find. It could perhaps be assumed that those teachers who had visited some childrens' homes, had only visited the homes of the respectable working-class, with whom they appeared to have most affinity. Teacher A, who appeared to have made the contact with more parents than most, admitted that 'It's very frightening to go to somebody's house and say 'I'm here to talk about your child'''. Some confirmation of the social/cultural ignorance could be the teachers' insistence of the lack of books, etc., in the homes. The prerequisites for what the Head calls 'introduction to literacy' i.e. 'being familiar with books and enjoying stories and that being very much built into the home life and enjoyable time with one or both parents'. The Head denied that there was any evidence that those 'educational' material goods were becoming more evident in working-class homes. However, the researcher in the process of participant observation in the school, was informed voluntarily by several children that they had many books at home that the school was using as part of an integrated reading scheme. In the ensuing conversations between children, and the children and the researcher, it was evident that many children — particularly of Caribbean and African heritage — were being given considerable help at home with reading and writing. Considering the dearth of bookshops in the area, the parents must have made considerable effort to purchase 'educational' books and equipment. Joan Moon (1979) also provides evidence of books and traditional story telling in the homes of what were regarded as 'poor West Indian' homes. The researcher's own experience would also endorse this. The problem here, and to a lesser extent with the white working-class children, is the teachers' ignorance of the 'poorer children's' home backgrounds which increases the class distance and prevents them from seeing as positive, factors in the home environment and experiences. The problem is further exacerbated by racial issues. For, as Jean Moon's study unwittingly demonstrates, black children tend to be regarded as of one class — an 'underclass'. This is re-affirmed by their presence on what are regarded as 'rough' working class estates. However, as her study revealed, and even a passing acquaintance with the black community would also reveal, there are similar class differences within and between different elements of the black community as there are in the white community. Thus, one consequence of her study, of which she appeared unaware, was to show that high achieving 'Afro-Caribbean' children came from very respectable working-class or lower middle-class homes, where they were given much support and help in their schooling. To ignore these differences is to ignore the actuality of racism in society, which relegates all black people to the conditions of an 'underclass'.

Considerable evidence has been provided to demonstrate that teachers continuously make implicit class distinctions in their perception of, and response to, the parents and children, and that much of the teachers' ideology is based on implicit class assumptions. This point has been pursued at some length, since it is considered to be a crucial and pervasive element in teacher ideology and in the reproduction of the formal educational system in this society. These internal contradictions in the teachers' ideologies could be described as 'limited consciousness' or 'partial truth'. To the extent that the teachers take this *partial* explanation to be the *total* explanation, or this partial perspective to be the *whole* situation, then it might be argued that their perspective approximates to false consciousness. The majority of the teachers claim that the environment — in particular the housing

— is the most significant factor in explaining the failure or 'lack of success' of their children in the educational system. Yet they fail to associate these factors with the structural conditions in society that produce them and help perpetuate an hierarchical order. Many of the teachers indicated that they had never considered seriously the apparent failure or underachievement of working-class or black children in the educational system. Teacher C's reasoning exemplifies this:

> *I:* 'Do you think that working class or black children generally fail or underachieve in the educational system?'.
>
> *Teacher C:* '(i) I don't think that's true; (ii) I suppose it depends where they live - that has a lot to do with it. Perhaps that's true of a place like Southdown; (iii) a lot of their failure is due to home circumstances; if there's failure in the home, then perhaps they do fail in our system; (iv) I don't really think about it — they're children, so I probably don't associate them with being black or working-class; (v) they're just children and the area's quite rough!'.

This reasoning was typical of the teachers: firstly, they deny the importance of heredity. Secondly, they then see the cause of variations in educational achievement as due to environmental features. Thirdly, having denied the existence of wider structural features and heredity, they must inevitably find the answer in 'individualism'.

This 'limited consciousness' would appear to be fuelled further by three other aspects of teacher ideology: (i) the autonomy of education, (ii) the status of infant teachers, and (iii) teacher professionalism. The teachers believed, and relative to other stages in the educational system had good reason to believe, that education was a relatively autonomous institution in society. Some thought it was autonomous at all stages; others (the Head and Teacher D), were conscious of the constraints of the examination system on secondary education. Only Teacher A was more cynical, implying that it was only because the infant stage was less powerful that it enjoyed a measure of autonomy: 'Infants isn't regarded as important, so it's left'. The teachers were unanimous as regards the low status of infant teachers. They described their status variously as 'the lowest of the low'; 'a bit more than child-minders'; 'the underdog'. Teacher B felt that they used to have a higher status but could not provide an explanation. The teachers on the whole, were not aware that the Government or the DES brought any pressure to bear on them. Their concern was limited to the LEA and the parents.

It was evident that *all* the teachers experienced conflict with the parents over the education of their children. These findings are very similar to those of Sharp and Green (1975) as regards the progressive pedagogy, but the general conflict would appear to be more a function of the infant teachers' status. For example, Teacher B remarks that even if parents want to help the teachers, 'they should come in and ask *what* they can do to help, not blindly go on making their kids read (as some of them do), pages and pages at night because they think they're not learning to read properly'. J. and E. Newson (1977) also found considerable evidence of help with reading from parents of all classes as did Sharp and Green. The conflict with the parents over *general* aspects of infant education (i.e., not over the specific progressive method of teaching) was further explicated by Teacher C:

> 'Most parents see the value in and want education. They always want better for their children than they had themselves; they want them to achieve more. Even here the general parents' view of education is not the same as teachers. They tend to think that as long as they're sitting down quietly learning their ABC and how to count up to twenty, their two times table, that they're doing sums. They don't see the value of play and what you can get from that. It's the same with reading books. When children are starting they need every clue (pictures, etc.) to get the words but parents don't realise that and cover up the pictures. There are constant examples'.

Bernstein (1975) in discussing the 'invisible' pedagogy covers these points and argues also that: 'The infant school teacher will not necessarily have high status, as the compentences she is transmitting are, in principle, possible also for the mother'. He goes on to argue that the consequence of a different 'theory of transmission and a new technology' entails that the power relationships have changed between home and school. 'Indeed whichever way the working class mother turns the teacher has the power' (Bernstein 1975 pp. 138–139). The teachers *imply* this apparent status conflict, whilst the Head states explicitly:

> 'Yet probably most people have the sort of feeling that they could teach better than the teacher if they were given the chance'.

This low status is compounded by the fact that infant teachers are almost 100% women and are seen therefore to be perpetuating their role as wives and mothers; a status or class position they hold in common with the mothers of the children. However, as Weber claims: 'class distinctions are linked in the most varied ways with status distinctions'. (Worseley 1970 p. 395). It would be argued then, contrary to King (1978) and Hartley (1985) that the status distinctions of the teachers do not cut across the class distinctions but are part of the teachers' consciousness in their claim for professional status. It could be argued that it is precisely because infant teachers are not so far removed from the class position of their 'clients' that they have emphasised their professional status in terms of the division between mental and manual labour, and their distance from the parents, etc. As Finn, Grant and Johnson (1977) argue: '. . . teaching has been ideologically constructed to emphasise differences from the working class' (p. 167). All the teachers asserted that professionalism was important, although, again, to varying degrees. Teacher

D is being the most sceptical, since she regarded that the teachers' response to the 'threat' of accountability, etc. meant that: 'They seem to be closing ranks and developing an almost war-like stance against everything else'. Teacher A saw professionalism as 'a safety guard ... we're fed up with being the underdogs — particularly infant teachers'. However, it is Teacher C and the Head, who really reinforce Finn *et al.*'s statement: 'I would say that we have to have a 'calling'; a special commitment that you wouldn't (I assume) if you were a dustman' (Teacher C).

'People who teach and survive have *got* to be doing it because they are the type of people whose particular satisfaction is in teaching. Teachers themselves have got, at some stage, to do something about behaving like a profession' (Head). These statements demonstrate historical continuities with the 'missionary ideology' of the 19th century, and the role of education in society and vis-à-vis parents' perspectives.

In summary then, it would be claimed that the teachers are falsely conscious as regards the concept of class and moreover that their class interests are pursued under cover of the ideology of professionalism. This last point is expressed lucidly by Finn *et al.*:

'The ideology of professionalism has been used by the teaching organisations to either defend their middle class status, or to assimilate themselves into that class. Trapped between the developing power of monopoly capital and the advance of the working class, professionalism can be understood as a petit-bourgeois strategy for advancing and defending a relatively privileged position'. (Finn, Grant, Johnson, 1977, p. 167).

Some Concluding Comments

The evidence of this research forces one to conclude as Sharp and Green (1975) did, that: 'The processes we have observed in the classroom ... can be seen as the initial stages of the institutionalisation of social selection for the stratification system' (p. 221). The role of teacher ideology in promoting hegemony is also apparent. Gramsci regards hegemony as involving the successful mobilisation and reproduction of the 'active consent' of dominating groups by the ruling class through the exercise of intellectual, moral and political leadership (Gramsci, 1978). Thus, as Grace (1978) suggests, despite many changes in the surface structure of education (pedagogy, curriculum, building design, etc.) the deep structure is characterised by continuities with those existing in the 19th century. By this means the particular form of schooling that was developed has been to serve as a non-coercive ideological apparatus of social control. So whilst the *content* of education may have been challenged, the *control* of the education by the ideological apparatus of the state has not been significantly challenged.

There must, however, be a constant problem of legitimating that authority at the classroom level at least. It is at this juncture that concepts of conflict and resistance can be most influential. Moreover, ideological forms such as schooling develop and maintain a relative autonomy in relation to the 'economic' and the 'state' spheres. This too exposes conflict and resistance. To relate these statements to present-day schooling, it is apparent that many contradictions exist within the infant-school system: contradiction between the developmental and instructional function; and the custodial, moral and preparatory traditions in the development of infant schooling; contradictions between family and community and the occupational system; contradictions between theory and practice; contradictions between the needs of the 'providers' and the needs of the 'provided'. These are manifest at the level of classroom practice in such dilemmas as the teaching of 'basic skills' versus developing individual growth and development. Increasingly, however, classrooms are faced with a crisis of 'management' where the urban working-class — particularly some black working-class pupils — are perceived as disrupting the smooth-functioning of the school system. Previously, these children have been syphoned off into various categories of 'special' schools where they are systematically disenfranchised. However, with policy decisions post-Warnock, implementing an integrated policy, how will the schools cope with the ensuing affront to their subtle forms of coercion? Does this mean that schools will be forced to play an increasingly explicit role in overt coercion? However, given the relatively autonomous ideological role that schools have assumed and that teachers have assimilated, will there not be considerable resistance from the teaching profession *per se*?

The needs of the providers and the needs of the provided appear to be coming into sharper relief especially in the inner-city where urban 'uprisings' are threatening traditional forms of legitimation in the society: school is one of the sites of this struggle. Teachers' responses to this conflict are being increasingly curtailed by the centralisation of the education system to better suit the needs of the 'providers'. Thus the relative autonomy of the ideology of schooling is also under attack. The control of the education system itself which has become increasingly centralised during the late 1970s and 1980s is undoubtedly facing some resistance from the teachers as evidenced by the on-going dispute over pay, conditions, and structure of the profession and appraisal. Whilst the motivating force for the teachers may be to protect their professional status, it is apparent that the ensuing conflict is enabling a potentially more political consciousness to develop. In particular, the way in which the present government is using the language of the factory in this dispute and is clearly demanding 'increased productivity' is in itself pushing teachers closer to the experience and status of the majority of their 'clients', i.e., white and black working-class. However, at the same time the teachers are being expected to take on increasing 'professional' duties. In the past 7 years teachers have been under increased pressure to be more accountable; to involve parents and the community in the schooling process (but which parents and which community? — The inner city is not an homogenous unit like surburbia may well be); to put greater emphasis on the 'core curriculum'; to attain higher standards in basic skills. The Secretary of State, Kenneth Baker, has just announced his intention to set up a new committee to look into language in schools because he has evidence of pupils' failure in reading (see *Teacher*, 21.11.1986). In addition, there are many other curriculum and policy innovations: science and maths teaching to be developed; developmental writing and reading approaches; introduction of computers; health education; equal opportunities initiatives; integration of special needs. Thus expectations of teachers have risen enormously — but since many of these innovations and initiatives emanate from different sources such as the LEA, DES, parents, ministerial dictate, they impose conflicting demands upon the teacher. All this in an economic climate where until recently, schools have been closed and staff redeployed. Promotion in primary schools has become a rarity; resources and equipment are increasingly scarce and buildings need repair and renovation. The following statement by a teacher perhaps reflects the present 'mood' amongst teachers:

> 'The general climate of ill-informed criticism, the proliferation of 'experts' and 'reports', the feeling of insecurity and the technique of commercial-style evaluation which is being adopted has produced a widespread despondency among the most valuable and experienced teachers, who normally would remain buoyant in difficult times'. (NUT, 1982, p. 40).

Primary school teachers in the inner-city are now faced with severe shortages of teachers particularly in nursery and infant classes. Given that the inner-city acts as a litmus paper for the national scene it can be expected that this shortage will spread in future years. It is an apt comment on the perceived status of primary school teachers and the perceived role of education in society that much is made in both Government and media about the shortage of science, maths and CDT teachers; whereas some *classes* of infant-age children in the inner-city have no teacher at all. Furthermore, the Coventry agreement perpetuates the inequality within the education system by not challenging the absurd weighting of points accorded to different age children in schools and thereby excluding a great many primary schools from being able to have principal teacher posts.

It is apparent then the ways in which the dominant groups within the economy have affected and are continuing to affect the organisation and curricula of schools in sustaining and reproducing the social relations of work. It is also apparent that schooling conditions and constrains the expectations and practices of both teachers and pupils but it is possible to see that there are contradictions, resistance, mismatch and therefore potential conflict and change in this attempt at cultural and social reproduction through the schooling system. As Bash *et al.*,

(1985) state 'What is apparent, especially in urban schools where the gap between the dominant ideology and the experience of pupils is frequently at its widest, is that the precise opposite (i.e. to cultural reproduction) has often been the result'. (Bash, Coulby and Jones, 1985, p. 63).

There are of course ways in which teachers can attempt to ameliorate the most inegalitarian aspects of education. Pederson (1986) gives details of research into the practice of two teachers in inner-city, multi-racial schools in a large North American city. He concluded that: 'What teachers believe and do in the classroom has enormous potential for influencing the quality of life of their students' (Gundara *et al.*, 1986, p. 74–75).

However, many good intentions are likely to be distorted, as with the 'progressive' teachers in the present study, unless the structural location of schooling is clearly analysed and understood. Ignoring or being unaware of such a structural and therefore political context will render most well-intentioned practice as ineffective and tokenistic as is the majority of 'multi-cultural' practice that occurs in classrooms. Sharp and Green express this lucidly:

> 'Unless or until educators are able to comprehend their own structural location and develop theories of the limits of feasible political action to transform that location, they will continue to be unwilling victims of a structure that undermines the moral concerns they profess . . .'(Sharp and Green 1975, p. 227).

Race, class and gender inequalities are *structural* inequalities as well as having personal manifestations. The 'individualistic' ethos that is both the experience and the underlying philosophy of the majority of teachers must be replaced by collectivism, collaboration, communality and political action. As Madan Sarup (1986) states: 'As schools can contribute to social change only to a limited extent, teachers should intensify the struggle on a large number of sites. They should be developers of 'critical consciousness' amongst their communities. We have to convince the black community that to subordinate the class struggle to the race struggle leads to barren cultural separatism, while at the same time convincing the Left that it is wrong to subordinate the race struggle to the class struggle' (Sarup, 1986, p. 122).

If Gramsci's point is taken that state power rests upon force but which is rarely used overtly, it is possible to see the interdependence of both the forces of coercion and consent. It has been stated that education has been one of the major means of legitimating this consent through promotion of the hegemonic order. There is, however, evidence to suggest, viz. the feverish activities of the Government in its attempts through centralisation to ensure greater control of education, that there is a crisis of the hegemonic order. It could also be postulated that the media has become another pervasive means of control by consent and that it too is under attack (viz. Tebbit's recent paper on BBC coverage of the bombing of

Libya). A hegemonic crisis requires a shift towards coercion. This is evidenced by the increase in police powers and police methods and responses to uprisings which are particularly well exposed in Lord Gifford's report (1986). Since this then provokes a problem of popular consent, a new consent has to be engineered. If, as it seems likely, a hegemonic crisis is apparent or imminent, it is crucial that teachers understand their class location and political location within the social structure and prohibit as far as possible the further use of education as a tool for the covert legitimation of invidious and inegalitarian social practice. Social change has to take place on both the structural and personal plane. As Gramsci states:

'It was right to struggle against the old school, but reforming it was not as simple as it seemed. The problem was not one of model curricula but of men (sic) and not just of men (sic) who are actually teachers themselves but of the entire social complex which they express'. (quoted in Ogden 1974).

References

ALEXANDER, R. (1984) *Primary Teaching*, Holt Education.

BASH, L., COULBY, D. & JONES, C. (1985) *Urban Schooling. Theory and Practice*. Holt Education.

BELL, A. and SIGSWORTH, A. (1987) *The Small Rural Primary School: A Matter of Quality*, Falmer Press.

BENNETT, N., DESFORGES, C., COCKBURN, A. and WILKINSON, B. (1984) *The Quality of Pupil Learning Experiences*, Lawrence Erlbaum.

BERNSTEIN, B. and HENDERSON, D. (1969) 'Social Class Differences in the relevance of language to socialisation', in *Sociology*, Vol. 3 No. 1 pp. 11–20.

BERNSTEIN, B. (1975) *Class, Codes and Control Vol. III Towards a Theory of Educational Transmissions*, 2nd edition RKP.

BOUDON, R. (1974) *Education, Opportunity and Social Inequality*, Wiley.

BRICE HEATH, S. (1983) 'What no bedtime story means: Narrative skills at home and school', in *Language Society* 11, pp. 49–76.

CORRIGAN, P. (1979) *Schooling the Smash Street Kids*, Macmillan.

DALE, R. (1977) *The Structural Context of Teaching* Course E202 Unit 5 Block 1. Open University Press.

FINN, D., GRANT, N. and JOHNSON, R. (1977) 'Social democracy; Education and the Crisis, in Centre for Contemporary Cultural Studies *On Ideology* Hutchinson.

FUCHS, E. (1973) 'How Teachers Learn to Help Children Fail' in Keddie, N. (Ed.) *Tinker, Tailor ... The Myth of Cultural Deprivation*, Penguin.

GALTON, M., SIMON, B and CROLL, P. (1980a) *Inside The Primary Classroom*, RKP.

GALTON, M., and SIMON, B. (1980b) *Progress and Performance in the Primary Classroom*, RKP.

GALTON, M. and WILLCOCKS, J. (Ed.) (1983) *Moving From the Primary Classroom*, RKP.

LORD GIFFORD (1986) *The Broadwater Farm Inquiry*, Karia Press.

GRAMSCI, A. (1978) *Selections from The Prison Notebooks* (edited by Hoare, Q. and Noel-Smith, G.) Lawrence & Wishart.

GRACE, G. (1978) *Teachers, Ideology and Control: A Study in Urban Education*, RKP.

GUNDARA, J., JONES, C and KIMBERLEY, K. (1986) *Racism, Diversity and Education*, Hodder & Stoughton.

HALSEY, A. H. HEATH, A. F. and RIDGE, J. M. (1980) *Origins and Destinations*, Oxford Univ. Press.

HARTLEY, D. (1985) *Understanding the Primary School*, Croom Helm.

HOLLAND, J. (1981) 'Social Class and Changes in Orientation to Meaning' in *Sociology*, Vol. 15 No. 1.

ILEA (1983) *Race, Sex and Class* 1–6 ILEA.

JOHNSON, R. (1976) 'Notes on the Schooling of the English Working Class', in Dale, R. (Ed.) *School and Capitalism*, Routledge & Kegan Paul.

KING, R. (1978) *All Things Bright and Beautiful?* Wiley.

KIRBY, N. (1981) *Personal Values in Education*, Harper & Row.

LEE, J. (1980) *Teacher Ideology and the Realisation of Pedagogy: A study in a Progressive Inner-City Infant School*, MA dissertation King's College, London.

LOWE, R. (Ed.) (1987) *The Changing Primary School*, Falmer Press.

MARRIOTT, S. (1985) *Primary Education and Society*, Falmer Press.

MARSDEN, W. E. (1977) 'Social environment: school attendance and educational achievement in a Merseyside town 1870–1900', in McCann, P. (Ed.) *Popular Education and Socialisation in the 19th Century*, Methuen and Co. Ltd.

MOON, J. (1979) *A Study of the variables that might contribute to the success or failure of West Indian children in the English School system*. MA dissertation, Kings College London.

NEWSON, J and E. (1977) *Perspectives on School at Seven Years Old*, Allen & Unwin.

NUT (1982) *Schools Speak Out*. The effects of expenditure cuts on primary education. NUT.

OGDEN, G. (1974) 'Changing Reality', *Radical Education* No. 1.

PEDERSEN, E. (1986) 'Socialisation in Schools in Multicultural Societies' in Gundara, J. *et al* (Eds.) *Racism, Diversity and Education*, Hodder & Stoughton.

POLLARD, A. (1985) *The Social World of the Primary School*, Holt Education.

RAMPTON: (1981) *West Indian Children in Our Schools* (The Rampton Report) London: HMSO.

RICHARDS, C. (Ed.) (1982) *New Directions in Primary Education*, Falmer Press.

RICHARDS, C. (Ed.) (1984) *The Study of Primary Education: A Source Book*. Vol. 1 Falmer Press.

RICHARDS C. (Ed.) (1985a) *The Study of Primary Education: A Source Book*. Vol. 2 Falmer Press.

RICHARDS, C. (1985b) *The Study of Primary Education: A Source Book*. Vol. 3 Falmer Press.

SARUP, M. (1986) *The Politics of Multiracial Education*, RKP.

SHARP, R. and GREEN, A. (1975) *Education and social Control. A Study in Progressive Primary Education*, RKP.

SILVER, H. (1974) *The Education of the Poor. The History of a National School 1824–1974*, RKP.
SWANN: (1985) *Education For All* (The Swann Report) London: HMSO.
WILLIS, P. (1977) *Learning to Labour. How Working Class Kids Get Working Class Jobs*, Saxon House.
WOODS, P. (Ed.) (1980) *Teacher Strategies. Explorations in the Sociology of the School*, Croom Helm.
WORSLEY, P. (Ed.) (1970) *Modern Sociology: Introductory Readings*, Penguin.
WRIGHT, C. (1985) The Influence of School Processes on the Educational Opportunities of Children of West Indian Origin, I: Learning Environment or Battleground?; II: Who Succeeds at School — And who Decides?, in *Multicultural Teaching*, Vol. 4 No. 1 Autumn.

6
Prisonhouses

Carolyn Steedman

Those who live in retirement, whose lives have fallen amid the seclusion of schools and other walled-in and guarded dwellings, are liable to be suddenly and for a long while dropped out of the memory of their friends, the denizens of a freer world ... there falls a stilly pause, a wordless silence, a long blank oblivion. Unbroken always is this blank, alike entire and unexplained. The letter, the message once frequent, are cut off, the visit, formerly periodical, ceases to occur; the book, paper or other token that indicates remembrance, comes no more.

Always there are excellent reasons for these lapses if the hermit but knew them. Though he is stagnant in his cell, his connections without are whirling in the very vortex of life ... The hermit — if he be a sensible hermit - will swallow his own thoughts, and lock up his own emotions during these weeks of inward winter ... (Charlotte Brontë, *Villette*, 1979: 348)

Great numbers of women have taught for a century and a half now — teaching became a woman's job, both statistically and by reputation, some time before the First World War (Widdowson, 1980; Corr, 1983) — and, rare for work performed by women, they have written about it. They write, but they reveal very little about it as a process of labour, a job of work. Lucy Snowe in *Villette* performs a still-recognizable miracle of classroom control and this is recorded, but not the detail of daily routine that makes up the work for which she says she feels a passion. We know she is good at it: she says so; but we do not see how. Her lover buys her a school, neatly equipped, commodiously arranged; he has advertisements printed for her. It is a recognition of her passion, his declaration that he *sees* the passion, and thereby sees Lucy Snowe. But the schoolroom, the place where this no one will surely became a someone, is the uninscribed conclusion to the novel, not its scene of action.

The narrator of Ruth Adam's *I'm Not Complaining* (1983) turns her back on the grimy blur of Standard II, gazes down from the Board School window at Depression-time Nottinghamshire, thinks her own thoughts: love, gossip, wretchedness; the company of women in the staffroom. Five hundred miles away in a Glasgow Infants' Department Jeanetta Bowie watches her children with a pawky wisdom, the feminized irony of the lad o'pairts. The bairns are the subject of funny stories in the staffroom, and their toothless decaying parents are bit-part players in the Comedy of Life (Bowie, 1978).

Sylvia Ashton Warner (1980) said what she did. Out of the myriad lives lived out in classrooms, minutes, days, weeks, multi-foliate activity, enforced stillness, a universe of human relations, there emerges an image; a Maori child holds in his hand a small piece of card on which his teacher has written 'car'. It is his word; he clutches it; a word in the hand is worth a thousand in the reading primer. It connects with his unconscious, and with infinity. Soon, he learns to read.

I was a teacher. I never wanted to be, and now that I've stopped, I never will be again, but for several years it took my heart. I entered a place of darkness, a long tunnel of days; retreat from the world. I want to explain, to tell what it is I know. Teaching young children must always be, in some way or other, a retreat from general social life and from fully adult relationships, a way of becoming Lucy Snowe's dormouse, rolled up in the prisonhouse, the schoolroom. The woman who teaches (ignore the generic 'he' in Charlotte Brontës description) must know:

> that Destiny designed him to imitate on occasion the dormouse ... make
> a tidy ball of himself, creep into a hole of life's wall, and submit to the
> drift which blows in and blocks him up, preserving him in ice for a season
> ... (1979: 348)

I loved my children and worked hard for them, lay awake at night worrying about them, spent my Sundays making workcards, recording stories for them to listen to, planning the week ahead. My back ached as I pinned their paintings to the wall, wrote the labels with a felt-tip pen, a good round hand, knowing even then the irony with which I would recall in later years the beacon light of the martyr's classroom shining into the winter's evening, the cleaner's broom moving through the corridor of the deserted schoolhouse.

Simone de Beauvoir calls the having of children the swiftest route to a woman's slavery (Schwartzer, 1983: 73–4, 76, 114–5). I know that you do not need to bear children in order to have them. As in most primary school classrooms, they rarely left me. We stayed together in one room most of the day long. Shabby, depressed, disturbed social-priority children learned to read under my care: the efficacy of affection. I admired their stoicism under disaster; I lost my temper with them: they longed for my approval again. I could silence a room with a glance. I was good at jokes, the raised eyebrow, the smile, the delicate commentary on the absurdity of things that is the beginning of irony in eight-year-olds.

We laughed a lot, cried a lot, wept over all the sad stories. An on-going show of human variety: what the old people forget as they rehearse their infant rebellion for the oral historian is that classrooms are places of gossip, places for the observation of infinite change: new shoes, new haircuts, a pair of gold ear-rings for pierced ears; passion, tears, love, despair (Humphries, 1981). No one goes into a classroom in the morning without the faint anticipation of something happening, that something made more eventful by the smallness of the stage, and its remoteness from the real theatre of life.

My days were passed in the most extraordinary watchfulness: the management of time and space. I never interrupted a child, though I struck a few. I took it all, the nightmare insoluble adult conflict, the hard lives, hard times that produced the children's passion washing over me. I didn't sleep properly in seven years. When I left the class of children of whom I had grown the fondest of all, I wrote a poem (all the bad, abandoned poems) in which the children jumped and played in the windy yard, the girls' skirts caught in the frozen triangle of a child's wax-crayoning, hair flying stiff-shaped, the shouting very distant like that of a water-erased dream. It was a poem about affection: all our bondage is bought by the soft pressure of fingers, the child's arms slipped unthinkingly around the adult's waist, the head resting, momentarily, listening to a heart-beat, the darkening November afternoon outside.

Or: there is the other way. She moves from her desk to the window, looks down at the yard, the gates, the streets, the fields beyond; smooths an eyebrow with a finger, corrects the setting of a belt. She thinks of: not being here, of love, a housefull of furniture, of marriage, the meeting of bodies, a new winter coat. The children's murmur rises behind her; she turns to quiet them, and they bow their heads to their books in obedience. It is a crenellated Board School in Deptford in the 1890s, Glasgow in the 1930s, now, anywhere. In an Italian nursery school she is shown sitting at her desk thinking over her own affairs, smoothing her hair: real life, marriage, this time next year — as she gazes out over the heads of the children (Belotti, 1973). At the window she stands, looking out. She is a woman liberated, a woman who has escaped all our fate: she is a woman who is not a mother, a woman who does not care: *a woman who has refused to mother.*

There was no other way to write this: only the ironies of self-dramatization available for narration; and indeed, the story itself could only achieve the status of ironic proposition after I had found a history that allowed me to understand the place where I had stood for so many years. To present a summary of that history now is to perform a deliberate act of disjuncture, to suddenly turn a story into another small piece of historical or literary evidence, to add to examples of earlier ones.

The daily detail of teaching and my experience of it directed all my reading, all my research, furnished my imagination, helped me to see the classrooms of the recent past. But the history I am about to present seems to mask what went into its making. What follows then, is framed by two problems, which are not disconnected from each other. The first is to do with the kind of concealment that the writing of history involves, the way in which, as a narrative form, it does not reveal the pictures the historian sets up in her head to think by:

> This concealment, this silence envelops — the choice of which subjects to treat, which questions to ask, and which not to; the process of reasoning by which the historian arrives at the positions she or he holds; and the structures within the text by means of which the answers are presented to the reader ... The result of this concealment, which makes the historian appear the invisible servant of his materials, is to endow him with a massive authority over the reader (Ashplant, 1981: 107–9. See also Mason, 1978: 14–15).

It is important to at least attempt to write a history that at some point reveals the processes of its production.

The second problem is the history of education which, like much writing about education in general, treats its field of inquiry as separate from general social and political life, and which remains largely institutional in focus (Silver, 1983: 17–24). To write any history of women in classrooms means an encounter with that kind of history, an encounter in which the first priority must be to shift the perspective, see the prisonhouse in the light of history and politics, infinitely connected with the world outside, whose artifact it is.

There have been explanations advanced for the peculiarities of educational history, and for its tendency to present evidence about classrooms and teaching as disconnected from wider historical issues. It has been suggested that this closing of frontiers between education and other disciplines has served to increase its mystique and status for practioners whose intellectual education is different from and, within our class system, bound to be seen as inferior to that of the traditional academic disciplines (Taylor, 1969: 12). The effect of this enclosure on the history of education is quite simple, and quite deadening. Information about pedagogic change, or about changes in the background of recruits to the job are used as facts that do one thing: illuminate the development of an institution. Thus: in the early years of the nineteenth century the majority of teachers of infants were male; as compulsory state education advanced, more and more women were recruited to the ranks of the profession — in the 1870s, the numbers of men and women teaching in elementary schools were roughly equal, and by 1914, in a striking reversal of earlier figures, women made up 70 per cent of the teaching force[1]. So is progress towards the present illuminated.

Yet it has recently become clear that the job changed from being a predominantly masculine one not only because of the obvious economic reckoning of various local authorities faced with recruiting teachers on a large scale, but also because of certain societal shifts in the idea of family government, and the decreasing status of the father as a patriarch (Clarke, 1985. See also Vincent, 1981: 62–75). In the early nineteenth century overt reasons for selecting men as instructors of infants had to do with assumptions about the ordering and disciplining of families, with the practice of judicious tenderness that such domestic practice helped acquaint men with, and that was seen as so vital an experience for the successful management of large numbers of small children (McCann and Young, 1982: 175). Towards the end of century women could be seen to occupy this position of authoritative watchfulness.

A sociological perspective like this, however cursorily it employs historical evidence, immediately makes the educational outline more interesting. But there are perhaps even more radical and interesting things to be done with the outline. The last ten years has seen the development of wide-ranging work on the subject of mothering. Psychoanalysis has been wedded to sociology to produce an account of how the need and desire to mother is reproduced in little girls (Chodorow, 1978: 199–201); serious attempts have been made to outline the particular thought processes that result from mothering small children (Ruddick, 1980: 341–67; Rich, 1979), and several accounts, by using content analyses of books and magazines of advice to mothers have pointed out how very recent a historical development our ordinary, everyday, common-sense understanding of mothering actually is (Helterline, 1980: 590–615).

The features of this everyday understanding are a belief in the efficacy and importance of attention to the child and a responsiveness to her needs; a belief in the practice of child-care as the responsibility of natural mothers; and a belief in the psychological effectiveness of love. The central and overriding feature is a conviction about the importance of a significant other, that is, the consistent presence of a reliable and loved adult (ibid: 611–612). Particularly important and pervasive is this last; it has crossed class barriers, and Ann Oakley found many working-class mothers in the early 1970s defining themselves as good by virtue of their constant presence in their children's lives (1974: 177).

Yet this ideal of constant attention to children, is a very recent historical development, its origins probably no older than the period immediately before and after the Second World War. The 'good' nineteenth-century mother was a guide and exemplar to her children, but in order to be good, only her intermittent presence was required. Child-care manuals, women's magazines and the like did not emphasize the effects of mother-child separation until the 1940s, and it seems that the pervasive beliefs about mothering that are being questioned today are no more than forty years old (Helterline, 1980).

The arena for this development of ideas about mothering is the middle-class home (and indeed, most modern investigations of mothering and the reproduction of mothering are restricted to the same milieu). And yet the children of those nineteenth-century mothers who, in Marilyn Helterline's description in 'The

Emergence of Modern Motherhood', acted as distant moral exemplars to their children, who saw them once a day for half-an-hour before dinner, who enjoyed the occasional romp with them in the garden, were looked after by other women, who washed them and fed them, and in whose company they passed the night. Up on the nursery floor the quality of attentive watchfulness was developed, and the fourteen-year-old nursemaid could truly say that she never left the children — because it was in the terms of her employment to be with them in this way. It may be that the lineaments of modern good mothering were developed by women who were not the natural mothers of children in their care, and because they were paid to do so. In this light, it is illuminating to look at the schoolroom as an arena for this kind of development, as a place where attention, empathy, watchfulness and enforced companionship were the dimensions of a job of work and became the natural-seeming components of the relationship. The classroom may be one of the places where the proper relationship between mothers and children has been culturally established.

This kind of relationship obviously existed long before it became a matter of recommendation in the magazines and manuals of the 1940s and 1950s, and it is for this reason that the infant and elementary school classroom (now the primary classroom) is of such importance, and why the secondary school and the relationships constructed within its classrooms remain outside the scope of the argument. In secondary schools children receive an education that is subject-based, and they encounter several teachers in the course of a day. Though *Villette* begins this article, it is a novel about what is essentially a secondary school, and the relationship between Lucy Snowe and her pupils cannot be used as evidence.

The essential feature of the primary school is that one woman (sometimes a man) stays in the same room all day long with the same group of children. They will leave her occasionally, perhaps for a music lesson or to go swimming, but essentially their teacher is responsible for them throughout the school day, and generally she works alone. The outline of an educational history that can be called the feminization of a trade, can be turned right round, and we can see that in classrooms, as in the middle-class nurseries of the nineteenth century, the understood and prescribed psychological dimensions of modern good mothering have been forged — and forged by waged women, by working women — by nurses, nannies and primary school teachers.

The emotional dimensions of the relationship that 'good mothering' implies — attention, identification, empathy with the child — have been encouraged as a pedagogic device since the early nineteenth century, particularly within the school of thought that has developed out of the work and writing of the German educationalist and philosopher of the kindergarten movement, Friedrich Froebel (1782–1852). Good mothers did naturally, observed Froebel in the 1840s, what the governess, the good nurse, the good teacher, must extrapolate from her practice, must make overt and use. She must:

waken and develop in the Human Being every power, every disposition
... Without any Teaching, Reminding or Learning, the true mother
does this of herself. But this is not enough : in Addition is needed that
being Conscious, and acting upon a Creature that is growing Conscious,
she do her part Consciously and Consistently, as in Duty bound to
guide the Human Being in its regular development (Hertford, 1899:
34–5).

Frobel's mother-made-conscious had a predecessor, in the work of Johann
Pestalozzi, the Swiss philosopher and pioneer of education for the poor, whose
Lienhard and Gertrude published in 1781 used the fictional Gertrude's upbring-
ing of her children to outline a pedagogy[2]. Both Pestalozzi and Froebel used
naturalistic observation of mothers interacting with their children to delineate
maternal practice as the foundation for a new educational order. Froebel knew
Pestalozzi's work, had spent time at his experimental school at Yverdun, and used
the older man's insight that 'mothers are educators of their children and that we
can learn from their methods' (Martin, 1982: 135).

It was peasant mothers, observed in 'the cottages of the lower classes' interacting with babies and young children, whose behaviour was used to establish 'the
tendencies of the maternal and infantile instincts' as the basis for a pedagogy (von
Marenholz-Buelow, 1855: 6–7). The feature of developments within this
pedagogy, developments made by Froebel himself during his lifetime, and in the
much later transmission of his ideas within teacher training in this country, was
its application to older children (Lawrence, 1952). The psychological principle
involved was the idea of growth as a natural unfolding, a kind of emotional logic
of development; and what was asked from the mother, the nurse, and the teacher
was empathy, a felt identification with the child. The romantic movement, and
its particular manifestation in mid-nineteenth-century Britain in the figure of the
sentimental, Wordsworthian child, and the cult of this child in literature, as well
as in the publicity machine of the Frobelian movement, all ensured a substantial
middle-class audience for Froebel's philosophy of education. In family magazines,
books of advice to mothers and in late nineteenth-century translations of his work
for the educational market, his ideas were immensely influential in the establishment of a British school of child-centred education (Coveney, 1957; Whitbread,
1972: 34). The late nineteenth century also saw the application of Froebel's ideas
to working-class children in schools, both through the establishment of private,
charitable kindergartens in the inner-city in the 1860s and 1870s, and through the
adoption of 'kindergarten' as part of the official school timetable, endorsed by the
Board of Education from the 1890s onwards (Lawrence, 1952: 34–94). Child-
centredness, which is the educational philosophy endorsed by the Board of Education and the Department of Education and Science since the First World War, and
which is the dominant view of childhood and learning presented to teachers in

initial and in-service training, has been nourished by these Froebelian roots (Walkerdine, 1983; Galton *et al.*, 29–58).

The literature that this article started by very briefly surveying — the autobiographical writing that has generally been ignored as educational evidence — indicates how very hard it has been for some women to make the prescribed act of identification and empathy with working-class children, children so very unlike themselves and those children they might possibly have one day for themselves. The children of the poor have always looked wrong to the investigative eye: tired, dirty, old before their time, their faces showing only an absence of childhood (Walvin, 1982: 15). What nineteenth-century investigators saw is seen still in classrooms occupied by working-class children, their teachers saddened and distanced by the difference between how those children actually are and what the text books and their own children at home tell children are really like. 'There was a gap or discrepancy between the "ought" and the "is", reported Ronald King from a Social Priority Infants' School in the late 1970s. 'The children were not as children should be. In the teachers' terms, they had few "ordinary" or 'normal" children . . .' (1978: 110–26, 102). It is hard to make an act of identification with a person who is so very different from the way you are yourself (Steedman, 1985).

This fragmentary evidence suggests that one of the most interesting aspects of the history of classroom life may be this overt and bored resistance displayed towards a set of ideas — an official pedagogy — a resistance displayed by women who have refused to take on the structures of maternal thinking in the classroom. Ruth Adams has her heroine brusquely dismiss notions of child-centredness in *I'm Not Complaining*:

> 'Don't you think that children ought to have to go to school?' asked Enid.
> 'I think that school ought to be such a happy place that they don't need any Attendance Officer to dragoon them into going'.
> 'It's evident that you've never been a teacher,' I remarked. I had talked that sort of stuff myself at college, but I thought he ought to have got over it at his age (Adam, 1983: 129).

Two factors need to be highlighted in the continued transmission of and developments within the idea of teaching as a kind of mothering. Administrative changes and the development of a system of secondary education in the years before the Second World War began to make the elementary/primary school classroom a more enclosed and separate place. For increasing numbers of children it became a stage on the route to further schooling, not a system that fed them directly into the labour market. This growing separation between primary and secondary education was formalized in the Education Act of 1944, and the 1940s and 1950s saw wide publicity given to new ideas of motherhood that in some cases drew analogies between the attention and empathy that both mothers and teachers in schools could provide for children (Davis and Wallbridge, 1983: 96–142; Winnicott, 1964: 179–239). The best known popularizer of such ideas for an educational market was Donald Winnicott, and we need quite badly to know how soon his work was made prescribed reading in the psychological training of teachers. But whatever the point of maximum transmission turns out to be, what is certain is that Winnicott's outline of the good-enough mother and the good teacher fitted into a pre-existing format, that had been developed within teacher education for at least a century past.

I didn't know this history when I entered that enclosed place, the primary classroom. I didn't know about a set of pedagogic expectations that covertly and mildly — and *never* using this vocabulary — hoped that I might become a mother. And yet I became one, not knowing exactly what it was that was happening until it was too late, until I was caught, by the pressure of fingers, looks and glances. In the story I tell now *Villette* provides a romantic substructure: my narrative is about another place, almost another country, where I hide myself from view, like Lucy Snowe was unseen, roll myself into the dormouse ball, yet expend vast passion in the classroom. (The streets outside shine with rain; I am alone; I almost don't understand what they speak, like a blur of voices in the streets of Villette.) The romantic vision is allowed to women who teach (Steedman, 1982: 7). Yet *Villette* itself is the romantic transmutation of Charlotte Brontë's loathing for the work of the prisonhouse, expressed fifteen years before the novel was completed, in the school at Roe Head:

> I had been toiling for nearly an hour with Miss Lister, Miss Marriott and Ellen Cook to teach them a distinction between an article and a substantive. The passing lesson was completed, a dead silence had succeeded it in the school-room and I sat sinking from irritation and weariness into a kind of lethargy. The thought came over me am I to spend all the best part of my life in this wretched bondage forcibly suppressing my rage at the idleness apathy and the hyberbolical and most assinine stupidity of those fat-headed oafs and on compulsion assuming an air of kindness patience and assiduity? Must I from day to day sit chained to this chair prisoned within these four bare walls, whilst these glorious summer suns are burning in heaven and the year is revolving in its richest glow, and declaring at the close of each summer's day, the time I am losing, will never come again? Stung to the heart with this reflection I started up and mechanically walked to the window ... an uncertain sound of sweetness came on a dying gale from the south, I looked in that direction — Huddersfield and the hills beyond all bathed in blue mist, the woods of Hopton and Heaton Lodge were clouding the water-edge and the Calder

silent but bright was shooting among them like a silver arrow . . . I shut the window and went back to my seat . . . just then a Dolt came up with a lesson. I thought I should have vomited (Quoted in Gerin, 1967: 103–4).

My recovery of a history, in which disgust and disdain are the hidden counter-point to identification, empathy and love, and my writing of that history were part of my long process of detachment from teaching, a way of leaving, of getting out. In fact, quite a different historical narrative carried me to the primary classroom. Like this: in the town of *X*, in the year of 197–, a child was killed, a slow death at the hands of a parent. I, through the exigencies of life, found myself in that city looking for work, and humble work at that, I thought, because I had recently become, in my own eyes, a spectacular failure, having had a thesis rejected by an ancient university, and what I had understood to be a future dissolved before my eyes. In the early 1970s it was as easy to get a job teaching if you had a degree as it was to find work filling the shelves of supermarkets, and I walked into the Education Offices, and went out on supply.

In the city a committee of inquiry investigated the circumstances of the child's death. I went and sat in the gallery on the days when schools didn't need me. One morning — fate led me, I had been meant to arrive at this place — I was sent to the school where the child had been in intermittent attendance at the time of death. From the high building, the crumbling, stained houses ran in lines over the horizon. I came home in this place of poverty. I had been an historian of the nineteenth century, had never really spoken, I think, to a child under ten. Swift vision, sudden new perspective, the denizens of ragged schools sat there in this twentieth-century classroom, tired workers educated by their union, Keir Hardie scratching his letters on a slate deep in the mine, the little watercress girl intently telling her story to Henry Mayhew (Steedman, 1982: 110–31, 38–39). I fell in love; they were my children; I couldn't ever leave them.

I don't care any more about sounding pretentious, so now I tell people who ask at parties why I did it for such a very long time, that it did seem a way of being a socialist in everyday life. I believed immensely in their intelligence, thought I could give them peace and quiet, a space of rest from the impossible lives that many of them had to lead. I read everything there was to read, later was to make myself a minor expert on children's writing. No one cared — indeed, no one knew — what social and political theories informed my classroom practice: all I looked like was a very good teacher, doing all the things that the textbooks said were right. I think with great fondness now of my little socialist republic, that intensity of use of time and space, the pleasure of its workings, my clear sighted refusal of all the liberal notions of false democracy that the official pedagogy of child-centredness presented me with. What mattered most was they believed that I knew that they could do it — learn, learn to read, defy the world's definition of them as deprived, pitiful social priority children. And I kept the door shut, and the children quiet.

I didn't know what was happening to me. My body died during those years, the little fingers that caught my hand, the warmth of a child leaning and reading her book to me somehow prevented all the other meeting of bodies. One woman who worked as a teacher noted this: the body's death, frantic burgeoning, then denial, provide the structure of *I'm Not Complaining*, a narrative course that we may disapprove of as women, but which has something to say about the teaching of small children, and its effect on the teacher.

I never left them: they occupied the night-times, all my dreams. I was very tired, bone-achingly tired all the time. I was unknowingly, covertly expected to become a mother, and I unknowingly became one, pausing only in the cracks of the dark night to ask: what is happening to me? Simone de Beauvoir tells you how to avoid servitude: she tells you not to live with men, to work, to attain financial independence; but above all she says, women should not have children, women *should refuse to mother* (Schwartzer, 1984). Children make you retreat behind the glass, lose yourself in the loving mutual gaze. The sensuality of their presence prevents the larger pleasures: the company of children keeps you a child.

Now, look, up on the balcony over the playground, a woman watches. In the room behind the boxes are packed, she is leaving, the walls are bare of the children's drawings. She turns, goes back for a moment through the door, removes her gaze. The stiff skirts swing into folds, a rope turns and the children run and jump, the volume of their voices rises: released, the children go on playing.

Notes

Warm thanks to Gill Frith for reading successive drafts of this, and for discovering at the last moment, Charlotte Brontë's walking in disgust to the window of the prisonhouse.
1   The material presented in this section summarizes a much longer argument in Carolyn Steedman, ''The Mother Made Conscious'': The Historical Development of a Primary School Pedagogy'.
2   Johann Pestalozzi, How Gertrude Teaches her Children. See p. 214 for Gertrude's model in a good and faithful female servant.
First published in Feminist Review no. 20, June 1985.

References

ADAM, Ruth (1983) *I'm Not Complaining* London: Virago (first edition 1938).
ASHPLANT, Timothy (April, 1981) 'The New Function of Cinema' *Journal of the British Film Industry* 79/80.

BELOTTI, Elena Gianini (1973) *Little Girls* London: Writers and Readers.
BOWIE, Jeanetta (1978) *Penny Buff: Memories of a Clydeside School in the Thirties* London: Arrow.
BRONTË, Charlotte (11 August 1836) 'Roe Head Journal' quoted in GERIN.
BRONTË, Charlotte (1979) *Villette* Harmondsworth: Penguin (first edition 1853).
CHODOROW, Nancy (1978) *The Reproduction of Mothering* Berkeley: University of California Press.
CLARKE, Karen (1985) 'Public and Private Children: Infant Education in the 1820s and 1830s' in STEEDMAN, URWIN and WALKERDINE.
CORR, Helen (1983) 'The Sexual Division of Labour in the Scottish Teaching Profession, 1872–1914' in HUMES and PATTERSON.
COVENEY, Peter (1957) *Poor Monkey: The Child in Literature* London: Rockliff.
DAVIS, Madeleine and WALLBRIDGE, David (1983) *Boundary and Space: An Introduction to the Work of W. D. Winnicott* Harmondsworth: Penguin.
GALTON, Maurice *et al.*, (1980) *Inside the Primary Classroom* London: Routledge and Kegan Paul.
GERIN, Winifred (1967) *Charlotte Brontë* Oxford: Clarendon Press.
HELTERLINE, Marilyn (1980) 'The Emergence of Modern Motherhood: Motherhood in England, 1899–1959' *International Journal of Women's Studies* vol. 3 no. 6, pp. 590–615.
HERFORD, W. H. (1899) *The Student's Froebel* London: Isbister.
HUMES, Walter M. and PATERSON, Hamish M. (1983) (Eds.), *Scottish Culture and Scottish Education* Edinburgh: John Donald.
HUMPHRIES, Stephen (1981) *Hooligans or Rebels? An Oral History of Working Childhood and Youth, 1889–1939* Oxford: Basil Blackwell.
KING, Ronald (1978) *All Things Bright and Beautiful? A Sociological Study of Infants' Classrooms* Chichester: Wiley.
LAWRENCE, Evelyn (1952) *Friedrich Froebel and English Education* London: Routledge and Kegan Paul.
MARENHOLZ-BUELOW, Bertha Maria von (1855) *Women's Educational Mission* London: Dalton.
MARTIN, Jane Roland (1982) 'Excluding Women from the Educational Realm' *Harvard Educational Review* vol. 52 no. 2,
MASON, Timothy (1 December 1978) 'The Writing of History as Literary and Moral Art' *Times Higher Educational Supplement*.
McCANN, Philip and YOUNG, Frances A. (1982) *Samuel Wilderspin and the Infant School Movement* London: Croom Helm.
OAKLEY, Ann (1974) *The Sociology of Housework* Oxford: Martin Robinson.
PESTALOZZI, Johann (1894) *How Gertrude Teaches her Children* London: George Allen and Unwin (first edition 1801).
RICH, Adrienne (1979) *Of Women Born* London: Virago.
RUDDICK, Sara (1980) 'Maternal Thinking' *Feminist Studies* vol. 6 no 2 pp. 341–67.
SCHWARTZER, Alice (1983) *Simone de Beauvoir Today* London: Chatto and Windus/Hogarth Press.
SILVER, Harold (1983) *Education as History* London: Methuen.

STEEDMAN, Carolyn (1982) *The Tidy House* London: Virago.

STEEDMAN, Carolyn (1985) 'The Mother Made Conscious': The Historical Development of a Primary School Pedagogy', *History Workshop Journal* no. 20.

STEEDMAN, Carolyn, URWIN, Cathy and WALKERDINE, Valerie (1985) editors, *Language, Gender and Childhood* London: Routledge and Kegan Paul.

TAYLOR, William (1969) *Society and the Education of Teachers* London: Faber and Faber.

VINCENT, David (1981) *Bread, Knowledge and Freedom: A Study of Nineteenth-Century Working-Class Autobiography* London: Methuen.

WALKERDINE, Valerie (1983) 'Its Only Natural: Beyond Child-Centred Pedagogy' in WOLPE and DONALD.

WALVIN, James (1982) *A Child's World: A Social History of English Childhood 1800–1914* Harmondsworth: Penguin.

WARNER, Sylvia Ashton (1980) *Teacher* London: Virago (first edition 1963).

WHITBREAD, Nanette (1972) *The Evolution of the Infant/Nursery School 1800–1970* London: Routledge and Kegan Paul.

WIDDOWSON, Frances (1980) *Going Up into the Next Class* London: Women's Research and Resources Centre.

WINNICOTT, Donald (1964) *The Child, the Family and the Outside World* Harmondsworth: Penguin.

WOLPE, Ann Marie and DONALD, J. (1983) (Eds.), *Is There Anyone Here from Education?* London: Pluto.

Part Three
The Politics of Work

7
Part of the Union : School Representatives and their Work

Jenny Ozga

'In this authority you have to make a straightforward choice between pursuing a career and working for the Union. If you choose to work for the Union you know you'll never be a headteacher. It's as simple as that'. (NUT[1] Divisional Secretary).

This chapter examines what it means to be an NUT school representative working in an LEA with a tradition of hostility to teacher unionism, in a period where bad relations between teacher unions and local management worsened, and eventually deteriorated into open conflict. The purpose of the chapter is to explore the pressures under which school representatives work, and, by examining the strategies with which they respond, to challenge certain assumptions about local teacher union (NUT) membership. One significant assumption is gender-related; i.e., it is assumed that as local union membership is predominantly female, it is therefore, apathetic. (Roy 1968, Ginsberg, Meyenn and Miller 1980). This study, therefore, will concentrate on women school representatives, and will take issue with the use of gender as an 'explanation' of the apathy of local union members. It will be suggested that local 'apathy' is not proven because

(a) the indicators of activism conventionally deployed are inappropriate,
(b) the extent of hostility to organized teachers in some authorities needs to be considered, and
(c) research into teacher unionism has been dominated by the idea of a simple dichotomy between professionalism and militancy which has obscured more than it has revealed.

The context of local 'apathy'

The idea of local teacher union membership 'apathy' has its antecedents in studies of organized teachers which stressed their commitment to 'professionalizing' strategies and their reluctance to align themselves with militant trade unionism. (see, for example, Parry and Parry 1974, Ginsberg, Meyenn and Miller 1980, Roy 1968, Gosden 1972, Coates 1972). The assumption of apathy at the local level was more readily made by ignoring the context in which local teacher unionism had to operate. This context included both hostile local employers, with an ever-extending repertoire of strategies for managing local activists available to them as the political climate hardened, and the complex organizational structure of the NUT, designed to ensure local democracy, but itself a hindrance to local member-ship participation. The research which forms the basis of this article was under-taken to explore these contextual factors further.

The project covers three contrasting LEAs, but the material here is mostly drawn from the study of one of them, a shire county. I have not identified the authority as the interviews with union members on which the article draws were confidential, for reasons which will become apparent, and which are signalled in the opening quotation.

The authority in question has a history of poor relations with organized teachers, and is one of those which embraced with enthusiasm the influx of cor-porate management ideas following local government reorganization. It is Conservative-controlled, with the ruling party divided between the traditional shire county conservative and the new Thatcherite model of local councillor. The latter now dominate the policy process. It is not an authority with a history of strong officer control: the Chair of the Council is well known, the Chief Education Officer is not.

The authority is not a 'straightforward' shire county — (though it is hard to think of any that are, after local government reorganization) — it has a large, rural, sparsely populated hinterland, a number of small market towns and some industrial towns, now in decline. It is not a homogenous entity, but for geographical and historical reasons is divided into relatively self-contained areas where education policy is determined largely by the structure of provision in the past. The factor which has imposed a certain uniformity of the county's provision has been the ruthless search for economies in the education service, which has resulted in levelling down in standards of provision. The revival of standards and selection as central principles in education policy has allowed the authority to preserve its selective system, and the gap between different types of school has grown as a consequence.

This, then is the context in which the union must operate: always a fairly unfriendly climate, but increasingly hostile since the early 1980s. Nor is the local operation of the NUT made any easier by the local structure of the union.

The — shire[2] Division of the NUT

The Division is a fairly complex example of a local Division. It is co-terminous with the County and made up of nine associations; which not only form an unwieldy number of associations, but are of widely contrasting character. The relatively self-contained town-based associations obviously differ considerably from the scattered rural associations.

In fact the east of the Division, like the east of the County, differs markedly from the rural west. It is difficult to imagine that teachers from the rural west would feel themselves at home in the urban schools. Some of the County's problems are reflected in problems for the Division, where the associations are divided between what may be broadly characterized as 'inactive' rural teachers and more active urban teachers, with, in between, the county town teachers who may be well organized but who cannot be readily located politically. Indeed these generalizations are far too simple, as more detailed discussion of the research evidence will show. They are only included here to give a general image of the broad divisions of character existing in the one area. As well as the obvious geographical differences, the county's school population has been affected by cut-backs in widely differing ways. Thus there are wide variations in type of membership and these differences may be expressed as differences among the associations which make up the Division. The associations relate to the Division through the Divisional Executive, which is composed of

(1)   Union Officers,
(2)   The Secretary of each affiliated local association (or a substitute)
(3)   Members of the JTSC (Joint Teachers Staffing Committee)[3],
(4)   NUT Teacher Representatives on —county Education Committee,
(5)   Any member of the NUT Executive who is also a member of an association affiliated to the County Division.

There is also a Divisional Council which is made up of the Divisional Executive plus representatives of each affiliated association on a proportional representation basis — e.g. 1–150 members: four representatives, 151–200: five representatives, over 201: six representatives.

The Annual General meeting of the Council is held in March, at which the Annual Report, audited balance sheet, etc., are considered. The Divisional Council meets a minimum of once a term, and considers reports and recommendations from the Divisional Executive and affiliated associations. All Divisional Council meetings are open to the general membership who have the right to speak but not to vote.

The Divisional Executive meets monthly, and has to have fifteen members present before a quorum is reached. Procedures for the election of the Union Officers are also clearly established.

Representation on the Teachers' Consultative Committee[4] is through the Officers ex-officio — the President, the Ex-President, Vice President and General Secretary of the Divisional Council as far as possible in such a way as to provide an even balance of representation for primary/secondary/middle school etc. delegates.

Representation on the JTSC is through appointment made by the Divisional Executive and includes the General Secretary. The rules of debate are set out in a code of standing orders, which seem, from the evidence of the minutes, to be fairly strictly adhered to, at least in terms of procedure if not in length of time allowed to each speaker.

Organizational Problems

The formal description fulfills the useful function of demonstrating the complexity of organization. Such a structure obviously depends heavily on efficient communication and co-ordination. But there are ambiguities built into it — particularly in the relationship of the Divisional Council — the superior body — to the Divisional Executive — and, perhaps more importantly, — in the relation of the Divisional Executive to the constituent associations. The general secretary of the Division described the Divisional Executive as fulfilling two main functions. In the first place it was the negotiator, entering into negotiations with the employers on behalf of the local membership. This is in line with the 'model objects' for a division issued by Union Headquarters, which specify the following objects (among others):

'(c) To secure direct representation on behalf of all members of the Union in the Division in those committees or bodies where negotiations of a collective nature are conducted'.

'(e) to be solely responsible for negotiating on behalf of the members of the Union in the division with the employing authority on all matters affecting the professional work and conditions of service of members'.

However, he saw the other function of the Divisional Executive as more problematic — this function he described as that of *gatekeeper*. For example any resolution from any of the associations to the authority had to receive approval from the Divisional Executive. The local associations, then, do not have a direct line to the authority, but have to go through the Division. This obviously causes problems, especially over an issue like school closures, which the General Secretary quoted as a source of friction between some local associations and the Divisional Executive. Following national union policy, the Divisional Executive had accepted that some schools would have to be closed, often on educational grounds, where a broad curriculum could not be guaranteed, or where there was too much across-class teaching. However, the members in individual associations — and especially those in threatened schools — went to their own association for help in fighting closures. Thus in some cases the local association was attempting to communicate a message to the authority in direct contradiction to the Divisional Executive's acceptance that some closures were inevitable.

As relations with the employers became more strained throughout 1981 and 1982, when the authority attempted to back out of its premature retirement compensation scheme, and initiate compulsory redeployment, the divisions in the Division became more apparent. Some of the Associations whose membership was directly affected were pressing for action — half-day strikes, demonstrations etc., but the General Secretary calculated that these represented only about 20 per cent of the membership of the Division. He then had to counsel moderation on one hand while trying to organize support for action among the less affected, less vocal members.

The general secretary saw the extent of Association autonomy as a major problem for the local organization of the union, as the Association could undermine the Division in its dealing with the authority (and provide the authority with yet another difference among teachers which could be exploited).

The complexity of the organizational structure and the problem of overlap and/or conflict between Division and Association is exacerbated in an authority like this where the Associations vary so much in character. One of the greatest problems for the officers of the union in the 1980s, in the lead-up to the Teachers' Action of 1986, was ensuring at least the appearance of agreement among the various Associations in the Division. In fact there were, of course, considerable differences, with some of the urban teachers calling for strike action while in the rural areas support even for Executive policy on no-cover action could not be taken for granted. It is a reflection of the strength of feeling among all teachers that the Action was supported so strongly throughout the Authority, in the face of threats to teachers' futures from the employers, who made public their intention of identifying all teachers taking part in the Action, and demanded that Heads identify any teachers engaged in 'dispute activity'.

Recent work has uncovered the forgotten history of teacher union militancy in the 1920s (Lawn 1982), when teachers in some authorities were willing, despite dismissal threats, to take strike action in a period when cuts were seriously damaging the education service. Given the lack of recognition of organized teachers, their exclusion from local education policy-making, and their dependence on their employers, it is remarkable that the minority of activists described by Lawn were willing to take such action. The strength of the employers readily explains the 'apathy' of the majority, and the strength of some local employers, willing to take on the teachers in the political climate of the 1980s must be recognized as an important factor in explaining local membership behaviour.

In — shire, as the 1980s progressed, the employers moved from reluctant acquiescence in local joint negotiations to effectively ignoring the conventions of consultation and negotiation. In confronting the unions they also relied on their heads, who were constantly reminded of their responsibility to the LEA for the 'efficient management' of their schools, and who were expected to identify with management and keep their schools open throughout the action.

Hostile Management and the School Representative

'I never had any time in school for union business, or any of the facilities we're supposed to have. I couldn't even talk to members of staff in the car park — the head accused me of organizing a union plot against him. We used to meet at my house after school or at weekends'. (Mrs W., School Representative.)

Interviews with school representatives in one Association of this division have so far revealed a degree of management hostility to the normal operating of the union at school level which, even if it should prove untypical, should still be borne in mind when conclusions about membership apathy and local inefficiency are drawn. The division between the authority and the union is perhaps most seriously apparent in the relation of some Heads to the School Representatives. These Heads are unequivocally part of management: their allegiance is to the Authority, which holds them responsible for the efficient functioning of its schools. For some Heads this apparently rules out any accommodation of the union; just as, at the level of negotiations in the various joint committees, the management groups refuse to recognize the union, so too do some heads. This has a number of effects, but one severe one is to drastically reduce union authority and organization. Only very committed individuals are prepared to work for the union in such circumstances, and the 'apathy' of much of the membership may be more accurately expressed as a realistic assessment of future employment prospects. One of my informants said that she was only able to pursue a long-held commitment to NUT activity on moving to —shire because her husband had a good income:

'I haven't been absolutely dependent on the money I earned in school and I was able really to stand up for myself and colleagues knowing that at worst if I lost my job it didn't matter that much . . . I mean these days when jobs are so difficult to find I think that you're terrified to stand up for your rights really'. (Mrs W., School Representative)

This school representative attributed her redeployment to her union activities

'Yes, it would be very difficult to prove, but I had sat in as a witness at so many interviews with the head and colleagues and I knew far too much . . . and I stood up to him. There were two representatives but the other was looking for promotion and although she's a very courageous person it would have been foolish for her to stick her neck out'. (Mrs W.)

She provided numerous examples of harassment where it was apparent that all the conventions established by one teacher union relating to grievance procedures, etc., were simply ignored.

Her description of the way in which she was forced to operate painted a picture of the NUT as a clandestine, proscribed organization, treated with a cavalier disregard of established procedures and negotiated agreements which might have been thought belonged more in the 1920s than the 1980s. How such a fragile organization survived throughout the 1986 Action is something which demonstrates both the commitment of teachers to the fight and the extent of their alienation from their employers and management.

One of the consequences of a confrontational stance is that it hardens attitudes on both sides; the membership in this authority, though initially divided over strike action, faced with a completely hostile management which threatened a 'lock out' perhaps did not experience the same conflict of loyalties involving their headteachers which teachers elsewhere describe.

The preceeding pages should have conveyed some impression of the difficulty of maintaining union activity in a hostile authority which uses its headteachers as a front line management force whose primary objective is efficient management of the schools. The difficulty is compounded by the fragmented local organization and by the vulnerability of the school representative. Membership 'apathy' in this context can be seen as a rational response to the situation, rather than something inherent in the nature of the membership itself.

The Apathetic Membership

Discussions of NUT membership have tended to follow Roy's (1968) lead, assuming apathy because of evidence of low attendance at meetings, low polls in the election of local national union officers, and because of the female gender of most of the members. A further 'finding' which has reinforced the belief in the non-militancy of teachers is that their commitment to professionalism weakens their commitment to union activism (Ginsberg, Meyenn and Miller 1980). The assumptions behind both these sets of conclusions need further investigation.

Roy's study came to the following conclusions about the membership:

1. Most members join the union for insurance and security purposes, for instrumental reasons, the majority are inert or apathetic.
2. Membership participation in the local structure of the union is weak, attendance at local union meetings, for example, is poor.
3. Local union activity is dominated by a small number of committed activists who may not be typical of the membership.
4. The apathy of the membership to some extent *derives* from the fact that the majority of the members are women.

5. The apathy of the membership to some extent derives from a conflict between active unionism and professionalism.

Other ideas about the membership which appear in the union's own literature and elsewhere are concerned with the conflict between democracy and efficiency in the union. There is, on the one hand, the belief that the local union machinery may be under control of people who are not typical of the membership — a comment often made about some of the inner London associations — while the rather contradictory view, that apathy represents contentment with executive leadership, is also expressed.

Obviously, some of these ideas are closely tied up with particular periods and episodes in the union's history. The fear of untypical elements gaining control of local associations stems from the period of Rank and File activism (see Seifert 1985), while Roy's uncritical acceptance of gender as an *explanation* of apathy is, one hopes, also a product of its time.

Generalisations about membership apathy are often based on information about low attendance at meetings. Certainly my own research revealed instances of delays to meetings of the Division in the absence of a quorum (15). The minutes show an average attendance of 15–20, these same regular attenders turn up for meetings. Roy argued that women 'tend to be less active than men ... it is not surprising that social functions are more attractive to them than ordinary business meetings'.

Ordinary business meetings after a hard day's work may not be attractive to anyone, and union meetings may well be less attractive than most. And we should not forget the well-documented evidence of women teachers' experience of the 'double-shift' of work and housework/family responsibilities (see Evetts, 1986, Davidson, 1985). A further factor in explaining low membership participation is the content and conduct of the meetings themselves.

These are conducted according to an agreed and established procedure, which is relatively simple once you are familiar with it. To the uninitiated it is not simple, without experience it is difficult for the new member attending a meeting to grasp such essential points as how to get an item on the agenda, how to speak to a 'motion', how motions are proposed and seconded, how amendments may be proposed, etc. These terms are a second language to the experienced union activist, but present difficulties for the new member, who may even be afraid to participate because of fear of making an error in procedure, and may lose interest in attending as a consequence.

The insistence on formal procedure is partly explicable in terms of the history of the union, but may also owe its uncontrolled survival — and indeed growth — to the fact that it serves the interests of established union stalwarts very well. Access to and expertise in the formal organization of union procedure is, for some activists, almost an end in itself.

'Engendered Apathy'

In this context Walker (1981) has referred to the 'unconscious institutional sexism' of the NUT. Although women in membership outnumber men by 2–1, men officers in the union outnumber women by 3–1.

In 1980 the following figures indicated the gender division in local union post-holders:

	Total	Male	Female	Percentage
Presidents	343	232	111	(32.26)
Treasurers	546	378	168	(30.77)
Secretaries	549	406	143	(26.05)

[Source: Brigid Walker: *Women and the NUT.* Unpublished M.Ed. thesis, University of Bristol.]

Walker found that single association Divisions were more likely to have women secretaries, and she also found a high attendance by women at local meetings (half to three-quarters of attenders). Interestingly, the women in her study were motivated in their union work by 'a sense of moral obligation' and were reluctant to seek office beyond that of School Rep. One claimed that the whole mode of operation of the NUT locally was hostile to women, as they were unwilling to spend time wrangling over procedure and listening to routine reports.

Here they may be a genuine gender-based difference. Those who make careers in the union — mastering procedure, running meetings and standing for election locally and nationally — are mostly men. Explanations of this which are couched in terms of women's 'failure' to come forward, or male prejudice, do not take account of womens' perceptions of procedure and formal processes. Many of the school representatives who were 'active' in my study defined their commitment to the union in broad educational terms. These women were not interested in the rather ritualistic element of local union business, but spent their time on individual membership problems and on protecting and fostering the union in their school. Thus womens' low attendance at meetings, and their absence from the ranks of local officials may not denote 'apathy' but a different definition of what union activism means.

This definition puts the emphasis on the 'caring' aspects of the School Representative's job; the women activists I surveyed often stressed their role in protecting staff from unfair and arbitrary management pressures (usually headteacher-generated), and in looking after probationary or inexperienced teachers.

These people acted as workplace representatives and their role in making teachers' working lives more tolerable was extremely important. It would be difficult to demonstrate that they had influence — instances where they achieved a change in policy are rare — but they are important in that they do provide staff with sympathetic support, and help staff to protect themselves; accompanying them to meetings with the head, and bringing in local union officials in the last resort.

It has been noted that the 'shop steward' function has developed in the public service sector in recent years and research on school representatives in another teachers' union has suggested that the shop steward model is an increasingly appropriate one. The NUT representatives discussed here present an interesting variant of the shop steward model, one modified, it seems, by gender.

However the difficulties of generalizing about School Representatives, even in this small scale research exercise, must not be underplayed. Their role and status varied enormously: in some city schools, in strong associations, and where the Head is often an active NUT member, School Representatives carry out a wide variety of promotional tasks for the union, and are give time and space to recruit members and to advise on members' problems. Workshops and discussions of union policy may be held. However, some of my findings in — shire suggest that there this would be exceptional. A number of difficulties were identified by the School Representatives in my survey, who themselves exemplified the diversity of this group.

Some of them saw themselves only as 'post boxes' for the union: in the remoter rural areas, in head-plus-one schools, the 'School Representative' disclaimed the title, as he or she (more often the latter) did not regard herself as an activist, but was prepared to distribute material for the union, or pin notices on noticeboards. Some of these people were anxious not to be identified as School Representatives, a few expressed opinions — particularly in relation to the undesirability of taking 'no cover' or strike action, in terms which were contradictory to national union policy. The local association Secretary in an area where the 'School Representatives' were mostly of this type was reluctant to let them be interviewed or even to distribute a questionnaire to them. His dilemma was that they were often long standing NUT members, who, he felt, might well be alarmed by enquiry into their functions, which might reveal their somewhat limited conception of their role. This might lead them to refuse to act as 'SRs' in the future, which would leave him with greater problems in a scattered rural area with no population/communication centre.

This example demonstrates an extreme in the findings, but other evidence supports the generalisation that there is no clear understanding among School Representatives of their role and function. A number of School Representatives said they spent little or no time on union business, and never initiated discussions on union matters in school. At the other extreme were very active School Representatives, who spent four to five hours per week on union business, who saw other members of staff regularly to advise them on union related matters, who brought up union business as a matter of course in the staffroom.

Clearly the School Representatives' position must have been affected by the prolonged teachers' action. Certainly during the Action, pressure on School Representatives was very severe. They were responsible for channelling the union's instructions to staff, for explaining strategies which changed — at least initially — at short notice, and for getting information on the latest stage in the interminable rounds of negotiations across. They had to cope with a membership often reluctant to implement 'no cover' action or half-day strikes, they had to keep up morale in a lengthy campaign, where teachers did not get a sympathetic press. They also bore the brunt of parental criticism, had to attempt to find some way of working with the Head throughout the dispute, and had to negotiate with the other unions in the school, including the non-teacher unions. This was all required of a group of individuals most of whom had no training. In areas like the western, rural part of this LEA, this was demanded of school representatives who had, perhaps, taken on the job because no-one else would, and who were not 'activists' in the traditional sense. These representatives also had to cope with the outright hostility of heads and employers, a hostility which took the form of threats to their continued employment and career development. In the cities, it may have been easier for representatives and heads to find a way for the school to survive the Action, if the Head understood the procedures for negotiation with the union and did not try to break the action in his or her own school.

Recent interviews with women School Representatives in another Authority indicate that during the action they became more committed and stronger in their activism; as they gained experience of negotiation, and as attitudes hardened during the long dispute, so their identification with the Union and their willingness to go on the offensive in defence of the Union's position increased. One school representative described how attendance at an NUT training course had made her much more confident, not just in terms of her union career, but in relation to her work and career generally.

The Action may well have fostered strengths in negotiation, organization and resistance among school representatives, strengths which they will certainly need in —shire in the uneasy time following the end of the campaign, as management reasserts its 'right to manage'.

Professionalism v. Unionism

The assumption that teachers experience a conflict between professionalism and unionism which weakens their commitment to unionism has been supported by research evidence gained from questions like this:

'. . . how do you see the NUT? Do you see it primarily as a trade union or as a professional body?'
'. . . do you think this poses any problem for you as a member of a union, being also a member of a profession?' (Ginsberg *et al.* 1980).

Interviews with teachers which allow them to discuss professionalism and unionism in a much less simplified, antagonistic way show that teachers hold many different views about professionalism, not all of which militate against union activism. It has been argued elsewhere (Lawn and Ozga 1981) that professionalism is a complex term, capable of many interpretations, and often used ideologically: by the local and central state as a means of managing teachers and distancing them from the labour movement, and by teachers to enhance their control over their work and as a means of defence against employers' attempts to worsen their working conditions and reduce standards in the service.

Unfortunately much of the literature on teachers is dominated by functionalist definitions of professionalism which uncritically accept certain historical features of the rise of the professions as immutable, and thus conclude that union activity runs counter to attempts to professionalize. Critical analyses of professionalism (Larson 1977, Johnson 1972) have had little impact, nor has historical research aimed at exploring the strategic use of professionalism by the state in the management of teachers (Lawn 1987). Ironically, attempts to locate teachers' class position have reinforced the ideas of contradiction, ambiguity and distance from the working-class and from unionism. (Ginsberg *et al.* 1980, Harris 1982).

The strength of the hold of restricted definitions of professionalism has led the academic study of teachers away from the potentially very fruitful examination of teachers as workers, and the exploration of their particular problems — including unionisation and resistance to management controls, workplace bargaining and so on — in the same way as these have been explored in the study of industrial relations and organizational sociology (Tipton 1973, 1985).

The categorization of schools as education 'plant', the separation of management from workforce, the concern with efficiency and the measurement of performance are all clear signals of the way school management is likely to develop. A situation in which 'professional' agreement and consultation is likely to be replaced by a contractual obligation and rule-following may strengthen the 'unionateness' of the teaching force; ironically, the confrontational stance of local employers and the central state alike may well have fostered those aspects of professionalism which support unionism — defence of skills, protection of standards and mutual support. The use of professionalism as a management device is no longer possible, and in an authority like — shire, where the accompaniments of professionalism — consultation and negotiation — never featured prominently, it is possible that teachers are more clearly aware now than at any other time since the 1920s of the division of interest between themselves and local management.

Conclusion

The evidence on which the arguments in this chapter are based is drawn from only one authority, and data have not yet been gathered from all the associations in the division[5]. It is possible that the hostility shown to the union by management is not duplicated, or at least not so strong, in other associations of the division. It is probable that — shire is not representative of LEA-Union relations, though more research needs to be done on this subject, and it is hard to believe that it is unique.

The prolonged and often bitter struggle of the teachers in 1986 revealed a strength and determination among the local union membership which challenged conventional assumptions about membership apathy. I believe that this study indicates that these assumptions were themselves based on assumptions about gender as an 'explanation' and professionalism as antagonistic to activism which are questionable. They also ignored the extraordinarily difficult climate in which local unions often had to work, further handicapped by a complex local organization which could exacerbate divisions among the membership.

The different definitions of activism and union involvement offered by the women school representatives in this study demonstrate yet again the androcentric bias of studies of unionism, and point to the more general need to explore and understand differences, not just in this context, but in school management, career development, and in all aspects of the work of teaching.

Notes

1   The NUT is the largest teachers' union in England and Wales, and represents teachers in all sectors of the education service, though the majority of its membership are female primary teachers.
2   I have referred to the authority as —shire, rather than select one of the fictional names commonly used in case studies of this kind (for example, Barsetshire or Wealdshire), because it is difficult to find a name which is not associated with a particular geographic area.
3   The JTSC is a local forum for negotiation between the employers and the teachers on matters concerning teachers' conditions of service.
4   The TCC is another forum for negotiation between teachers and the LEA on general educational issues and is supposed to provide a point at which teachers can make a contribution to local policy-making. However, the extent to which genuine consultation takes place varies considerably from authority to authority.
5   The research on which this chapter is based was supported by the School of Education, the Open University.

References

COATES, R. D. (1972) *The Teacher Unions and Interest Group Politics*, Cambridge University Press.

DAVIDSON, H. (1985) 'Some unfriendly Myths about Women Teachers' in Kant, L. and Cruickshank, M. (Eds.) *Girl-Friendly Schooling*, London, Methuen.

EVETTS, J. (1986) 'Teachers' Careers, The Objective Dimension', in *Educational Studies*, Vol. 12, No. 3.,

GINSBERG, M., MEYENN, M. and MILLER, H. (1980) 'Teachers' Conceptions of Professionalism and Trades Unionism: an ideological analysis', in Woods P. (Ed.) *Teacher Strategies: Explorations in the Sociology of the School*, Croom Helm.

GOSDEN, P. H. (1972) *The Evolution of a Profession*. Basil Blackwell.

HARRIS, K. (1982) *Teachers and Classes* R.K.P.

JOHNSON, T. J. (1972) *Professions and Power*, Macmillan

LARSON, M. S. (1977) *The Rise of Professionalism: A Sociological Analysis*, University of California Press.

LAWN, M. A. (1982) *Organized Teachers and The Labour Movement*, Unpublished Ph.D. thesis, The Open University.

LAWN, M. A. (1987) 'The Spur and the Bridle: Changing the mode of curriculum control', in *Journal of Curriculum Studies*

LAWN, M. A. and OZGA, J. T. (1981) *Teachers, Professionalism and Class*, Falmer Press

PARRY, N. and PARRY, J. (1974) 'The Teachers and Professionalism: the failure of an Occupational Strategy', in Flude, M. and Ahier, J. *Educability, Schools and Ideology*, Croom Helm.

ROY, W. (1968) *The Teachers' Union*' Schoolmaster Publications.

SEIFERT, R. (1985) 'Some Aspects of Factional Opposition: Rank and File and the National Union of Teachers 1967–1982'. *British Journal of Industrial Relations*, 1985.

TIPTON, B. F. (1973) 'The Hidden Side of Teaching: The Teacher Unions'. *London Educational Review*, Vol. 3, No. 2.

TIPTON, B. F. (1985) 'Educational Organizations as Workplaces', *British Journal of the Sociology of Education*, Vol 6, No. 1.

8
The Politics of Teacher Appraisal

Kieron Walsh

Introduction

The teachers' dispute of 1985–86 was as much about how the teaching force is to be managed as about levels of pay. Local Education Authorities (LEAs) and the Department of Education and Science (DES) were concerned about what would be delivered in return for higher pay, and how they could ensure control over teachers and the teaching process. Appraisal of the performance of individual teachers was seen as crucial in ensuring control, particularly by the Secretary of State for Education and Science and the DES civil servants. The introduction of an appraisal system was made a condition of Government funding of any salary settlement. The Education Act 1986 gives the Secretary of State the power to introduce a national system of appraisal should the LEAs themselves fail to deliver satisfactory schemes. The Act abolishing the Burnham Committee will give him the power to specify conditions of service, on the basis of which teachers will be appraised.

The pressure for the introduction of performance appraisal for teachers derives from a number of sources, but the most important is the desire for greater central control of education, which has been apparent since the mid-1970s. The Government and the DES are trying to make education conform to new social, economic and political purposes[1]. The centre wishes to see a curriculum that it considers more relevant to the world of work, and to life after school more generally, and that is more fitted to the capacities of students. The present curriculum is seen as too academic, and not sufficiently adapted to the needs either of the most or the least able. As many commentators[2] have argued the DES has, since the 1970s, developed a clear strategy for re-orientating the education system and for asserting its dominance over the LEAs, the school and the teachers. In the thirty years immediately after the Second World War, the 'partnership' of central government, the LEAs and the teachers controlled education, with no one of the three parties exercising monopoly control. Since James Callaghan's administration, the desire of the Department of Education and Science for control over the LEAs and the teachers has become public in white and green papers, in legislation, and in changes to the system of finance. The LEAs, in turn, have been attempting to assert more control over the schools and teachers, and within the school the managerial roles of headteachers and other senior staff have been emphasised. The notion of teachers as independent, autonomous professionals has been eroded, and the importance of management and hierarchical accountability emphasised.

This essay examines one aspect of the development of managerial and employer control — performance appraisal. I shall argue that the development of teacher appraisal has taken two main forms, both deriving from the desire for more centralized control of the education system. The first is the attempt to rationalize teachers' work through influencing both the teaching process, notably through control of the teacher training and in-service training systems, and the content and output of teaching through influence over the curriculum and examinations. The second form is the attempt to formalize the employment relation, by specifying much more closely teachers' conditions of service. Employer and DES control of teachers' work would be limited without control of the employment contract. The teacher-employer relationship is to become one of exchange rather than of trust. In manufacturing industry, and in many service industries, management control can normally be asserted through control of the work process and of the product, as well as by direct surveillance, for example, through the use of technological systems, and the design of work. In teaching, the potential for such control is limited and there is a prior need for the employer to develop control of the employment contract. The changed labour market conditions that confront teachers have allowed the employers to assert a form of bureaucratic contractual control that fits ill with the notion of professional autonomy. I shall argue that there are fundamental weaknesses in the teachers claim to professional status, which have made that formalization possible.

The managerialism that has come to characterize education in the last decade was made possible by the change from growth to decline that has faced the service in that period. The form that managerialism has taken reflects the balance of forces that operate in education. I shall argue that the teachers' claim to professional status and autonomy is weakly grounded and has become weaker in the last decade. But, as has been apparent in the recent teachers' action, trade unionism is strong in education. In the United States, where teacher unionism is much weaker, states such as Texas have been able to impose rigid forms of appraisal and, in some cases, to relate pay to performance. A survey by the American Association of Colleges for Teacher Education found that 44 of the 50 states have introduced some form of standardized test[3]. In Britain, though partnership no longer operates, power is still distributed between the Department of Education and Science, and the Government generally, the LEAs and the teachers. Differences in power and interest have influenced the way that appraisal has developed and the pattern that it has taken. Employers have not simply been able to impose their preferred form of appraisal. But nor have teachers been able fully to assert professional independence and peer control.

The attempt to introduce performance appraisal is an aspect of the formalization of the employment relation. The employer is to make a more explicit contractual statement of what is expected of the teacher, but there will inevitably be strong elements of discretion in performance, and appraisal can be seen as a means of controlling the exercise of that discretion. In discussing appraisal I shall distinguish between three dimensions:

Focus: appraisal may focus upon the individual teacher or upon the unit within which education takes place, that is at the collective level — the department or the school, or even the whole LEA

Purpose: appraisal may be used to assess the development needs of teachers, or to pass judgment on their performance, especially in the exercise of discretion (sometimes called 'summative' appraisal)

Form: appraisal may be performed hierarchically by management, or cooperatively, through a process of peer review, possibly involving students, parents and the community.

These three dimensions allow us to distinguish two basic forms of appraisal; managerial, control-oriented appraisal, which is individually focused, judgmental and hierarchical; and participative appraisal, which is collectively focused, developmental and cooperative. Guidelines for the Review and Internal Development of Schools (GRIDS) provide an example of the participative approach. The employers and the DES have been concerned to develop control-oriented appraisal, but the outcome, so far, has been a hybrid of the two basic types, because teachers have been able to resist control, and influence the pattern of appraisal adopted. They have been able to ensure that the systems of appraisal adopted are not wholly control-oriented, but contain elements of the participative approach.

This paper examines the development of teacher appraisal. It first considers the rise of central control. Secondly, it examines the development of the movement for the appraisal of the performance of individual teachers. I shall then develop the argument that the weakness of the teachers' claim to professionalism makes them vulnerable to attempts to develop control-oriented appraisal. At the same time as the nature of the teachers' work makes it difficult to create systems of control oriented appraisal, it also makes it difficult for them to claim the right to independent, professionally-controlled, participative review. I shall conclude this article by considering the positive arguments for appraisal, and possible future developments.

The Rise of Control

Political criticism of the standards and relevance of education has been strong since James Callaghan's speech at Ruskin College in October 1976, and has intensified under the present government. The desire to assert more direct control over the teachers, and specifically to introduce performance appraisal, has its origins in the political wish to ensure that the education system carries out national political purposes. The belief that teachers and schools were failing society and the economy, based more in prejudice than in evidence, has led to moves for assessment of the performance of the education service, embodied, for example in the establishment of the Assessment of Performance Unit, and the publication of examination results by schools and of HMI reports. There has been general pressure for more accountability in education. Financial constraint has led to an emphasis on 'value-for-money' and to financial assessments of performance, reflected in the enhanced role of auditors and the creation of the Audit Commission, which has carried out three specific studies of education[4].

In the long period of post-war growth, teachers were in control of their own career structures to a much greater extent than had previously been the case. The present concern for central control contrasts strongly with the autonomy that was allowed to teachers or, at least, which the centre was unable to prevent. The expansion of the service meant that teachers could move from school to school and authority to authority with comparative ease. Indeed the DES operated a quota system to try to share out scarce teachers fairly. Career advance and mobility were directly linked. Those who moved most were those who were promoted most. The expansion of the number of scales in the Burnham structure after 1956 increased the extent and range of promotion. Teachers had careers rather than jobs, in contrast to the pre-war period when, as Spooner says, 'there was virtually no promotion ladder but a sudden jump to deputy or head'[5]. It was a sellers' market in which teachers could control their own professional lives and employer power was limited.

The curriculum that was taught in schools also came increasingly under the control of the teachers as education expanded, particularly in the secondary sector. Early Government attempts to gain some influence over the curriculum, through the establishment of the Curriculum Study Group, failed because of teacher and LEA resistance. The Schools Council, established in 1964 under the majority control of the teachers, institutionalized their dominating influence on the shape and content of the curriculum. The DES and the LEAs played little part in the control of what was taught, which, in practice, rested with the individual headteacher and teaching staff in school. As the Schools Council Constitution put it:

'... each school should have the fullest possible measure of responsibility
for its own work, with its own curriculum and teaching methods based
on the needs of its own pupils and evolved by its own staff'[6]

The place where curriculum policy was ultimately developed was seen as the individual classroom, and it was this belief in independent control that lay at the heart of the teachers' claim to professionalism. The claim to professionalism was a claim to autonomy in the determination of the form and content of work.

The result of these developments, by the mid-1970s, was a teaching force that was young, largely self-controlling, with good promotion prospects and high career expectations. Studies of teachers' lives have shown that attitudes to careers vary widely, but the post-war development of education had created individual teacher autonomy and self-determination.

Opportunities for mobility and promotion have been dramatically reduced by financial and demographic contraction. Teachers, whose understandings have been shaped by growth, now in the 1980s face the prospect of becoming old together, trapped on relatively low paid scales, with little opportunity for movement. Teachers have lost control of the employment relation and the DES and LEAs and headteachers have gained much more influence over careers.

From the mid-1970s the DES and the LEAs were taking more control over the context of teaching. Education was blamed for Britain's long economic decline; the curriculum was seen as insufficiently relevant and vocational, and teaching methods as not rigorous enough. Education was argued not to be accountable for its performance. The evidence upon which such judgments could be based was necessarily limited, given that knowledge about the process of education lay predominantly with the teacher and the school. But this, in itself, was a source of teacher weakness, for, while those who claimed that standards had fallen could cite little evidence, nor could teachers provide evidence to counter the claim. Some mud was bound to stick. The answer was seen as more centralized control of the curriculum, and systematic information on standards. The Assessment of Performance Unit was given a brief to develop criterion-referenced methods of assessment.

From the mid-1970s there was also growing pressure for accountability, which was linked to the concern over standards. Teachers, schools and LEAs were all to be held accountable for pupil achievement and behaviour. The 1977 Green Paper, *Education in Schools*, argued that:

'Much has been achieved: but there is legitimate ground for criticism and concern. Education, like any other public service, is answerable to the society which it serves and which pays for it, so these criticisms must be given a fair hearing'[7].

and that:

'growing recognition of the need for schools to demonstrate their accountability to the society which they serve requires a coherent and soundly based means of assessment for the educational system as a whole, for schools and for individual pupils'[8].

Under the Conservative Governments the desire for accountability has become stronger, being expressed in the provisions in the Education Act 1980, requiring schools to publish examination results, the publication of HMI reports and the increased powers of governing bodies. Performance appraisal is part of this movement for accountability and central control, as responsibility for performance has come to be focused upon the individual teacher.

Governments have been concerned to increase their own control of education while weakening the institutional power of LEAs, schools and teachers. The centre has taken an increasing interest in the content of the curriculum. Circulars 14/77, 6/81 and 8/83 have required Local Education Authorities to develop curriculum policies and make returns on the curriculum to the DES. Central government is increasingly concerned to develop a centrally specified core curriculum. Examinations are being developed which embody central purposes. The new GCSE, operating through a simplified system with fewer Examination Boards, must meet both general and specific subject criteria laid down by the Secretary of State. The 17 + examination has been subject to closer scrutiny than previous examinations by the DES. The Government has funded specific curriculum developments directly, notably the Technical and Vocational Education Initiative (TVEI). The powers of LEAs, schools and teachers have been reduced by a dual process of centralizing and decentralization. The financial powers of the centre have been increased by establishing direct grants for various specific educational purposes, as opposed to funding education wholly through the general rate support grant. A considerable amount of educational finance has been channelled through the Manpower Services Commission. The power of LEAs on governing bodies has been greatly reduced by the Education Act 1986. The power of schools has been reduced by increasing parental rights in choice of school. The teachers' influence has been reduced by the abolition of the Schools Council and its replacement by the Secondary Examinations Council and Schools Curriculum Development Council, which are more directly under the control of the Secretary of State. The Advisory Council on the Supply and Education of Teachers has also been disbanded. Most recently the Secretary of State has announced the establishment of City Technical Colleges, which will be directly funded by the DES and run by trusts independent of the LEAs.

The Education Act recently passed by Parliament radically reduces the power and influence of the LEAs and teachers, while increasing the powers of the centre. The Burnham Committee is to be abolished. Teachers' pay and conditions are no longer to be subject to collective bargaining. The Secretary of State is to set up a small advisory committee on pay and conditions but may set aside their advice if it is not to his liking. The advisory committee will not have to be representative of the teachers or the LEAs. The Act also contains the power for the Secretary of State to vary pay levels in different parts of the country. It will also allow him to specify conditions of service for teachers.

It is not only in schools that the development of closer control of the work of individual teachers is leading to increased surveillance of educational work. At the national level government is also introducing procedures that will involve considerations of teachers' performance and the content of their work. The Council for the Accreditation of Teacher Education has been given oversight of initial training and tighter requirements have been laid down for the content of training, and the relation between qualifications, and subjects and age groups taught. The Government is also introducing a specific grant for in-service training, which would require each LEA to:

'... submit information about its plans for in-service training and making good use of the teachers who had been released to engage in in-service training'[9]

National priorities are laid down for in-service training. The policy has already been partially introduced through the funding for TVEI Related In-service Training which is controlled by the Manpower Services Commission, and involves its own inspection system. Local Education Authorities are required to submit information on the methods used to ensure that the training offered to, and taken up by, teachers matches their identified needs; what information is available on the in-service training needs of individual teachers; and plans to ensure that training is part of a coherent programme of staff development for individual teachers. A clear line of responsibility and accountability from teacher and school to central government is being established.

The new approach to the closer control of in-service training by central government, implies that individual education authorities and the DES will have more detailed knowledge of what teachers are doing and their standards of performance. The evidence from the development of such policy planning systems, for example Housing Investment Programmes and Transport Policies and Programmes, is that coordination quickly becomes control[10].

The proposal to appraise the performance of the individual teacher, then, is only one aspect of the growing monitoring of the performance of teachers, schools and LEAs. Changes in the nature of educational work in the future may also mean more assessment and appraisal. Eggleston sees the possibility of assessment extending professionalism. He argues that the development of criterion-referenced assessment of pupils will:

'... make available a far wider range of a child's achievement and of a teacher's work to assessment ... Such moves, along with other associated techniques such as pupil profiling ... involve the active participation of the profession itself, so extending professionalism ... Together the new techniques present a prospect of a far more effective appraisal of professional achievement than heretofore — an appraisal that can be made available to the clients'[11].

But assessment may lay the base for managerial control not professional account-ability. Closer specification of the nature of teaching — as opposed to the content of the curriculum — may lead to the development of a competency-based testing, used in some parts of the United States. Competency-based appraisal involves specifying single discrete elements of knowledge or skill or professional value posi-tions required of teachers, for example, 'Reinforces and encourages learner involvement in instruction' is a competency specified in one American scheme[12]. While such approaches have had very limited success or impact, they illustrate the possibilities for the formalization and rationalization of the work of teachers. Requirements to be more accountable are also shifting schools towards providing more detailed information on performance, for example, in the case of Croydon LEA, where assessment is performed partly through regular, standardized tests of pupil performance.

Central government has, therefore, pursued control through asserting greater influence over the content of education. It is also attempting to influence the teaching process through control of initial and in-service training. Assessment at all levels is to be a key part of the process.

It is in the context of a weakening of the labour market position of teachers, and growing central control over, and concern for, the curriculum and standards that appraisal must be understood. The debate about teacher appraisal is a debate about accountability, quality, competence and professional autonomy. It follows from a desire to change the nature of educational work, and the employment rela-tion through specifying conditions of service. Given the lack of specific contractual commitments it is necessary, if central control is to be asserted, to develop a more specific contract.

The Development of Appraisal

The early origins of appraisal for teachers lie in the self-critical mood that developed in education from the mid-1970s. There were no immediate moves to introduce formal teacher appraisal as part of conditions of service as a result of the 'Great Debate'. But a number of schools and LEAs, starting with the Inner London Education Authority, introduced processes of self-assessment for schools. By 1983 self-assessment was operating in at least 56 LEAs. Such schemes involve schools evaluating their overall performance, normally on an informal basis, though sometimes involving LEA advisers and formal reports. Whole school self-assessment schemes have resulted in the development of individual teacher appraisal in some cases, though normally of an informal sort and with the purpose of development not judgment. James and Newman, in a survey of 233 schools, found that about half would have appraisal schemes by 1987[13].

Self-assessment procedures are based on a collegial view of the schools as a professional community. According to Her Majesty's Inspectorate, they have proved invaluable in primary schools because they:

> 'promoted professional discussion among staff; brought frustrations and disagreements to the surface; gave a voice to more members of staff . . .'[14].

In secondary schools HMI found that self-assessment has increased teacher commitment, created a common professional language, and enabled teachers to see their work in the context of the whole school. The forms of self-assessment that have developed embody the participative activity of professional peers.

In the early 1980s the focus shifted to the appraisal of the performance of individual teachers, in negotiations over the reform of the Burnham salary structure, which was almost universally recognised as inadequate at a time of falling rolls. The availability of 'points' for promotion depended upon the size of the school, and as numbers fell there were fewer points. Those in promoted posts frequently had to have their salaries protected as schools lost points. The focus was naturally on the individual, since the problem was the limits that financial and demographic decline placed on the individual teacher's career. But the individual focus fitted the market-oriented 'responsibility' ethic of central government under Mrs. Thatcher. The decline in promotion opportunities heightened the dissatisfaction of the teachers' unions, which had long been concerned about promotion procedures, and had argued for a systematic approach that would provide objective evidence on teachers' ability for advancement. The Burnham structure no longer provided the basis for the development of teachers' careers or for schools' management structures. It was clear, both to employers and unions, that reform was needed.

From the first the employers saw appraisal as part of any reorganized payment structure. The initial report of a group of officers appointed by the Burnham Management Panel in 1981, argued that pay should be related to performance. There were prolonged negotiations before the employers finally put forward their detailed plans in November 1984, in their document *A New Remuneration Structure for Teachers*. They proposed a three year probationary entry grade, a main professional grade for the classroom teacher, and principal teacher and assistant headteacher posts, forming about 20 per cent of the school establishment, which would have primarily management responsibilities. The proposals involved a threefold process of appraisal. Teachers could only move from the entry grade to the main professional grade by undergoing appraisal. Once on the main professional grade, teachers were to go through a twofold procedure: an annual performance appraisal by the 'senior professional and managerial colleague to whom the teacher is accountable'; every third year there was to be a 'performance review' involving LEA officers or advisors. Pay and performance were to be linked, the proposals stated that:

> 'If performance appraisal or review demonstrates that the performance of a teacher is unsatisfactory it would make little sense to increase the pay of that teacher ... thus progression to the next point in the teachers incremental scale will not be awarded to any teacher unless his or her performance is certified as satisfactory'[15].

A larger salary increment was to follow the three-yearly review as compared with the annual appraisal.

During the period of negotiation between 1981 and 1986, the DES and the Secretary of State were encouraging performance appraisal related to pay. Both the major white papers produced at that time gave it considerable emphasis. *Teaching Quality* argued that:

> 'the salary structure should be designed to offer relatively greater rewards to the best classroom teachers as well as to encourage good teachers to seek wider responsibilities in senior posts'[16].

Better schools saw the appraisal of teachers as the 'key instrument' for managing the relationship between pay, responsibilities and performance. So important was it, that the Secretary of State was to take powers:

> 'to provide (a) national framework in the form of statutory regulations ... it is proposed therefore that the Secretary of State's existing powers for regulating the employment of teachers should be extended to enable him, in appropriate circumstances, to require LEAs regularly to appraise the performance of the teachers ...'[17].

That promise has been fulfilled in the Education Act 1986. The issue was confused by Sir Keith Joseph who gave the impression that the purpose of the appraisal was to discover, and dismiss from the service, incompetent teachers. Sir Keith also saw dismissal of incompetent teachers as a means of reducing teaching numbers, which were well above the levels planned by the Government. He made the availability of money from central government to fund any revised salary structure dependent upon performance-related pay being introduced.

The employers' proposals, particularly on appraisal, were unacceptable to the teachers, and talks eventually broke down in Summer 1985. The talks that resulted in the Coventry agreement followed the acceptance by Sir Keith Joseph that pay and performance should not be linked through appraisal. He had been persuaded, in part, by the Graham Report[18], which examined various approaches to appraisal in Britain and overseas. The report emphasised the difficulties of appraising teachers' work. The necessary techniques are hardly developed and appraisal will require training especially in classroom observation. The report argued that appraisal was valuable, but that it should not be related to pay:

'We have concluded that the necessary conditions for success do not currently exist in England and Wales. Teachers manifestly believe their salaries to be poor: the criteria for determining a factual base for assessing (a) their classroom performance and (b) their total contribution to the school community as a whole, are largely undeveloped and in any case exceedingly difficult to construct. In these circumstances the introduction of merit pay for a sceptical and organized teaching force might, we suspect, be self-defeating'[19].

The Audit Commission also:

'reluctantly accepts the conclusion of the Graham Report regarding merit pay that the "necessary conditions for success do not currently exist in England and Wales"'[20].

There is no guarantee that the employers and the DES will not return to performance-related pay if conditions become more favourable. Strong teacher unions have been able to resist it. Any major change would require a weakening of the unions. The abolition of Burnham and collective bargaining might be seen as part of a move to weaken the teacher unions. The importance that the employers attach to appraisal can be judged from the costs involved. The Graham Report refers to a total of 8 to 12 hours effort for each teacher appraised. If an additional day of teacher time were allocated for every teacher appraised, the cost would be in the region of forty million pounds. Training costs and the costs of maintaining the system would need to be added to this. Through the Coventry Agreement, the Nottingham negotiations and the ACAS Agreement, the establishment of appraisal has been maintained as a key part of any settlement.

The teachers' successful resistance to the direct link between pay and performance should not obscure the fact that the employers and the DES have gained considerable control over the work of teachers. The settlement of the teachers' pay claim will inevitably involve tighter specification of teachers' duties. The dispute itself illustrated the intimate link between control of work and control of the employment relation, given that little is specified in the teachers' contract. Indeed in a court case arising out of the dispute, the employers' view that the teachers' contract implies much more than simply class teaching was upheld. The teachers' claim to professional status was used by the judge to undermine their position; he stated in his judgment that:

'the contracts are silent on the teachers' obligations on many (other) important matters. This feature of the teachers' contracts does not seem to me a matter of surprise. A contract for the employment of a professional in a professional capacity would not normally be expected to detail the professional obligations of the employee made under the employment contract'.

In future, duties will be more tightly specified and monitored, and the result will be tighter control of teachers. The formal appraisal system may be developmental, but closer monitoring and the gathering of more information on teachers will also involve judgements on performance.

Whether they are agreed with the employers or imposed by the Secretary of State, teachers' conditions of service will now be specified. While performance-related pay has been dropped for the moment, there is no reason why it should not be revived by the Secretary of State in the future. The more hierarchical career structure favoured by the Secretary of State also involves strong elements of payment for performance through the promotion process, as he has made clear. Appraisal is not a whimsical notion of the Secretary of State, but a crucial part of the process of control through specifying teachers' work in detailed contract conditions. It is the process that will ensure that central purposes are being fulfilled.

The appraisal of teacher performance is part of a much wider development of assessment, accountability and control. In many types of work greater control and monitoring is possible through technological change, deskilling, and fragmentation. Such approaches are much more difficult to adopt in teaching, given the problems in specifying the work, and especially when there is a concern to enhance the skill of the workforce. The approach to gaining control of teaching work has been different from what it might have been in the case of manufacturing work. The politics of the workplace are quite different, because the nature of teaching work is quite different. I shall now turn to an analysis of teachers' work and the implications for appraisal.

Appraisal and Teachers' Work

Littler[21], in his study of the development of work under capitalism, distinguishes between rationalization and control of the labour process, of the structure of managerial control and rationalization of the nature of the employment relation. We have argued that, given the particular nature of teachers' work, appraisal of performance is key to the process of rationalization and that reform of the employment relationship is crucial to the process of control. Part of the teachers' claim to professional status is that judgment is part of the educational process because teaching work is difficult to specify. But the teachers' claim to professional autonomy is weak, and given changed labour market conditions they find it difficult to resist change in the nature of the employment relation. More importantly, given their own interest in reform of the career structure and the position inherited from the period of growth, they cannot resist change in the employment relation, only the link of pay and performance.

Appraisal of the performance of individual workers by their employers may be thought to be inappropriate for professionals whose work can only be adequately assessed by other professionals, if at all. Much of teacher resistance to appraisal and to tight specification of conditions of service is based upon the notion that teachers are professionals. The assertion of professional status is typically based on a claim to one or both of two types of knowledge distinguished by Jamous and Peloille[22], technical knowledge and indeterminate knowledge. The claim to 'technicality' is the claim that one's expertise is based upon theoretical knowledge, which can be codified and passed on through training. In the case of teaching this might be specialist knowledge of one's subject, or theoretical knowledge of the teaching process. The work of Sikes and her colleagues[23] has shown the importance of the subject base to many teachers:

> '... relating to one's subject rides above the problems, intricacies, pitfalls, and blocked opportunities of the hierarchical structure. It is a countervailing force against bureaucracy, giving one a firm foothold in the semi-autonomy of the subject department, affording status within it and bolstered by a like-minded community'[24].

The post-war period of growth saw a rapid expansion of subject specialisms as the curriculum widened. More recently, pedagogical skills have received increased emphasis, for example in the study of teaching styles.

The indeterminacy claim is that there are aspects of one's work that can only be learned through considerable practical experience and which cannot be taught. These indeterminate skills constitute the professional secret. The extent of indeterminacy is particularly high in teaching because, to a considerable extent, it is done by the teacher alone with the students in the classroom. Teaching is still a private activity, and a skill that can only be acquired in the classroom.

Claims both to technical and indeterminate knowledge as bases for teacher professionalism have become weaker as we have moved from growth to decline, and, to a considerable extent, it has been the circumstances created by growth that have undermined those claims. The technical basis of professional autonomy in specifiable skills will be eroded as management is able to proceduralise such knowledge, and, perhaps, embody it in machines and proceduralised approaches such as curriculum packages. This is much less possible in teaching than in many other types of work, but, as some American experience has shown, can be developed.

The claim to professionalism based upon specialist subject expertise has been seen by Wood[25] as containing the seeds of its own destruction:

> 'The curriculum has been divided and sub-divided, the areas thus created tending first to ensure their own self-preservation, then gathering strength with a view possibly to some further fission. Thus have teachers become more and more 'expert' as their areas of preserve become increasingly digested in this rationalizing process'.

As Buswell[26] has argued, this fragmenting of the curriculum can be the basis of control through the setting of aims and objectives and the development of curriculum packages. Subject hierarchies can form the basis for 'oligarchic control of the institution, through formal and informal meetings of heads of department with the head or principal of the institution'[27]. The expansion of managerial structures in the period of growth created the basis for such oligarchic control.

Expanding career opportunities and control of the curriculum created a strong degree of independence and individualistic self-control. But the growth of specialization and managerial structures worked, implicitly, in the opposite direction. The growth in student numbers and in finance led to a set of managerial structures in schools, which, in a period of decline, could be used for control rather than coordination. The increase in pupil numbers and the comprehensive movement created large schools which made specialization possible. The curriculum expanded because big schools created economies of scale in pupil groupings, and larger teaching staffs made possible a broader spread of teaching expertise. Bigger schools also needed explicit pastoral systems to counter the anonymity that goes with size, and to compensate for the difficulty of maintaining the personal knowledge of, and relationship with, pupils that are possible in smaller schools. Both subject and pastoral structures enhanced career routes for individual teachers, but individual teacher-pupil links, which, along with subject expertise, lay at the base of the claim to professional status, were weakened. The claim to professional status was shifting from the professional relationship of teacher and student to technical knowledge and skill. But the more the professional claim to occupational autonomy is based upon technical skill, the more it is prone to the claim that standards can be checked through appraisal.

Bigger schools with more complex curricula and organizational structures, required more coordination and the Burnham structure, with its proliferation of scales, allowed the creation of a range of managerial posts. The approach to management was hierarchical in concept, though, as we have said, the autonomy of teachers that followed from the context of growth limited managerial authority in practice. The school was 'loosely coupled' but the conditions for future hierarchical management that would be able to exert real control had been created. Teachers had come to talk of 'the hierarchy'; in future they would come to experience it. The form of management that developed in the period of growth provides a base for appraisal as the teachers' autonomy is eroded.

Growth led to general teacher shortage, but it has always been difficult to recruit specialist teachers and the expansion of the curriculum and pupil rolls led to teachers teaching subjects for which they are not specifically qualified. The Secondary Staffing Surveys of 1977 and 1984 found considerable evidence of such mismatch, especially in English, physical education, mathematics, religious education and physics. HMI reports have continually related poor teaching to mismatch. Changes in the curriculum have weakened some of the traditional claims to technicality as new subjects have been introduced, and as in-service training has been limited. New claims to technical skill have been established in some cases, for example special education. But the growing use of computers, the Cockcroft Report, the emphasis on technical and vocational aspects of education, the integration of pupils with special needs and the requirements for multi-cultural education all serve to highlight perceived inadequacies in the technical skills of teachers.

The claim to autonomy based on indeterminacy is also weak in the face of accusations of declining standards and demands for accountability. The teaching process is complex and there are no standard outputs. It is, therefore, difficult for teachers to give an account of their stewardship that is adequate and understandable. There is the danger that parents and employers will then fall back on examination results and standard tests. The requirement in the Education Act 1980 to publish examination results is an instance of such a tendency.

Teaching requires skills that are ill-understood even by those who practice them. Hargreaves[28] has argued that:

'most teachers believe(d) teaching to be an intuitive act, one in which skills defy easy analysis and explanation and thus cannot readily be transmitted to the novice . . .'.

It is then difficult for teachers to defend themselves against arguments that there are bad teachers and that there is bad teaching, and that the bad teachers should be weeded out.

'. . . certainly there are good and bad teachers but there are very different ways in which one can be good or bad and there are few universally agreed criteria by which teaching can be judged good or bad. Teaching is thus replete with "endemic uncertainties" about competence'[29].

The privacy of teaching, and the unwillingness to talk about the problems of competence make it all the more difficult to give an account. Sikes[30] argues that it is much easier to talk about problems now than was the case in the 1950s or 1960s, but there are still taboos about admitting problems.

The teachers' claim to professional autonomy is therefore limited by the growth of specialization and hierarchy and by the inability to provide an accounting language. Managerial control rather than peer evaluation is therefore easier to assert, even though it may not be clear how managerially-oriented appraisal might be done. Further, the claim to and the notion of a right to a career, implicit in much of the recent discussion of the reform of Burnham, is essentially individualistic. The focus is clearly upon the individual teacher, underestimating the role of the school as an organic entity, and the teacher's membership of a collegiate body of colleagues. The work of Rutter and others has shown the importance of the influence of the school and its ethos, and illustrated the limitations of the government's individualistic focus in the development of appraisal. A more collective view would have two implications. First, appraisal of the individual would necessarily involve evaluation of the school. Second, it would imply that any appraisal would be reciprocal and involve all those who go to make up the educational community. As Sayer put it:

> 'schools and communities are organic. A teacher is responding to demands, pressures and needs among pupils, parents, colleagues, the local community, and personal perceptions of good practice. The response is in a context of a school responding to or creating demands from governors, central and local government and other institutions, including future places of employment or continuing education . . . the collegiality of a teaching community is not just a matter of style, but of mutual responsibility. Any systematic review of performance . . . has, then, to be mutual if it is not to undermine the spirit of the enterprise'[31].

It is difficult to see how much a process could be used to judge individual teachers, though the Graham Report, while acknowledging the collective nature of the evaluation enterprise, implies that it could:

> ' . . . provide a vehicle for a cohesive pattern of national education, which in some instances would flow all the way from the Secretary of State through the LEAs to every classroom teacher'[32].

The basis would be laid for management-by-objectives, and centralized influence based upon managerial control-oriented accountability. At each level — DES, LEA, school, department, individual teacher — aims could be specified. A collective orientation could be hierarchical.

Focusing upon the individual teacher also gives a false picture of the teachers' autonomy. HMI, in their paper *Good Teachers*, observe that:

> ' . . . A successful teacher may rise above some organizational barriers, may bring coherence to a teaching programme where a school or department provides little, and help to compensate for social deprivation or handicap among the pupils. But the contribution of even the best teachers can be limited by outside factors, and appropriate weightings need to be employed in assessing the effectiveness of teachers operating in highly favourable conditions, and those working against a backcloth of severe disadvantage, shortages of necessary resources, or inadequate management . . .'[33].

A strong focus upon the individual may be a means of evading responsibility by those who must provide the conditions within which the teacher must work. Teaching is a constrained activity, and for appraisal of any sort, the constraints must be understood and specified.

The developments discussed above all serve to make teaching more public. Professional appraisal may serve to make more open processes that have always been implicit. The British teaching structure, unlike the American seniority-based system, has come to contain a high assessment content through the promotion system. But this is essentially based round the individual case.

The individualistic emphasis that characterizes the teachers' claim to professional autonomy, makes it more likely that any attempt at assessment will involve accountability as well as development. It also means that, in practice, assessment of performance and reward are likely to be related. The HMI study of appraisal found that:

> 'Appraisal was also used to provide evidence of promotability. One head pointed to ten internal and eight external promotions in the previous 18 months. The information gained and the judgments made during the appraisal process were frequently used as a means of ensuring fuller, more accurate references and this was generally welcomed by the teachers . . .'[34].

There is much more likely to be a link between performance assessment and promotion in a time of decline, when the labour market is much looser and teachers consequently less able to determine their career progression. Kenneth Baker's proposed hierarchical career structure will, therefore, involve a closer relationship of pay and performance than the more egalitarian ACAS agreement.

As the teachers' unions have argued, the basis upon which evaluation for promotion is made must be questioned. Grace's[35] study of a number of inner-city schools has shown that teachers' competence was more likely to be assessed on the basis of features such as personality, relations with other teachers and pupils and bureaucratic efficiency than the ability to teach. Moreover, headteachers frequently claim to know who are the more and less competent members of their staff by a rather unclear, almost osmotic, process of being around in school.

The individualistic nature of the relationship between teacher and taught has served, according to Lortie[36], to undermine the teachers' ability to develop a claim to technicality. The consequence, as Becher *et al.*[37] argue, is that the process of assessment moves from teaching to non-class based activities.

> 'One consequence of classroom privacy and the lack of generally acknowledged criteria for evaluating teaching is that promotion is likely to be based on considerations other than classroom performance. Provided a teacher is sufficiently competent not to have major disciplinary problems it will be his qualifications, his age, his attendance at courses outside the classroom which determines his chances of promotion'.

Moving into the classroom presupposes a clear set of criteria on which a teacher's performance in class can be assessed. Such developed criteria do not yet exist.

Conclusion

The teachers are now being subject to two separate processes of control. Developing central control and influence over the curriculum is specifying what shall be taught and how it shall be taught. LEAs, for example through curriculum staffing, are also exerting stronger central control. Aims and objectives to be met by all schools are being laid down by LEAs and the DES. Second, teachers' contracts are now being more closely specified. Both the content and form of the educational process are therefore being more closely controlled. Teacher appraisal and assessment must be seen in this context. The appraisal process may be judgmental or developmental. In the former guise it is clearly aimed at the control of performance. Implicit or explicit standards established by employers rather than established by the teacher or his or her peers will have to be met. But developmental assessment also has elements of control, for as we have seen the LEA, the DES and other bodies such as the Manpower Services Commission, will control the planning of in-service training and state priorities for its content. The focus is not on individual, self-determined, development, but controlled development in line with central objectives and priorities. It is worthy of note that one of the key central government priorities is management training.

The ability of teachers to resist these moves towards central control is limited. The labour market is loose, except for certain specialisms like mathematics and physics. Ring-fences and falling rolls limit career mobility, so that teachers are likely to find themselves for long periods in the same authority and the same schools. LEAs and schools can now plan teachers' careers in a managerial fashion. The teachers' own resistance to financial cuts and salary decline has weakened their professional position. By working to a tight interpretation of contract conditions, they have changed the emphasis in their jobs from one of general professional obligation, to specific contractual conditions.

Professionalism is a dynamic concept, changing its meaning according to the claims that occupations generally acknowledged to be professions are able to make. Those professions are strongest in their claims to autonomy that can claim independent self-control both on the basis of technical knowledge and indeterminate, experience-based, skill. Doctors have been very successful in claiming both. Teachers' claims to technical control of the curriculum are no longer accepted, as central government and the LEAs have reasserted control. The claim to indeterminate knowledge has always been weak, because of a neglect in emphasis on the teaching process, and because outsiders have been critical of teachers' methods. The privacy and individualistic nature of teaching has made the development of a collective professional voice difficult.

The development of appraisal systems is part of the development of a more managerial approach to education. A dual process of centralization of control in the hands of the DES, MSC and LEA, and decentralizing of power from the school to the parents and governing body, is eroding the autonomy of the teacher. Schools and teachers are to be held responsible for producing education, according to closely specified aims and objectives. The danger is that the result will be the sort of bureaucratization that frequently characterizes attempts at appraisal. Wise has argued in the United States that the result is 'hyper-rationalization' — 'bureaucratic overlay without attaining the intended policy objectives'[38]. Clearly we have already moved into a cycle of mistrust in which emphasis is laid on contractual obligations and continually enhanced rule-systems to ensure that they are met. We may not have moved as far as some of the individual states in the United States, but we are clearly 'rationalizing'.

Appraisal need not be purely negative and controlling. In laying out various dimensions — focus, purpose and form — along which appraisal can vary, I argued that appraisal can be either controlling or participative. In the United States we have seen the development of the control form — with standardized tests and competency-based assessment. Teaching, in such approaches, is broken down into a set of individualized, potentially fragmented skills. By contrast, a positive approach emphasises the 'wholeness' of the teaching and learning experience. Participative appraisal can enhance that recognition of the wholeness of the teaching and learning experience. It can encourage a focus upon the school and its place in the community rather than the individual isolated teacher.

Appraisal may also have a role to play in the partnership-based government of education. It can be a part of the process of involvement of teachers as well as parents and students in the educational process. In that sense it might form part of a reciprocal form of accountability, rather than a hierarchical, managerial accountability. Appraisal might then be a process that involved all those that formed part of the school in the community.

Participative appraisal could also help overcome the sort of isolation, uncertainty and loneliness that characterizes a great deal of teaching. In that it could be a part of the learning process in the school. It could be used not to identify the successes and failures of the individual teacher, but the constraints that operated on the school as a learning community. Appraisal might also be part of the process of developing a language in which one could account for education, making possible more rational dialogue on its nature and development. Participative appraisal could contribute to a reassessment of the purpose of education.

Notes

1 See, for example, the discussion by S. Ranson, 'Towards a Tertiary Tripartism: New Codes of Social Control and the 17 + ' in P. Broadfoot (Ed.), *Selection, Certification and Control*, Falmer Press, 1984

2 See Ranson (note 1) and the various articles in S. Ranson and J. Tomlinson (Eds.) *The New Management of Education*, George Allen and Unwin, 1986.

3   *Times Educational Supplement*, 27.6.1986

4   Audit Commission, *Obtaining Better Value In Education: Aspects of Non-Teaching Costs in Secondary Schools*, HMSO, 1984
Audit Commission, *Obtaining Better Value for Money from Further Education* HMSO, 1985
Audit Commission, *Towards Better Management of Secondary Education*, HMSO, 1986

5   Quoted in R. Saran, *The Politics Behind Burnham; A Study of Teachers' Salary Negotiations*, Sheffield Papers in Education Management, 1985, p 159

6   Quoted in B. Salter and T. Tapper, *Education Politics and the State*, Grant Mcintyre, 1981, p. 119

7   *Education in Schools; A Consultative Document*, Cmnd, 6869, HMSO, 1977, p. 2.

8   *Education in Schools*, p 16

9   *Better Schools*, p 54

10 See V. Karn 'Housing' and C. K. Skelcher 'Transportation' in S. Ranson, G. Jones, K. Walsh (Eds.) *Between Centre and Locality*, George Allen & Unwin, 1985

11 J. Eggleston, 'Teacher Professionalism and Professionalization' in S. Ranson, J. Tomlinson (Eds) *The Changing Government of Education*, George Allen & Unwin, 1986

12 *Assessment Techniques and Approaches, Better Schools Evaluation and Appraisal Conference*, Birmingham, 14–15 November, 1985, pp. 70–71

13 Quoted in J. B. Whyte, 'Teacher Assessment: A review of the Performance of Appraisal Literature with special reference to the Implications for Teacher Appraisal' in *Research Papers in Education*, Vol 1, No 2, June 1986, p 154

14 Department of Education and Science, *Quality in Schools: Evaluation and Appraisal*

15 *A New Remuneration Structure for Teachers*

16 *Teaching Quality*, p 15

17 *Better Schools*, HMSO, Cmnd, 9469, 1985, p 56

18 Suffolk Education Department, *Those Having Torches … Teacher Appraisal: A Study*, 1985.

19 *Those Having Torches*, p 9

20 *Towards Better Management of Secondary Education*

21 C Littler, *The Development of the Labour Process in Capitalist Societies*, London, Heinemann, 1982

22 H Jamous, B. Peloille 'Change in the French University Hospital System' in J. A. Jackson (Ed.) *Professions and Professionalisation*, Cambridge University Press, 1970

23 P. Sikes, L. Measor and P. Woods, *Teachers Careers: Crises and Continuities*, Falmer Press, 1985

24 P Sikes *et al.*, p 21

25 P. Woods, *The Divided School*, Routledge and Kegan Paul, 1979, p. 254

26 C. Buswell, 'Pedagogic Change and Social Change', in *British Journal of the Sociology of Education*, Vol 1, No 3, 1980

27 B. Bernstein, Quoted in S. Ball and I. Goodson, *Teachers' Lives and Careers*, Falmer Press, 1985

28 D. Hargreaves, *The Challenge for the Comprehensive School*, Routledge and Kegan Paul, 1982, p 197

29 D. Hargreaves, *The Challenge for the Comprehensive School*, p 204

30 P. Sikes *et al.*, pp 33–34

31 J. Sayer, *What Future for Secondary Schools?* Falmer Press, 1985, p 160

32 *Those Having Torches*, p 10

33 HMI, *Good Teachers*, HMSO, 1985, p 2.

34 DES, *Quality in Schools*, p 29

35 G. Grace, *Teachers, Ideology and Control: A Study in Urban Education*, Routledge and Kegan Paul, 1978

36 D. C. Lortie, *Schoolteachers, a Sociological Study*, Chicago, University Chicago Press, 1975

37 T. Becher, M. Erault, J. Knight, *Policies for Educational Accountability*, Heinemann, London, 1981

38 E. Wise, *Legislated Learning*, Berkeley, University of California Press, 1979

9
The Teachers' Action, 1984–1986

Richard Pietrasik

A series of notices pinned up in staffrooms during the Spring and Summer Terms of 1984:

March: Burnham Latest — TEACHERS REJECT 3% PAY OFFER
        PAY TALKS ADJOURNED — Employers repeat offer of 3%
April: ACTION
May: PAY ACTION EXTENDED
June: THE ANGRY PROFESSION

At the bottom of the first three of these notices is the banner: 'THE NUT: THE PROFESSIONAL UNION'. For the May and June notices this has changed to: 'THE NUT: THE PROFESSIONAL AND CAMPAIGNING UNION'. In many ways the inherent contradictions between the headlines on these NUT notices and the proclamations at the bottom underly the feelings of many of the teachers in Britain's schools today.

The teachers' dispute began in March 1984, at virtually the same time that the National Union of Mineworkers began what was to become a year-long strike against pit closures. The Conservative Government, in its fifth year of power, was determined to maintain control on its spending and had held down pay increases for all public service workers. The then Secretary of State for Education, Sir Keith Joseph, is not mentioned a great deal in this narrative; however he was always there in the background, and as one of the main architects of the Government's monetarist policies, determined to keep down spending in his sector.

The dispute is viewed from within the NUT but the reader should be aware that the NAS/UWT were as involved in taking action in the schools during this time as the NUT. Also, an even more determined struggle was going on in Scotland involving the Educational Institute of Scotland (EIS), the union to which a majority of Scottish teachers belong.

The Background

The story of the teachers' pay dispute is one of a leadership, in the main union — and at the beginning of the dispute the majority union — the NUT, that has historically seen its role as the representative of the third 'partner' of the English and Welsh education system, the teaching 'profession'; the other two partners being the Department of Education and Science and the Local Education Authorities. In this role it has always been treated with respect and continually consulted by the Government on every aspect of schooling. This emphasis and belief in a partnership has dominated the education system since 1945. The NUT Officers, Executive, and full-time officials have always seen their role as negotiators on behalf of a profession and only in the most exceptional circumstances as organisers of trade unionists in industrial action. To quote from the NUT 1985 Report of the Executive (page 3):

> 'Whilst the dangers to the education service presented by the Government cuts in education expenditure, rate-capping measures and the financial penalties, were stark and obvious, 1984 also brought the clearest evidence to date of a more insidious threat to the education service — that presented by the extent to which the present Government seeks to exert influence and control over the education service from Whitehall, and thereby to destroy the partnership between central government, local education authorities and the teaching profession, on which the service traditionally has been based ... These menacing developments have been accompanied by a distinct and disquieting tendency on the part of the DES to set extremely tight deadlines for the receipt of responses from those being consulted ...'.

The 'Teaching Profession'

Many teachers meanwhile have been gradually moving away from a perception of their job as a profession comparable to doctors and lawyers. More often, when arguing for greater salaries, they compare themselves with the police, other public servants, or middle management in the private sector. The word 'professional' is certainly used but in a loose fashion indicating commitment, self-organisation, and a certain status. Since the election of the Thatcher Government in 1979 the word is often heard in an ironic context indicating teachers' feelings that they are expected to still give the commitment but without the reward. Increasing numbers of teachers see an improvement in their pay and working conditions coming via trade union action rather than special pleading as a profession. It is this contradiction between the different perceptions of the dispute of the leadership of the NUT and that of many of their members that underlies the development and organisation of the teachers action.

That is not to say that there hasn't been some reaction to this among many teachers seeing increased trade union militancy as the cause of both a loss in status for teachers and the consequent drop in salary. This is evidenced by the development of the Professional Association of Teachers (PAT), which was formed on the basis that it would never take industrial action. However the most significant change in teacher union membership has been the growth of the National Association of Schoolmasters and Union of Women Teachers (NAS/UWT).

Union Membership

This growth in the NAS/UWT, as shown in the table[1], has been to a great extent at the expense of the NUT. The NAS part of the NAS/UWT was formed as a breakaway from the NUT shortly after the First World War as a 'Men's Movement' opposing the NUT's policy of equal pay. The UWT was tagged on in the seventies in order to conform to anti-discrimination laws. Interestingly the NUT suffered another split in the twenties by the formation of the National Union of Women Teachers (NUWT), a union committed to equal pay and exasperated by the male-dominated NUT's lack of action on the issue; it was disbanded in the early sixties after equal pay was brought in; it has no links with the UWT of the NAS/UWT.

The NUT and the NAS/UWT are the only two of the teacher unions affiliated to the TUC. The NAS/UWT is a very centralised organisation with a reputation for a narrow but strong militancy on the national issue of salaries, but much less prepared to take action on a local basis, and with an authoritarian position on education policies. The NUT on the other hand, in maintaining its traditional role as representative of all teachers, has been much less militant nationally but much more progressive in its education policies. It has pursued its policies through negotiation and seldom through national action. At a local level the Local Associations and Divisions of the NUT have always historically had a lot of autonomy and because of this there has been more action on local issues by the NUT than the NAS/UWT.

There has been a steady erosion of NUT membership to the NAS since the early 1960s, mainly caused by the NUT's lack of success in salary negotiation. With the oil crisis of the mid-Seventies and the consequent cutbacks in public expenditure, accelerated with the election of the Conservative Government of 1979, the NUT's failure in negotiation continued. The NAS/UWT, always ready to use its militancy as a recruiting weapon, has as a result gained members.

Not only did the Thatcher Government cut back on educational expenditure, it also did so without consulting the NUT leadership. It abolished the School's

Council, the organization on which the NUT were well represented, which gave teachers an influential voice on all matters to do with the curriculum in England and Wales.

The Burnham Committee

Teachers are employed not by the State but by Local Education Authorities (LEAs) in Britain. Their pay was, until recently, negotiated by the Burnham Committee, first set up in 1919. This committee, consisting of representatives of the teacher unions and Local Authority employers, with just two seats for the Department of Education and Science (DES) representatives, met every year to decide teachers' wages from April. On the teachers' side, the NUT, representing as it did until 1984/5 the majority of teachers, held a majority of the teachers seats on the 'Teachers Panel' of the Burnham Committee[2].

The Houghton Committee

After another period of decline in teachers' salary levels in the early seventies, the situation was resolved in 1974 by the setting up, by the Government of the day, of the Houghton Committee. This Committee recommended altering the structure of teachers' salaries and substantially increased them with the pledge that the relative levels of teachers' pay with respect to comparable jobs would in future be maintained. However, since 1975, when the Houghton structure was fully implemented, teachers' salaries have continually declined in relative terms. By 1983 the NUT calculated that teachers' salaries had fallen behind by some 30 percent.

The Salary Structure

There was an additional problem — the salary structure[3]. Many teachers felt themselves 'trapped' on the tops of the scales, a quarter on the top of the bottom two — Scales One and Two. Already, the management side of the Burnham Committee were offering a change in this structure in return for changes in teachers' conditions with assessment and monitoring of teachers' work.

The 1984 Claim

After what was considered a poor increase of 4.98 per cent in 1983, further eroding the relative salary levels of teachers, and against a Government pay target of 3 per cent, an unspecified claim for 1984 was submitted by the unions in January of that year for 'substantial salary increases for all teachers'.

The Executive of the NUT had not prepared for any sort of a fight on the salaries claim: no publicity or meetings for membership, no talks on action with other teaching or non-teaching unions, a late claim, no precise figure to act as a rallying point, and a preparedness to accept a percentage figure further increasing the divisive differentials.

Action on the 1984 Claim

The employers offered 3 per cent in March 1984 and stated that there could be no increase on that figure. They also refused the unions' offer of recourse to an independent arbitration panel. The Easter 1984 Annual Conference of the NUT in Blackpool voted for industrial action. The intention was, interestingly enough, not to obtain a particular increase but to force the employers to go to arbitration to resolve the 1984 Claim. A contradictory position, taking action to force arbitration.

No Agreement on the 1985 Claim

The call for arbitration was not a universally supported move. At Blackpool, the Socialist Teachers' Alliance (STA), the main left grouping within the NUT, was defeated in an amendment opposing arbitration. More interestingly, the Executive's proposal for the 1985 claim was thrown out by the conference. This was on the basis that a majority of the delegates at the conference wanted a more egalitarian structure in the claim. The amendments that were carried called for the amalgamation of scales one, two, and three instead of the Executive's position of amalgamating only the first two scales, and for flat-rating the claim instead of a percentage increase. The conference finished in the end with no claim being decided for 1985, hence the need for the Special Salaries Conference in the Autumn to agree on a claim. The strength of the support for these amendments reflected what had been a growing force within the schools that the scale structure was divisive and unfair on the majority of classroom teachers, a disproportionate number of whom are women, 'stuck' on scales one and two. The Autumn Conference was to support a claim for a more egalitarian structure.

Summer Term 1984 — Action

From the second day of the Summer Term, following the Conference decision on action, all NUT members were 'called upon' to:

'● refuse to cover for the absences which are known in advance or for any other unexpected absences after the first day;

   • withdraw from lunchtime supervision of children and administrative and accounting tasks in connection with the school meals service;

   • refuse to attend staff meetings, departmental and year meetings ...

   • refuse to attend parents meetings ...

   • withdraw goodwill from any activities outside school hours connected with the administration, organisation or management of the school'.

There was to be a one-day strike on 9th May.

An offer by the employers of 4.5 per cent at the end of April was rejected unanimously by all the teacher unions and the NUT together with the NAS/UWT continued with their action. The NUT ballotted their members on strike action and started a series of three day strikes in selected areas on May 22nd. Four thousand teachers from 224 schools in 42 local authorities were called out. The NUT were to ballot their members 14 times during the two-year dispute.

Arbitration

On June 11th the employers agreed to go to arbitration and the NUT called upon its members to cease all action as from Friday June 22nd. The teachers, and in particular the Officers of the NUT, felt they had won a major victory. In an open letter to all NUT members, the four senior Officers said:

> 'Your determination and commitment, together with that of your colleagues in the NAS/UWT, has proved how effective planned action by teachers can be ....
>
> Teachers have learned that they can bring pressure to bear. The Employers have learned the same lesson and you can take pride in the part you played in helping the profession to stand up and be counted'.

When, at the end of the Summer, the three-man arbitration panel gave its decision there was bitter disappointment. Teachers were given an increase of 5.1 per cent with no restructuring and no flat-rating. The message from the NUT displayed on staffroom notice-boards throughout the country declared 'ARBITRATION FAILS'.

The 1985 Claim

With the miners strike still continuing, and against a background of the Conservative Government's attack on local government with the further introduction of ratecapping through the Rates Act, legislation to abolish the Metropolitan Counties, including the GLC, and with the Rate Support Grant from the Government based on pay increases being kept to 3 per cent, the NUT held a Special Salaries Conference at the end of September 1984 to decide on its claim following the stalemate of the Easter Conference.

The conference decided on a policy that was a considerable change from previous years. The leadership of the union, taking note of the successful amendments at Easter, put forward proposals for the amalgamation of scales one, two and three and the payments for extra responsibilities being in the form of extra increments above the basic scale rather than separate scales, so that teachers would all be on the same 'scale' but those in positions of responsibility would receive an extra £1000 or £2000, say, above the scale, the amount depending on the level of responsibility; for 'a minimum flat rate increase of £1200' for all teachers rather than the usual percentage claim; and for the rejection of any trade-off of conditions of service for increases in salaries. Significantly it required amendments from the floor of the Conference to insert into the claim a timetable of escalating action linked to the negotiations and for the rejection of any recourse to arbitration.

On November 1st the General Secretary of the NUT, Fred Jarvis, in his role as leader of the Teachers' Panel of the Burnham Committee, submitted the claim for 1985. This early submission was intended to avoid a late settlement of the claim, allowing plenty of time for negotiation, and possibly action, before April 1st 1985. The claim had been formulated jointly by the NUT and the NAS/UWT but conformed to the NUT Conference decision.

'Today's Teacher'

At the same time the NUT released a booklet titled 'Today's Teacher'. It was in fact the evidence that the Union had submitted to the arbitration panel in support of their 1984 claim. The booklet took the statement from the Houghton Committee, the official body that settled the 1974 teachers' salaries claim and ended a long period of decline in teachers' salaries: 'There is no doubt in our minds that teaching has become more demanding — the content and techniques of education are changing more rapidly than they have ever done before, requiring flexibility and new enthusiasm from teachers ...' and used quotes from teachers that showed that teaching had become a far more demanding job in 1984 than it was even in 1974.

The initiatives and changes in society that had led to an increase in the workload and stress on teachers were listed; curriculum developments such as environmental studies, multi-faith education, pre-vocational and social skills training, CDT (Craft and Design Technology), and Computer Studies; the pressure to improve the teaching of 'core' subjects from the Bullock Report on English (1975), the Cockcroft Report on Mathematics (1982), and the many reports of the Assessment of Performance Unit (set up in 1974); the more active role of Her Majesty's Inspectorate (HMI) as initiators of curriculum development, producing numerous reports, discussion documents and surveys.

A list of other factors increasing the complexity of teaching since 1974 was cited: microcomputers, the Technical and Vocational Initiative (TVEI), special needs legislation, education for a multicultural society, equal opportunities, new methods of assessment, social pressures, counselling, changing approaches to discipline, increased demands on accountability, the 1980 Education Act; the fact that teachers are expected to produce higher standards of performance against a background of serious shortcomings in material and resource provision throughout the service.

The quotations from teachers make salutary, if depressing reading and repeat what can be heard in any British school staffroom:

'... the never-ending round of assessments, reports, field trips ..., parents' evenings to which staff travel in their own time and their own expense. Staff meetings, departmental meetings, the pastoral care of pupils, marking and preparation of work, after-school clubs, the school production (staff using evenings and weekends for rehearsals), the after-school and weekend sports fixtures, the music department's rehearsals and concerts, the induction day for sixth years, held on a Saturday, the language department's treks abroad and in-service training to try to keep abreast of the latest methods'.

'Morale is also low at a time when unemployment is so high and often frighteningly inevitable; one can no longer encourage with "try and get some decent grades and you'll be o.k." — I have heard comments like "What's the point? There are no jobs." from second years!'.

'Children generally seem to be becoming more difficult to handle, livelier and less amenable to school discipline'.

'Increasing interest by those outside the teaching profession has meant that teachers have had to justify/explain/account for themselves more frequently and in more detail'.

'I am 41 years of age and had my first stress-induced heart attack four years ago'.

'Ten years ago, teachers retired reluctantly. My own Authority has been surprised at the sheer numbers applying for retirement, especially senior scale post holders, deputies and Heads. All of these cannot be inefficient or ill'.

'Last year a colleague who had spent 15 years in industry and five years in science teaching resigned and left teaching saying that the demands on him were too great compared with the time he spent in industry and the rewards were insufficient'.

A Productivity Deal

On November 15th Philip Merridale, the Conservative leader of the employers' panel on Burnham, presented a series of proposals to the Salary Structure Working Party, a joint union-management body set up by the Burnham Committee. These proposals amounted to a productivity deal for teachers:

a three-year Entry Grade, with the employers right to sack Entry Grade teachers at any time;

annual assessment of teachers by the headteacher with no progress to the next salary increment if the assessment is unsatisfactory;

three-yearly assessment of teachers by their local authority again linked to salary;

abolition of the 1968 School Meals Agreement, which ensured the voluntary nature of dinnertime supervision;

an obligation on teachers to cover for absent colleagues.

If teachers were not already aware of the fact that they were involved in more than a pay claim, then these proposals made sure that they understood what it was all about. With the background of increasing government intervention in the curriculum, the introduction of these proposals for 'managing the workforce' made it clear that the teachers were involved in a struggle for the whole future of education. Following the lead of the coal and car industries, the employers appealed to their employees, the teachers, over the heads of their unions by placing adverts selling the deal in the Times Educational Supplement.

In response to the management proposals, the NUT used its majority on the Burnham Teachers' panel to withdraw the teachers' side from the Salary Structure Working Party.

Questions and a Call for Arbitration

In the Burnham Committee, the employers' side, rather than rejecting the unions' claim as had been expected, played for time by tabling a series of questions to the unions on the distribution of the above scale payments. At the Burnham meeting of December 7th the unions were not able to answer the questions because of the difficulties in reconciling the different approaches of the NUT and the NAS/UWT. On December 14th the NUT Executive met, and despite demands from the left-wing Executive members, made no proposals either to meet with the NAS/UWT to hammer out their differences or to come up with a timetable for action for the coming term as outlined in the motion passed at the September conference.

At the Burnham meeting of January 28th the employers offered 4 per cent, and after discussing the teachers' unanimous rejection of the offer among themselves for five hours, announced that the negotiations were over and argued that the time had come for arbitration. On the teachers' side only the NAHT, SHA, and PAT supported the call for arbitration. The NUT requisitioned another Burnham meeting for February 11th and in the meantime started organizing action.

As from February 6th NUT members were called upon to take virtually the same action as they had the previous Summer Term, but this time it was in support of continued negotiation and an improved offer from the employers rather than to get arbitration. The employers indicated outside the Burnham Committee that there could possibly be another 7.5 per cent available for teachers' salaries if their structure package were to be accepted. The NUT's response as stated in the NUT News No. 4 in February was that '. . . teachers are grossly underpaid and undervalued for the work that they do now; they should be adequately paid for the additional demands already made of them without the imposition of a new and worsened contract . . .'. Sir Keith Joseph was soon to state in Parliament that there was never any prospect of this extra 7 per cent being made available anyway.

At the February 11th meeting, the Teachers' Panel offered the concession that although they couldn't agree to link negotiations on salaries with those on conditions of service, they would be prepared to negotiate in the local authorities standing committee on conditions of service at the same time as discussing salaries in Burnham. The employers rejected this proposal and reiterated their previous offer.

Three-day Strikes

In response to this the NUT began balloting members in order to start three-day strikes in selected schools as from February 26th. Support from members was described by the union as 'overwhelming' with 94 per cent of the teachers balloted voting in favour of the action. 4,000 teachers were selected to strike for the three days from the 26th, with 5,000 called out the following week. The action was organized centrally from the NUT Headquarters in Hamilton House, London. The Officers of the union together with the paid officials chose representative areas, spreading the action geographically and across all sectors. Local officers of the NUT in these areas were then asked to ballot the required members as quickly as possible and relay the results to Hamilton House where the final decision was taken, based on the ballot results, on who to call out.

NUT policy, an unusual one, probably linked to the traditional view that it is as much a professional association as a trade union, is to pay in full the teachers who are on strike; only national one-day or half-day strikes have been unsustained. The effect of this is two-fold: it encourages support for strike action from the doubters but severely limits the number of strike-days that the union can fund. The 3-day strike weapon, the days being Tuesday, Wednesday, and Thursday, was chosen in order to cause the maximum disruption for the minimum cost since if a teacher took strike action on a Monday or Friday s/he would be liable to have money deducted for the weekend as well.

Following the obtaining of a High Court injunction by Solihull local authority on the grounds of the possibility that teachers were breaking their contracts by withdrawing from lunchtime supervision, the NUT decided, 'to ensure it is acting within the 1984 Trade Union Act and to prevent a succession of injunctions in other authorities', to ballot all members on the withdrawal of goodwill and refusal to cover. Again, reflecting the NUT's 'professional association' status, the union has always shown great respect for the decisions of High Court Judges. Over 77 per cent of those who voted supported the imposition of the sanctions.

The 'withdrawal of goodwill' action together with the selective 3-day strikes continued until the Easter holidays with no movement from either side of the Burnham committee, except for some meetings with ACAS to explore the possibility of conciliation, and with Sir Keith Joseph keeping aloof from the whole affair except to say that there would be no extra money from him come what may. More than 29,000 NUT members were called out on strike during the last five weeks of the Spring Term. The hope on the management side was obviously that the teachers would be forced to go to arbitration by their own reluctance to prolong the action and by the weight of public opinion against them harming children's education.

Conference — Easter 1985

The Easter NUT Conference opened in Scarborough with press reports that Philip Merridale, the employers' leader, had likened striking teachers to orang-utans. This comment by the Hampshire Tory was condemned by Josie Farrington, Labour opposition leader of the Association of County Council's education committee. She was quoted in the Teacher (12.4.85) as saying that 'the remark was insulting and lowered the tone of the whole dispute'. Josie Farrington's rather weak comment probably reflected the lack of support for the teachers in the local councils, Labour as well as Conservative. A number of Labour councils had already threatened teachers with disciplinary action and pay-docking if they continued taking industrial action.

The NUT conference passed the motion put by the Executive which reiterated the demand for a minimum increase for all teachers of £1200 and called for an intensification of the strike action so as to make teachers' pay a major issue in the forthcoming May County Council elections. It was also agreed to hold a voluntary levy to raise an expected £3 million pounds for the strike fund. Members were asked to 'refuse to complete reports, school records or pupil profiles or to be involved in curricular innovations outside normal school sessions'. Closer co-operation in the campaign was sought with the other TUC-affiliated teacher unions: the EIS, NATFHE, and the NAS/UWT, and with other public service unions.

Amendments from the floor calling for the disruption of the Summer exams, for increasing strike action, for absolute 'no cover' action, and for the levy to be made compulsory, were all defeated.

The Conference passed motions opposing any form of teacher assessment linked to pay; opposing any linking of salary negotiations with those on conditions of service; and calling for a campaign, including action, on class-size.

Summer Term 1985 — More Action

The new term started with intensified action in the schools and with the NUT asking Local Authorities to express their support for a model statement calling on the authorities to convene a Burnham meeting to accept that the relative decline in teachers salaries since 1975 was over 30 per cent; that teaching was an important and demanding job to which the commitment of teachers had not diminished; and to make a substantially increased offer. Those Authorities that supported the statement were rewarded by the suspension of strike action in their area.

Local Elections

The County Council elections led to the Conservatives losing control in a number of authorities and hence on the employers' side of Burnham, but made very little difference to the position that the management side of the Burnham Committee took. Although it was now accepted that there would have to be an increased offer above the 4 per cent, it was only at the end of the term that any offer was made and that was an 'informal' one of 6 per cent tied to changes in conditions of service. Sir Keith Joseph at the DES kept on reiterating that there was no more money to come from him. The NUT continued to intensify its action, increasing the number of strike days until over 100,000 teachers had been involved in some form of strike action during the Summer.

The 'Four Principles'

The Teachers' Panel, led by the NUT, called for a settlement which:

' ● gives a total increase for the year at least equal to the increase in the cost of living;

   ● produces levels which do not further erode the relative salaries of teachers;

   ● contains an element towards the recovery of the decline identified by the Pay Data Working Party; ...

   ● involves a commitment for the future to further moves towards the restoration of Houghton relatives' (NUT News No 19)

The NUT were to refer to these as 'the four principles'.

Differences within Schools

There were bitter differences between teachers and between teachers and heads in the schools. Heads felt that they had to keep the schools running as normally as possible, but in trying to implement this, often strayed into the area of undermining the teachers action. In Secondary schools, senior members of staff, rather than allow pupils to be sent home, were doing all the cover, classes that teachers had refused to cover were herded into the hall with the Head or a Deputy supervising a number of classes at once. Teachers from AMMA or PAT, the teacher associations not taking any action, were often taking on the cover that members of the NUT or NAS/UWT had refused to do.

At lunchtime in many schools the headteacher would be alone in trying to supervise all the pupils. At the end of the Summer term the NAHT and SHA issued statements saying that their members would not be able to keep their schools running at lunchtime for much longer.

Teachers in the NUT and NAS/UWT were doing their teaching and nothing else, no staff-meetings, parents evenings, reports, or out-of-school activities. Meetings were held by the union groups in many schools to inform parents what was happening and why. The majority of parents gave their support to the teachers at these meetings.

The feeling among most NUT and NAS/UWT members was that, although they were fed up with the lack of progress in the negotiations, they were winning the arguments outside of Burnham and were certainly not going to give up this long struggle until there was a substantial increase in their pay.

Autumn Term 1985 — 'Top People' receive 46 per cent

There was no lack of determination by the teachers when they returned to school in September with the 1985 claim still in dispute. In particular, during the Summer the Government accepted the Top People's Salaries Review Body's recommendations and awarded increases of up to 46 per cent to top civil servants, high court judges, and high ranking army officers. These large increases were justified by the Government on the grounds of comparability while still refusing to provide any more than 3 per cent extra for teachers salaries. In the staffrooms even the teachers belonging to the associations not taking action were furious.

The NUT asked all members to vote in favour of 'extending the withdrawal of goodwill sanctions to do no more than teach their classes and undertake any necessary preparation and marking related to this'; this was in fact reiterating the situation that already existed in many schools. They were also asked to vote in favour of taking a half day strike to attend regional rallies in support of the campaign. These were ballots number 7 and 8 of 1985. Returns from these by the end of September showed a level of support respectively of 87 per cent and 74 per cent for the two ballots.

Employers offer 5.85 per cent

At the first Burnham meeting of the term the employers formally offered 5.85 per cent but tied to changes in teachers' conditions of service. The teachers' side unanimously rejected the offer. The NUT organised a ninth ballot in support of 3 more half-day strikes in the Autumn Term.

It was obvious to the LEAs that the teachers were determined to carry the fight on. John Pearman, the Labour leader of the employers, stated at the beginning of October: 'The fact is that the ballots and the demonstrations and the meetings have shown an overwhelming upsurge of support by teachers for continued action. Those of us who had said that the teachers' leaders were out of touch with their members have been proved wrong'. (NUT News No. 23).

The Management Panel now, in a letter, offered the teachers 6.9 per cent for the 1985/86 settlement, end loaded to produced 7.5 per cent by March 31st 1986. Management, as part of the offer, called for 'the setting up of a Royal Commission to report and make recommendations on pay and other conditions of service in addition to structure and negotiating machinery'. This offer was conditional on an immediate cessation of industrial action by the teachers. If the teachers indicated acceptance then a full Burnham Meeting would be held to ratify an agreement. The offer was therefore non-negotiable.

The Teachers' Panel, with the NUT using its majority, rejected the Management offer. The NUT expressed its willingness to meet in the full Burnham Committee to negotiate a settlement but insisted that this had to be based on the four principles passed by the Teachers Panel in the Summer. The flat-rate element in the teachers' claim appeared to have been forgotten by all sides. The NUT was alone among the teacher associations in supporting these four principles with the NAS/UWT calling them 'fatuous pre-conditions'.

NUT loses Burnham Majority

Tuesday, November 5th was a momentous day for the NUT. The Secretary of State for Education and Science, Sir Keith Joseph, reduced the NUT's representation on the Burnham Committee from 16 to 13 (see Note 2); the change was to reflect the fact that no longer did a majority of teachers belong to the NUT. This was the first time in the 66-year history of the Burnham Committee that the NUT did not hold the majority of the Teachers' Panel. The NUT negotiators were aware that the other associations, including NAS/UWT, would combine to use their majority to get a settlement with the employers based on their 6.9 per cent offer. There would be no commitment to the four principles and a trading-off of conditions of service for salary gains. The NUT News at the beginning of November, headlined 'SELL-OUT AHEAD?', referred to the NAS/UWT as collaborators.

As things turned out no agreement was reached at the Teachers' Panel meeting on November 11th due to the PAT representative abstaining on the crucial vote and the NATFHE representative, at his last Panel meeting before his removal, voting with the NUT. However, the NUT leaders were affronted by their removal from all the posts on the Panel. All the other teaching associations voted together to remove the NUT from holding both the Chair and the Secretary's position on the Teachers' Panel. It was felt by the NUT that the NAS/UWT membership would not agree to these manoeuverings by their negotiators in joining with all the other associations, particularly the NAHT that had not supported the action, to force an unsatisfactory settlement. The NUT through its newsletters began appealing to the NAS/UWT members to stop their leaders 'selling out'. NUT News No. 28 was headlined 'FIRM AND DETERMINED' and although subtitled 'an open message to NUT members' was clearly aimed at NAS/UWT members:

> 'As NUT members you have shouldered the responsibility for the salaries campaign. At staffroom level you have been joined by your colleagues in the NAS/UWT and to a lesser degree in the AMMA. Teachers in schools will therefore find it hard to comprehend the enmity and combined opposition arrayed against the NUT at this week's meeting of the Teachers' Panel.
>
> Above all, colleagues in the NAS/UWT will be appalled at the new alliances which their leadership have made with organisations that have throughout sought to undermine their own campaign — the NAHT, the SHA, and the PAT.
>
> The NUT will not be deflected from its path ....
>
> The NUT is firm and determined to achieve better pay for teachers and an agreement to the phased restoration of Houghton salaries over the next two or three years'.

The statement was signed by the four elected Officers of the union and by the General Secretary and his deputy.

At the Teachers' Panel meeting in December a motion accepting the employers 6.9 per cent offer as a significant improvement and seeking an interim agreement for 1985 was carried with only the NUT voting against.

The NUT Executive then called a Special Salaries Conference for January 18th and prepared a ballot (No. 11) for further half-day strikes in the Spring Term.

Spring Term 1986 — ACAS[4]

The new term began with ACAS offering to help the two sides of Burnham reach a settlement. NUT representatives met the Officers of ACAS and advised them that because of the 'fundamental differences' between the NUT and other teacher organizations they would wish to present their views individually to ACAS. These differences were the union's firm position on the 'four principles' and its opposition to any trade-off between salaries and conditions of service. ACAS from the beginning indicated that it was prepared to allow discussions to link salaries and conditions.

The NUT Special Salaries Conference expressed support for the union negotiators' position and for a continuation of the action pending a satisfactory settlement of the 1985 claim. The determination to continue the fight by the NUT membership was demonstrated by the fact that not one of the over 400 amendments submitted by Local Associations to the Executive's main motion before the Conference called for a reduction of the campaign. An amendment to boycott exams as part of the action was lost by 99,000 votes to 120,000; significantly, however, two amendments were carried despite the Executive's opposition: the first seeking a united approach with the NAS/UWT in Burnham and building joint action with them where possible, and the second calling for a one-day national strike and demonstration.

The Conference also agreed on the salary claim for 1986. Although the 1985 claim was still not finally settled, it was only just over two months to the settlement date for the 1986 claim. The union policy was for a basic salary starting at £8000 and rising to £16500, with ten increments of £850; additional allowances of up to £3400 for extra responsibility; Head's salaries to rise to a maximum of £31500. Houghton relativities were to be restored. No teacher was to receive less than £1700.

February 1986 — 6.9 per cent Agreed for 1985

At the beginning of February, the Teachers' Panel made a deal with the employers accepting the 6.9 per cent backdated to April 1985, with a further increase of 1.6

per cent for the day before the 1986 salary agreement was due to be made, March 31st 1986. Considering the level of involvement and continual action by the teachers that had taken place for almost a year, and in particular the support being shown by parents' groups up and down the country, it was a pathetic deal. But, much worse from the NUT's point of view was that the Teachers' Panel agreed, as part of the deal, to enter into negotiations with the employers, and facilitated by ACAS, on 1986's salary in which conditions of service would be linked to pay.

The 1986 Claim

Action Continues

The NUT balloted members on the continuation of action and called on other teachers, in particular NAS/UWT members to reject the deal. Certainly the membership of the NAS/UWT showed little support for the settlement; their local association meetings up and down the country expressed disappointment. In Lancashire, the Executive member and the whole local committee resigned in opposition. However in their ballot there was a two-thirds majority in favour of acceptance. As the NUT News stated:

> 'A third of the NAS/UWT members who voted expressed their op-position to the ACAS deal's terms, and together with those NAS/UWT members who opposed the deal but who could not out of loyalty vote against their leaders, less than half of the NAS/UWT could find it in themselves to accept the employer's deal'

NUT enters ACAS Talks

The NUT ballot (No 14) for continuation of the action received a strong vote in favour. The action went on until Easter and the NUT Annual Conference. As stated in the NUT News in March:

> '. . . the NUT has made the implications of the ACAS deal clear to its members: it means a trade off of inadequate pay for worsened conditions of service'.

However, despite the leadership's strong opposition to the ACAS talks, to quote Fred Jarvis speaking in the Burnham Committee of March 3rd:

> '. . . the ACAS deal gives the government and employers what they have been seeking .... The proposed procedures will effectively deprive representatives of teachers and employers of the opportunity to negotiate

with each other; they will hand themselves over to the control of the 'three wise men' from ACAS'.

At the Executive meeting three days later it was agreed to go into the ACAS talks.

The justification for joining these talks was that the NUT needed to be there to protect all teachers from any worsening of conditions of service and salary levels. However the NUT negotiators were unwilling, or felt unable, to call off the action and because of this were excluded from the talks.

Interim Settlement of 1986 Claim

The Easter Annual Conference endorsed the Executive's decision to enter the ACAS talks and the successful Executive motion offered a way into the talks by proposing an interim settlement of £800 flat-rate for all teachers in return for a cessation of action.

After the Conference, and with this offer on the table, the NUT balloted for strike action in 21 'key' Local Authorities. The intention was to force the employers to reach some agreement with the unions at a Burnham Committee meeting requisitioned by the NUT for May 9th. An agreement was reached. The employers agreed to pay teachers an interim settlement of £519 or 5.5 per cent, whichever was the greater, as from April 1st 1986. The unions in return agreed to stop all action and enter and support the ACAS talks.

NUT staffroom notices were headlined 'NUT TRIUMPH'. The interim settlement was described as 'money in the bank'. All action was to cease with the exception of lunchtime supervision. With regard to cover, the notices explained that the union's view was 'that cover for absent colleagues is not a contractual requirement and that voluntary cover for up to one day's unforseen absence only is acceptable'. In many areas, teachers continued to refuse to cover even for the first day, not so much as an industrial action on the pay front but more as an established gain in their conditions of service.

For many teachers in the NUT this acceptance of the ACAS talks was a surprising change of position by their union. After all the statements criticizing the talks and the condemnation of the NAS/UWT for bringing them about, here was the NUT leadership ending the action and accepting a deal that fully involved them in the ACAS talks linking salaries and conditions of service and with no statement from the employers on an intention to return to the Houghton relativities.

Summer Term 1986

The Summer term became one of the contrasts with regard to action. Many teachers in the cities, particularly London, continued the full range of sanctions.

In other areas teachers, hoping that the end of this demoralising time had come, stopped the action and returned to all the parents evenings, meetings, reports, etc., in anticipation of a large pay increase.

In May, the NUT received a High Court judgement on cover. The union had taken to court four Local Authorities that had docked pay from teachers who had refused to cover for absent colleagues. The NUT's case was that cover was not contractual. The judge, Mr. Justice Scott, didn't say that cover was contractual but ruled that teachers had a 'professional obligation' to cover. Up until this judgement the NUT had always advised teachers that they did not have to cover. The interesting contradiction of this judgement is that it labelled teachers as professionals, not to make sure they were paid accordingly, but to ensure that they did exactly as their employers demanded, not generally accepted as one of the characteristics of a professional.

As the ACAS talks rumbled on through the Summer, Sir Keith Joseph, viewed on all sides as having lost the propaganda battle on the teachers dispute, was replaced as Secretary of State for Education by a much more ambitious politician, Kenneth Baker.

In late July, after a final four days of virtually continuous negotiation in a Coventry hotel, an agreement was reached in the ACAS talks. 'The Coventry Agreement' offered teachers a new salary structure with a Main Professional Grade, with salaries ranging from £9600 to £14500, for the majority of teachers and two allowances of £750 and £2000 for those teachers, to be known as Principal Teachers, with extra responsibilities. All teachers were to receive a one-off lump sum of £750 on January 1st 1987. The agreement also introduced an 'Entry Grade' for new teachers, defined teachers' 'duties', and guaranteed non-contact time and maximum class sizes. The employers and all the teachers' organisations, with the exception of the NAS/UWT signed the agreement. Of course it would require the signature of the Secretary of State for Education for the deal to be implemented.

Autumn Term 1986

As teachers returned to schools, concern about the agreement grew. Many NUT Associations passed motions opposing the deal. Opposition was also voiced in the other teaching organisations. Although the Main Professional Grade salaries looked attractive, teachers at present on the maximum of Scale One would take at least nine years to reach the promised £14500; on the maximum of the MPG, it would take 8 years for those on the top of Scale Two. There were too few Principal Teacher allowances; teachers could now be directed by their headteacher to attend parents evenings, staff meetings, and to work for five days in the school holidays. For NUT members, the agreement went against the principles for which they had been fighting of a promised return to Houghton, and no linking of salaries and conditions of service.

On 'cover' an 'interim agreement' was reached just before the beginning of the term. It stipulated that the employers would provide supply teachers to cover after the first day of absence if they could, but should they be unable to, then teachers would continue to cover. In many areas, where teachers had not been covering at all or only for the first day, this agreement was not welcomed. Many Local NUT Associations voted to ignore the agreement.

Against this background the employers and unions began talks again to clarify those points left outstanding in the Coventry Agreement. Kenneth Baker, the Education Secretary, announced that he would not fund the deal and introduced a bill in the House of Commons allowing him to impose his own deal and removing from teachers the right, in future, to negotiate their salaries.

On November 15th the employers and unions reached a further agreement, the Nottingham Agreement. This was a refining of the Coventry Agreement but did not differ from it significantly. Only the NUT and AMMA finally endorsed this agreement.

The NUT held a Special Salaries Conference specifically to ratify the agreement but it did so with 45 per cent voting against. Three unions held ballots on the agreement at the end of the Autumn Term; the NUT and AMMA called for an endorsement and got it narrowly, the NAS/UWT called for opposition and obtained that. However, the total votes in favour from the three ballots were in fact slightly less than those against[5].

At the time of writing, morale in the schools is very low with teachers waiting for either the acceptance by Kenneth Baker of the unpopular Nottingham Agreement or the imposition of an even worse deal by Baker. Many NUT Associations are still refusing to cover at all or are only covering for the first day, not perceived as industrial action but as a gain that this dispute has brought in their conditions of service.

Conclusions

Against all the predictions, the determination of the teachers in this dispute forced concessions from the employers. The NUT probably lost about 5 per cent of its members through dissatisfaction with the dispute, but the loss in numbers has been far outweighed by both the increased militancy of those that remain and the union's greater effectiveness gained by the experience of the action.

The dispute is still not over and won't be, which ever of the two settlements outlined above come about. Teachers are finding it difficult to understand how, after three years of a dispute which until the end of the Summer Term 1986 they had no doubt they were winning, they have ended up with this unsatisfactory choice of a negotiated settlement or an imposed one, neither of which endorse the principles for which they fought the campaign.

The most obvious factor has been the way in which the leadership of the NUT, after strongly criticizing and refusing to enter the ACAS talks, embraced them, and indeed together with the Labour employers, forced a settlement through. They were no doubt unnerved by the loss of their majority on Burnham. The justification on the NUT side seems to be that the concessions are worth it to avoid the imposition of a settlement on Mr Baker's terms and hopefully will help the re-election of a Labour Government committed to increase spending on the public services.

The unions' effectiveness in negotiation has been undermined by the rivalry between the leaderships of the NUT and NAS/UWT. In the schools themselves relations between members of the two unions has been good, with a great deal of co-operation over the action. There are certainly differences between the membership of the unions but it must be asked to what extent the differences expressed at a national level are a true reflection of them.

The pretension to a professional status for teachers, if not abandoned in the course of the dispute, looks like disappearing with a settlement that will involve a close definition of the teacher's job and tighter management of the workforce.

Notes

1   MEMBERSHIP OF TEACHERS ASSOCIATIONS

	1960	1973	1984
NUT	244,664	320,000	216,138
AMMA	38,000	80,000	64,636
NAS/UWT	22,651	60,230	115,611
NAHT	13,750	—	19,952
SHA	2,953	—	3,939
PAT	—	—	21,260
Total	322,028	460,230	441,536

NAS/UWT was just the NAS, all male, in 1960.
AMMA was two separate organisations for men and women in 1960.
SHA (Secondary Headteachers Association) didn't exist in 1960 but there were two separate organisations representing men and women heads.
NAHT — National Association of Headteachers

Sources: Roy, *The Teachers' Union* (1968)
Kogan, *Educational Policy Making* (1975)
Saran, *The Politics Behind Burnham* (1985)
(the 1984 figures are those used by the DES to reconstitute the Burnham teachers' panel).

2 MEMBERSHIP OF THE BURNHAM COMMITTEE (PRIMARY AND SECONDARY)

Management Panel	1981	1985
Association of County Councils	13	13
Association of Metropolitan Authorities	10	10
Welsh Joint Education Committee	2	2
Department of Education and Science	2	2
Total Number of Representatives	27	27
Teacher's Panel		
National Union of Teachers	16	13
Assistant Masters and Mistresses Assn.	4	4
National Association of Schoolmasters/		
Union of Women Teachers	7	7
National Association of Head Teachers	2	2
Secondary Heads Association	1	1
Professional Association of Teachers	1	1
Professional Association of Teachers	1	1
National Association of Teachers in		
Further and Higher Education	1	—
Total Number of Representatives	32	28

3 The Salary Structure

The salary structure for teachers, other than Heads and Deputies, is based on five scales. Each school is allocated promotion points according to the number and age of the pupils. Each point represents one 'jump' up the scale for a teacher, so that for instance a teacher on the middle scale, Scale Three, takes up two of these points since s/he has made two jumps up from Scale One, the basic Scale. Within each Scale there are a number of increments, yearly increases in salary, which each teacher receives automatically in September until the maximum is reached. With the drop in pupil numbers there was a proportional drop in the number of promotional points in the schools. This means that in many schools teachers have much less opportunity to increase their salary by promotion and therefore look to an overall improvement in the teachers' salary structure.

4 ACAS — Arbitration, Conciliation, and Advisory Service

5 NOTTINGHAM AGREEMENT BALLOTS

	FOR	AGAINST	TURNOUT (percent)
AMMA	32,871	16,747	55.1
NAS/UWT	5,178	41,994	42
NUT	60,912	44,216	55.3
TOTAL	98,961	102,957	

Part Four
Teachers and the State

10
Teachers and the State in Britain:
A Changing Relation

Gerald Grace

Questions to do with the relations of organised teachers and the state in Britain are of great contemporary concern. Walter Roy, a leading member of the NUT, in a book significantly entitled *Teaching under Attack* (1983), has argued that the teaching profession in Britain finds itself in an increasingly hostile environment. There is, in Roy's view, a crisis in the relations between organised teachers and the state which has been precipitated by the growth of central state intervention and an attack upon the central principles of teacher professionalism, particularly that of autonomy. The argument is expressed in this form:

> 'The attack on teaching.... has its roots in a philosophy resting on the belief that it is central government, its ministers and civil servants, that must determine not only the shape of the school system but of the curriculum and the methodology of the teaching process. Teachers must therefore be subordinated to a political will based on the notion that only an all powerful state knows what is best for its citizens ...' (p. 1).

and

> 'Alongside the attack on the material fabric of the education service there is a more dangerous and far reaching attack on the profession itself, the freedom of the teacher to do his (sic) job in the best interests of the children, using curricular patterns and methods most appropriate to his circumstances, free from political interference and petty tyranny is itself under threat, a threat which represents the greatest challenge to the teaching profession since the introduction of state education in 1870'. (p. 4).

Roy calls upon organised teachers in Britain to resist what he sees as the encroachment of politics on the teaching process and to 'answer the attack on the profession by enhancing their own professionalism' (p. 2). The sense of urgency which is present in this analysis arises not simply out of the recognition that the vested interests of an occupational group are under attack but out of a more profound realisation that an established policy position in education has been decisively broken. That policy position has clearly involved, from Roy's perspective, a concept of the non-interventionist central state, a strict separation of politics and education and a strong sense of the British teacher's professional autonomy and professional integrity. All of these crucial elements are now seen to be the objects of radical change or radical reappraisal and this, ironically, in a period of Conservative rather than of Socialist government.

How is this to be explained? I want to suggest that our understanding of these contemporary developments cannot be found simply in a present crisis perspective. The present balance of social, political and ideological forces in education arises out of, and can only be properly appreciated in, a longer socio-historical perspective. Socio-historical inquiry can be a powerful and illuminating mode of educational policy analysis. From sociology it can derive theoretical frameworks and fundamental theses concerning the role of the state and of political and class relations in the structuring of educational policy and process. From history it can derive a sense of the complex and changing nature of these relations in different periods of social and economic change. Most importantly, socio-historical inquiry sensitizes us to the principles and procedures which have been dominant in the past, and why they have been dominant, so that we become more keenly aware of the correlates of contemporary change.

The intention of this paper is to provide an outline of the changing relations between organised teachers and the state in Britain from the 1900s, to the 1980s. (Although the term 'Britain' is used throughout, detailed material relates in the main to England and Wales only). Such an ambitious venture within such a limited space runs the risk of over-simplification and this danger is admitted. On the other hand, it may be claimed that the necessity to make sense of these relations within a limited space may produce a focused clarification which the rich elaborations of more extended socio-historical scholarship sometimes obscure. The analysis will concentrate primarily on the cultural and political relations between the state and the dominant organisation of teachers within state schooling, i.e., the National Union of Teachers (NUT). This focus will necessitate an examination of what is to be understood as 'the state' in education in different historical periods. It will also involve a clarification of the dominant preoccupations and orientations of state agencies when dealing with teachers and the strategies employed in the light of those preoccupations. At the same time, the occupational, cultural and political strategies of teachers both as initiating or responding to state action will be scrutinised. A central element in the analysis of these relations will be a making visible of the complex set of assumptions and meanings associated with notions of teacher professionalism. As I have argued in *Teachers*,

Ideology and Control (1978) and as Ozga and Lawn have suggested in *Teachers, Professionalism and Class* (1981), ideologies of professionalism can be made to serve the interests of the state for control and containment of teachers or they can be effectively deployed by teachers to improve their terms and conditions of service and their enjoyment of social status and occupational autonomy.

In one sense the whole story of teacher-state relations in Britain this century has been an extended war of position[1] over the terrain of professionalism and its assumed correlates. It will be suggested later that the present crisis in these relations has arisen because the state has achieved, as a result of wider socio-political and economic change, a series of major tactical advantages to which Roy's appeal to British teachers to enhance their professionalism will be no effective defence.

The State, the Teachers and Educational Settlements

The Centre for Contemporary Cultural Studies (CCCS) Education Group (1981) has suggested that educational policy should be viewed as the provisional outcome of a continuous socio-political struggle. In that struggle state agencies, the labour movement, 'the needs of capital', class and gender interests, teachers and educationists, and parent organisations are involved. The advantage of this formulation is that it refers to a dynamic historical process in which the balance of forces can be seen to change over time as new alliances are formed. This can be a useful counter to those forms of analysis which by presenting education as a 'huge and marvellously intricate apparatus of social control'[2], over-emphasise structural determination and under-emphasise agency, strategy and resistance. The Education Group want to stress that 'the power of dominant interests is never secure; it always has to be won' (p. 32). Applying this to education, they have suggested that educational policy can be seen as a series of crises and settlements. The crises occur when the power and interests of dominant groups are challenged or threatened by the strategies of subordinate groups. Educational settlements refer to those situations where a crisis has been temporarily resolved through an acceptable compromise or balance of forces. These theoretical constructs can be fruitfully applied to the analysis of the cultural and political relations between organised teachers and the state in Britain this century. In the socio-historical account which follows it is hoped that their utility will be demonstrated.

However, before proceeding to that substantive analysis it is essential to clarify the nature of the two major contenders in the struggle, from the point of view of this study. Particularly, what is to be understood by 'the state' in education and what are the characteristics of the organised teachers under examination? Dale (1982) pp. 129–130) has pointed out that 'focusing on the source and nature of control over education and schools entails focusing on the immediate provider of education, the State and it is in the analysis of the State that we may begin to understand the assumptions, intentions and outcomes of various strategies of educational change'. How to analyse the state then becomes the problem.

The great advantage of using a concept of the state in educational analysis is precisely, as Dale suggests, that it focuses attention upon the locus of power and control in the system. Given the tendency of so much educational analysis to be innocent of the major politics of education as opposed to the minor politics of education, this emphasis upon the state is a useful corrective. However, the great disadvantage is that references to the state in education can easily become over-simplified (e.g., the state as a single power entity), too conspiratorial (e.g., the state as omniscient planner and controller) and too abstract (e.g., the state not examined in relation to specific historical contexts). Some recent and important contributions to our understanding of the wider politics of education have perhaps been exposed to some of these disadvantages.

If the state in education is understood not as a single and unified entity but as a set of 'agencies, departments, tiers and levels, each with their own rules and resources and often with varying purposes'[3], then it becomes possible not only to avoid conspiratorial explanations but also to trace the dynamics of state action in different historical periods. The state in education *is* the locus of power and con-trol but the mode in which these are expressed and the agencies through which these are mediated change in relation to wider socio-political development. It is clear that the elected government can claim a broad mandate for initiating certain policy positions in education. The designated minister for education can activate or emphasise certain features of that mandate and can make further initiatives which represent his/her own preoccupations in the field. The elected government and the designated minister represent the formal embodiment of the state in education at the highest level. However, there also exists another power level represented by 'the state apparatus' or the various categories of educational bureaucracy and administration, in which senior officials, particularly Permanent Secretaries, have a crucial role. The power relations between these two levels can and do change over time as a result of wider political developments; the energy and ideological commitments of particular ministers and the experience, skills and vested interests of the senior officials. The central state in education is also in a dynamic relation with the local state as constituted by the local education authorities and this relation has had considerable importance in the politics of education in Britain this century.

It will become apparent in the socio-historical account which follows that the active agency in mediating teacher-state relations in Britain has sometimes been a powerful and influential bureaucracy and sometimes an energetic and ideologically committed minister representing a strong political mandate. The agency of the state in this sense has not been a constant. However, while agency and strategy change over time, the control objectives of state policy can be seen to have remained constant. These objectives had to do with the forging of a mode of socio-cultural and political control of an occupational group which (theoretically, at any rate) was perceived as having the capacity to contribute towards the legitimation of the existing social order or to threaten in various ways its existence. Throughout an important part of the historical period under examination, teachers in the state system of schooling were regarded as crucial agents in the structuring of popular consciousness. The structuring and formation of their own occupational consciousness and their relation with other social and political groups was therefore always a significant matter.

Of all the various categories of organised teachers with which the state has had to forge a cultural and political relation, the National Union of Teachers has been pre-eminent. From its foundation as the National Union of Elementary Teachers in 1870 (NUT from 1889) it has represented the largest number of teachers in the state system of schooling. The NUT can be seen to be central to the formation and to the contemporary dynamics of teacher-state relations in Britain. The reason for its importance is not simply a function of its size but also because of its socio-political features and strategies. The Union has a crucial class relation which has been expressed both pedagogically and in terms of social origin. Pedagogically, NUT members have always constituted a most significant sector of the formal teachers of the working class, whether that class has been schooled in elementary, primary, all-age, secondary modern or inner city comprehensive settings. In that sense the teachers of the NUT have been a key sector of the organised 'teachers of the people'. But they have also been teachers of the working class derived very much from the working class, albeit historically from its more religious, respectable and aspirant sectors.

It will be argued that this particular class relation of the NUT, i.e., the pedagogic and the demographic relation with the working-class in Britain has been, until recently, a major element in the determination of state policy vis-à-vis the Union. What has always been at issue, from the viewpoint of various agencies of the state, is whether this large and strategically placed occupational group, having what might be called intrinsic connections with the working-class, might in the course of time develop extrinsic connections, i.e., some form of explicit social, cultural and political alliance. The 1920s represented a critical period in the resolution of this issue and notions of teacher unionism on the one hand and teacher professionalism on the other were central to its determination.

Teachers in the NUT have not however been the passive objects of state policy or of state intentions but, on the contrary, an active agency. It is useful here to follow E. P. Thompson's (1963, 1978) example in the wider field of socio-historical scholarship where he insists that the British working class was an active force which shaped events through struggle. As the CCCS Education Group (1981, p. 16) put it, 'without abandoning a notion of the state as a means of control, Thompson presents popular struggles as actually constitutive of state policies and state forms. They are a principle of movement in the whole system'. If we apply this insight to the history of the NUT, it is possible to discern the ways in which through its organisation, resistances, initiatives and socio-political strategies, the Union was 'constitutive of state policies' and 'a principle of movement in the whole system'. What is of some moment to the understanding of contemporary education policy and its trends, is whether that historical agency of the Union has been as effectively deployed in recent times as it undoubtedly was in the past. What is particularly at issue here is the changing relation between 'political' strategies and 'professional' strategies in affecting the active agency of the NUT.

One further comment about the NUT as a major contender in this analysis must be made. Just as it was pointed out earlier that to use a unitary conception of 'the state' in education is to over-simplify the sets of interests present within that notion, so there are also dangers in the unproblematic use of 'organised teachers' as a category, even if this is restricted to the NUT. The NUT represents an aspiration to professional unity for schoolteachers but within its own organisation, viewed both historically and contemporaneously, it does not itself embody that unity in any straightforward or absolute sense. Throughout its history the Union has had to deal with sectional divisions arising out of hierarchical and power differentials, differences in training and formal certification, regional and institutional affiliations, gender categories and ideological groupings. The NUT has at various times been an alliance of disparate interests within the state school teaching force. In one sense, if the concept of educational settlement can be usefully applied to the resolution of crises between the Union and the state on the cultural and political front, then it can also be applied to the internal relations of the Union.

Teachers in the NUT have had to face not only crises precipitated by state policy in education but also internal crises arising out of differences of interests between headteachers and class teachers, men and women, professional certification groups and also the varying ideological and political commitments of the membership. For these internal crises, organisational settlements had to be found if the Union was not to be weakened or out-manouevred in its wider relations with the state in education. Sometimes these settlements have not been possible and the Union has been structurally weakened as a result. In all cases these internal divisions have limited the range of options which the NUT has been able to pursue in the war of position with the state.

It is now possible to look substantively at teacher-state relations in Britain this century in the light of these considerations. Four phases of these relations can be suggested:-

1   a period in which state policy in education was experienced initially by the teachers as one of cultural and professional condescension which they bitterly resented and a period in general marked by

a vigorous politics of confrontation between organised teachers and the central and local state (1900–1920)

2 a period in which the key issue was the political and union identification and role of organised teachers as opposed to their professional identification and role (1920s–1930s)

3 the partial resolution of these questions in the making of a social democratic and professional consensus between organised teachers and the state (1940s–mid-1970s)

4 the breaking of this social democratic and professional consensus and the return of a politics of confrontation (1970s–1980s)

The periodisation outlined above is intended to be broad and indicative of policy trends rather than of exact historical chronology. However it is maintained that these periods do constitute significant transitions in teacher-state relations in Britain this century. A form of educational settlement, as already defined, marks each of the first three phases. The fourth represents a radical breaking of these settlements and a return to policies of cultural and professional condescension and to the politics of confrontation. In the space available it is only possible to elucidate main trends and to characterise the general features of these relations.

Cultural and Professional Condescension and the Politics of Confrontation (1900–1920)

Simon (1974, p. 10) refers to the establishment of the Board of Education in 1899 as bringing into being 'a department of state consolidating central direction over the educational system and not only along lines defined by legislation but by administrative measures which shaped the course of developments imperceptibly without open discussion of the implications . . .' and he notes the early formative influence in state policy of 'that masterful permanent secretary to the Board from 1902 to 1911, Robert Morant . . .'. Similarly, Tropp (1957, p. 183) has argued in relation to this period that 'the development of education was determined not by Parliament but by the Board of Education in conjunction with the new LEAs. From 1902 until 1911, Sir Robert Morant was Permanent Secretary of the Board of Education and it was his will which was mainly operative in shaping English education in those key years'. While it would not be correct to suggest that the policy of the central state in education at this time can be reduced to the prejudices of a single individual, it does seem accurate to say that Robert Morant in his role as Permanent Secretary was able to give expression to a wider ideological position within the dominant social group. That ideological position, in relation to organised elementary school teachers, grew out of concerns in the dominant social order that this occupational group brought into existence by the state was becoming too powerful and too assertive. There had been hostile references in the latter part of the nineteenth century to the growing 'army' of elementary schoolteachers. The Times in 1880 called the National Union of Elementary Teachers 'a Frankenstein's monster which has suddenly grown into full life'[4]. The elementary teachers had shown themselves to be active and effective in educational politics. They had mounted a campaign of resistance to curriculum and inspectorial control as represented by a centrally-imposed Elementary Code and a system of 'payment by results' related to it. The NUT had interpreted the ending of payment by results in 1895 as the successful outcome of its long campaign of opposition and it now saw enhanced prospects for the growth of teachers' classroom autonomy.

Organised elementary teachers were active in local educational politics especially in the elections for the School Boards in the large cities. This activity had a very definite wider political connotation because these urban School Boards were widely perceived as 'citadels of Radicalism'[5]. At the national level, the NUT was becoming a political force in its own right through the sponsoring of members of parliament.

In addition to active political involvement in the formation of policy, organised elementary schoolteachers were asserting with growing confidence their claim to be regarded as a profession with the accepted correlates of that status in terms of social respect, appropriate salaries and pensions and degrees of autonomy and self-government.

While educational policy at this time arose out of a complex of cultural, political, bureaucratic and religious interests, elementary schoolteachers were an important category in the constituting of state policy. The ideological position to which Morant gave vigorous expression from 1902 to 1911 was, among other things, a response to the activity and the aspirations of elementary schoolteachers. This position was premised on two general notions, i.e., that the pretensions of the elementary schoolteachers needed to be cut back and that their relative power and independence needed to be transformed and constrained. Johnson (1976), writing of an earlier period of popular schooling, has suggested that one of the major intentions of the providing-classes was the 'class-cultural transformation' of the working-class. A similar intention, it may be argued, can be detected in Morant's relation with organised elementary schoolteachers at the beginning of the century. A form of class-cultural transformation of organised elementary schoolteachers involved an attempt to distance the teachers from active political involvements on the one hand and to incorporate them culturally in a more effective way during their own education. At the same time they needed to have a more realistic understanding of their own 'professional' status when compared with university graduates. The distancing of politics was one of the consequences of the 1902 Education Act which replaced the School Boards with Local Education Authorities based upon county and county borough units. It was difficult for the teachers to play so central and integrated a role in the educational politics of these larger and literally more distanced institutions of the local state[6], as they had done in the politics of the School Boards.

Cultural transformation was facilitated by ensuring that the route into elementary schoolteaching passed through the new publicly provided secondary schools (of which Morant was a strong advocate). This had the advantage not only of strengthening the secondary school sector vis-à-vis the elementary sector but also of incorporating future elementary schoolteachers into a middle-class social and cultural institution. The hoped for effect was 'to bring the pupil-teachers under the influence of a wider outlook and a more humane ideal of education than has been possible in the past' and to facilitate the development of 'trained intelligence and refinement of character'[7]. The state, through the agency of the Board of Education, implemented this policy and as Tropp (1957, p. 189) notes, 'the period from 1902 to 1914 saw the complete transformation of the method of recruitment to the profession'. At the same time, the state assumed tighter control of the training college system itself. The Training College Regulations of 1904 increased the control of the Board of Education over appointments to training colleges in terms of approval of academic qualifications held by potential lecturers and tutors.

These central state initiatives in the reconstruction of the local educational state (with a distancing of teacher politics) and in the changes in occupational recruitment and education (with greater cultural incorporation) were opposed by the organised elementary schoolteachers but in each of these changes they saw possibilities for their own future action and interests and although the situation was contested no crisis situation emerged.

A crisis was precipitated, however, out of a growing recognition by the teachers that the whole orientation of state policy, as mediated by Morant, was one of cultural and professional condescension with a refusal to take their claims to professional status seriously. Their desire to see a Teachers' Register with a Teachers' Registration Council to administer it, represented a long held aspiration towards greater professional unity and a measure of social recognition. Gosden (1972, pp. 252–253) notes that 'Morant did all he could to impair their unity and to play off one group of teachers against another in order to prevent progress being made. A series of papers published by the Board of Education in these years bears witness to the mixture of hostility and contempt which the Permanent Secretary felt towards the teachers' associations'. This contempt for the cultural and professional status of elementary schoolteachers had been mediated to the teachers in various ways but its most explicit and public statement came in the Holmes-Morant Circular of 1910. This Circular was concerned with the bad results that were seen to arise from the appointment by local authorities of inspectors of the wrong type, particularly former elementary schoolteachers. It was leaked to the press to become the most explicit statement of official cultural and professional condescension:-

> 'Apart from the fact that elementary teachers are as a rule uncultured and imperfectly educated, many, if not most of them, are creatures of tradition and routine ... As compared with the ex-elementary teacher usually engaged in the hopeless task of surveying, or trying to survey, a wide field of action from a well-worn groove, the inspector of the 'varsity' type has the advantage of being able to look at elementary education from a point of view of complete detachment and therefore of being able to handle its problems with freshness and originality'[8].

This produced a crisis that had been inherent in teacher-state relations since 1902. A major parliamentary contest developed in 1911 in which the full force of the NUT's political agency, in alliance with civil service unions and other political interests was brought to bear upon the Board of Education. So effective was this campaign that it resulted in the resignation of the President of the Board (Runciman) and of Morant as Permanent Secretary. The events of 1911 were the most dramatic manifestation of the NUT's capacity to mobilise political power against the agency of the central state in education, if that agency treated elementary schoolteachers with obvious contempt[9]. It was an episode in teacher-state relations not to be quickly forgotten by the permanent officials of the Board or by subsequent Presidents of the Board. Tropp argues that the NUT 'had driven Morant from office and the new Permanent Secretary (Selby-Bigge) had adopted a policy of conciliation and consultation' (p. 206). The events of 1911 had made it clear that the agencies of the central state had to find a strategy in relation to the teachers' aspirations towards professionalism which was altogether more subtle and indirect than that which had characterised the regime of Morant[10]. However, the attempt to formulate that strategy was impeded by a vigorous politics of confrontation conducted between the teachers and various LEAs over terms and conditions of service. A series of disputes on salary levels beginning in West Ham in 1907 and culminating in a major strike in the Rhondda in 1919 demonstrated the extent of teacher militancy. The teachers protested at 'the meagre and capricious nature of local payment'[11] and called for the establishment of national salary scales. What was more threatening was a tendency for these local disputes to begin to form alliances between organised elementary teachers and sections of the labour movement, a development made most explicit by the Rhondda teachers' call for support from 'the people' as fellow exploited workers (Ozga and Lawn 1981, p. 95).

The significance of these developments was not lost on the representatives of the central state in education, particularly H.A.L. Fisher, the President of the Board of Education from 1917. Fisher had a lively awareness of the socio-political significance of elementary schoolteachers and this awareness was sharpened by the revolutionary ferments of the time. He 'saw clearly enough that an underpaid, restless and resentful teaching profession was a menace to the stability of the State'[12], and he was able to communicate this realisation to other leading political figures.

These political considerations were related to some important policy initiatives intended to make it clear that the central state took seriously the teachers' claim to be professionals. In introducing the Education estimates in 1917 Fisher had said 'An anxious and depressed teacher is a bad teacher, an embittered teacher is a social danger .... The first condition of educational advance is that we should learn to pay our teachers better'[13]. It would be too crude to say that the central state at this time was 'buying' the loyalty of the teachers but it would not be inaccurate to say that there was an important connection between these material improvements and the political considerations made explicit by Fisher and by Lloyd George. These material improvements took the form of the Teachers' Superannuation Act of 1918 which introduced a generous non-contributory scheme which had the effect of making teachers eligible for pensions on much the same basis as civil servants. National salary scales were brought into existence through an appropriate agency (the Burnham Committee) by 1921. In a comparatively short time the economic position of teachers had been given some of the correlates of professional status.

When this first phase of teacher-state relations is reviewed it can be discerned that the agencies of the state had for their part made a temporary educational settlement with teachers following a crisis period. This settlement involved an end to the stance of obvious cultural and professional condescension[14] which had alienated elementary teachers since the nineteenth century. The permanent officials of the Board of Education had learned that this stance was counter-productive. The settlement also involved some acceptance of the teachers' professional claims in relation to terms and conditions of service without having conceded any real power over the administration of the occupational group.

For their part, the teachers had demonstrated that despite changes in the organisation of the local educational state they were still, at a national level, a political force to be reckoned with. They had shown a willingness to make alliances with civil service unions on the one hand or with the labour movement and 'the people' on the other, to achieve their ends. By 1920 some sort of truce situation had been arrived at between organised teachers and the state but it had no sooner emerged than it was to be immediately threatened by the volatile social, economic and political conditions of the 1920s.

Teachers: Political Subversives or Trusted Professionals? (1920s–1930s)

The 1920s was a period in Britain in which the contradictions that it can be claimed are always present in educational arrangements and policies[15] became particularly visible. The wider social context of education was characterised by a sense of economic crisis (with associated strategies for cuts in public expenditure) and from the viewpoint of the dominant social order, a sense of political crisis (arising from fears of the growing influence of Bolshevism and socialism). Policies which involved proposals to cut back public expenditure at a time when fears about popular socialism were growing had their obvious contradictions and the agencies of the central state were placed in the difficult position of attempting to mediate these contradictions.

Teacher-state relations were caught up in this network of contradictions arising out of the wider social context. These contradictions affected three inter-related sectors of the educational settlement which had emerged by 1920. In the political sector, the contradictions focused around the question of whether organised elementary teachers should be regarded as politically unreliable (and at worst potentially subversive) and treated as such in policy terms, or whether they should be regarded and treated as loyal professionals. In the economic sector, the contradictions to be faced were just how far could the now-required cuts in teachers' salaries and the reductions in their conditions of service go, without provoking a dangerous reaction from the NUT. In the cultural and professional sector the question of how much classroom and curriculum autonomy could be permitted for the teacher in a time of ideological ferment, was central.

It must be stressed that the various agencies of the state did not have a unified or conspiratorial plan of action in relation to these issues but rather that various agencies had different policy intentions and that contradictions were in some cases generated *by* state agencies as well as by the wider socio-political context.

The state in education faced one of its most critical periods in formulating relations with organised teachers in the 1920s. However, it had some advantages in that the sectional divisions of the NUT had by this time made themselves very apparent; also the ideological and political differences among the membership had similarly become explicit. The NUT had been structurally weakened by the secession of activist and political women teachers who had in effect broken away in 1920 to form the National Union of Women Teachers (NUWT)[16]. This secession had been prompted by the NUT's cautious position both on women's suffrage and on equal pay. Although the NUT Conference in 1919 adopted the principle of equal pay for women it was clear that the male leadership of the Union remained lukewarm on the issue and regarded the principle of equal pay as 'only symbolic'[17]. The fears of activist women teachers were confirmed when it became apparent in the early 1920s that the Burnham salary scales did not include the principle of equal pay. The Union was seen to have betrayed its commitment and the effect was a further secession of activist women members from the NUT to the NUWT[18]. Despite the NUT's lukewarm position on equal pay the fact that there was a conference commitment to the principle was enough to cause the secession of a sector of militant men teachers to form the National

Association of Schoolmasters in 1922. The gender struggles within the NUT were sharp in the early 1920s and they resulted in greater fragmentation of elementary teachers as a group. While polarisation was occurring in relation to gender, sharp divisions were also appearing in relation to political identification. A formal proposal that the NUT should affiliate with the Labour Party had been lost in a referendum vote (29,743 to 15,434)[19]. The size of the pro-Labour vote did not go unnoticed and it was considerably greater than had been expected, given the Union's traditional policy of no party political affiliations. Labour members of the NUT formed a Teachers' Labour League in 1923 which became in the eyes of contemporaries more explicitly Bolshevik over time. The League was associated with the organisation of workers' councils on education, with attacks on the class bias and imperialist bias of the elementary school curriculum and with calls for wider alliances with the working class. The impact of the Teachers' Labour League on the ideological climate of the time was considerable despite its comparatively small membership. Through its journal 'The Educational Worker' (1926–33) and in sponsoring resolutions at the Labour Party Conference in 1926 that the next workers' administration should investigate how 'a proletarian attitude and outlook'[20] might be cultivated in the schooling system, the League and its activities appeared to suggest that a sector of organised elementary teachers had become politically subversive. The existence of the Teachers' Labour League provoked Conservative teachers within the NUT to form their own organisations in 1927 to 'combat the teaching of Socialism and Communism in schools and frustrate generally the activities of the TLL'[21].

The key question for state policy in these years was how to deal with the political radicalism which was evident among the teachers and it was a question which preoccupied the Conservative President of the Board of Education (Lord Eustace Percy) between 1924 and 1929. From within his own party, Percy received a stream of suggestions all of which involved proposals for greater state control of, and surveillance of, elementary schoolteachers. There were proposals to make teachers into civil servants and to require them to take an oath of loyalty to the state[22]; attempts to get the Commons to pass a Seditious Teachings Bill[23], and requests for inquiries into alleged political indoctrination in schools[24]. In dealing with all of these proposals for visible and explicit control and surveillance, the President of the Board of Education was certain that such policies would be counter-productive as well as being 'un-English'. In correspondence with a persistent critic (Sir Charles Yate), Percy made this position clear:-

'I am horrified by your assumption that teachers are to be regarded as State servants. This may be a conception quite proper to Republican France, to Communist Russia or to Kaiserist Prussia, but anything more alien to the whole Public School tradition of this country cannot be conceived .... The fact of compulsion in Education does put a heavy responsibility on the State but what could be worse ... than to encourage a conception that teachers are servants of a Government in the same way as Civil Servants and therefore must teach in their schools precisely what any future Labour Government may tell them to teach....

I still believe that the best safeguard against irregularities is to give teachers a sense of reasonable independence and not to subordinate them too much either to Central or to a Local Authority .... The membership of the League (Teachers' Labour League) is quite insignificant and in the main I believe the Teaching Profession itself will see to it that the League's activities are properly checked'[25].

Eustace Percy in his role as President of the Board of Education mediated an ideological position from within the dominant socio-political group which was very different from that mediated by Morant as Permanent Secretary in an earlier period, and very different from that being urged upon him by backbench Conservative MPs. In the critical period 1924–29 this ideological position involved a strategy of 'trusting the teachers' (and marginalising groups such as the Teachers' Labour League)[26]; of emphasizing the point that true professionals did not mix politics with their practice and of looking for other ways of influencing, controlling and winning-over the teachers, a mode of 'indirect rule' (Lawn and Ozga 1986) rather than of visible distrust and constraint[27].

The events of the General Strike in 1926 were to give this position considerable credibility. For all of the expressed alarm about the Bolshevik tendencies of elementary schoolteachers, no significant support for or solidarity with manual workers was forthcoming from organised teachers in 1926. The NUT's newspaper, 'The Schoolmaster' (sic), printed in May 1926 a message from the President of the Board in which he thanked the teachers for carrying on their duties 'without interruption during this emergency' and conveyed the Government's appreciation 'of their loyal service at this time'. The editor of 'The Schoolmaster' took the opportunity to note that elementary schoolteachers could claim some of the credit for the generally 'orderly behaviour' which had characterized the strikers and for the general spirit of 'self-control', 'moderation' and 'good humour' which had prevailed despite the Strike[28].

Although periodic scares about communist infiltration of the NUT were to continue in the 1930s and beyond, the 1920s marked the decisive turning point. Organised teachers in the NUT emerged from this period of ideological and industrial struggle with a reputation for being loyal professionals (or more precisely, aspirant professionals). This outcome was not achieved without the experience of certain contradictions in state policy. The winning of teachers to notions of loyal professionalism or true professionalism had to contend with a countervailing tendency to cut their salaries and to reduce their conditions of service. As a result of the Committee on National Expenditure (the Geddes Committee) the teachers saw cuts in their salaries and pensions in 1923 and again in 1932. The outcome of this particular contradiction was that while teachers, along with other 'public servants', had to accept salary cuts their magnitude was limited (by political decision) and the cuts were ultimately restored by the mid 1930s. While the material rewards of the teaching profession were for a time reduced in this period, its relative security of employment was not seriously affected and Tropp (1957, p. 225) notes that 'the teaching profession as a whole was spared the horrors of mass unemployment'. State policy at this time was uneasily balanced between a view that the country could not afford financially to support armies of teachers and civil servants and a view that it could not afford politically to have armies of embittered and unemployed teachers and civil servants[29]. The attempt to resolve this contradiction came in the form of a muted retrenchment of public expenditure.

In the cultural and professional sector of teacher-state relations, organised teachers encountered what appeared to be a much more positive stance towards their cultural and professional aspirations. They found themselves with the potential for greatly enhanced classroom and curriculum autonomy when the Board of Education relaxed its controls in 1926 over the elementary school curriculum. In 1926 the Board swept away the remnants of the Code prescription in elementary schooling by eliminating all mention of the subjects (except for practical instruction) which were expected to be taught in elementary schools. Eustace Percy and others in Conservative party circles were aware of the dangers inherent in centralized control of the system of popular schooling (as has already been shown) and this major policy change was undertaken for political reasons. As White (1975, p. 28) has put it:

'If Parliament still controlled the content of education, the Socialists would change the Regulations . . . they would be able to introduce curricula more in line with Socialist ideas. To forestall this it was no longer in the interests of Conservatives to keep curriculum policy in the hands of the state . . . . If they could devise a workable system of non-statutory controls, the Conservatives had everything to gain and nothing to lose by taking curricula out of the politicians' hands'.

It seems clear that the 'non-statutory controls' to which White refers were to be looked for in a particular version of teacher professionalism. This conception of professionalism, in which teachers were being immersed, crucially involved the separation of education from politics. It involved the construction of the idea of the non-political school, the non-political teacher and the non-political curriculum. The policy of 'trusting the teachers' which Percy and others endorsed at this time was premised on a view of the great majority of teachers as conservative, respectable and anxious to be seen as 'true' professionals whose concerns would be pedagogic, moral and inter-personal, but not political. In other words, despite earlier scares, it appeared that elementary schoolteachers could be given greater autonomy in the schools without any serious danger to the interests of the dominant social group ensuing.

These political considerations were not expressed in the public language of policy change. As far as the teachers were concerned the changes had all the appearances of a progressive recognition of the professional status which they had long claimed. Other evidence seemed to confirm this, when the Board of Education also relaxed its controls over the training colleges and the examinations for the teacher's certificate and began to encourage closer working relationships between the training colleges and the university system. Similarly, the Teachers' Registration Council (which had been formed in 1912 after the fall of Morant) was dignified in 1929 with the title of the Royal Society of Teachers[30]. Organised teachers in the 1930s had come a long way from the cultural and professional condescension of the Morant era.

State policy in the 1920s and 1930s towards organised elementary school teachers was in effect one of incorporation rather than of confrontation. The teachers were incorporated over time both professionally and culturally and the incipient dangers of alliances with the labour movement and the working-class were attenuated and defused. This was not due to any exceptional prescience or wisdom in the agencies of the state (although the preoccupations of Eustace Percy were important) but rather because of a particular conjunction of circumstances. The NUT had been shaken by its gender divisions and struggles and it had lost some of its most active members, both men and women, to rival organisations. It was threatened with the possibility of internal political splits unless it could find a strong occupational ideology which would be cohesive. This occupational ideology which can be called the *ethic of legitimated professionalism* provided a solution not only to the socio-political concerns of the state but also to the organisational concerns of the teachers' leaders for unity. The legitimated professionalism which emerged in the 1930s was a form of educational settlement which implicitly involved an understanding that organised teachers would keep to their proper sphere of activity within the classroom and the educational system and the state, for its part, would grant them a measure of trust, a measure of material reward and occupational security, and a measure of professional dignity. By the late 1930s the teachers in Britain seemed to have attained to respectable white collar/white blouse security as one of the accepted (lesser) professions. Tropp (1957, p. 228) notes that an idea of partnership in the administration of education was beginning to emerge in Britain in the late 1930s with close working relations between the National Union of Teachers, the Association of Education Committees and the Board of Education. Such involvement in the planning and administration of education was a source of professional pride to the teachers' leaders. From the viewpoint of the Teachers' Labour League, however, it was evidence that the NUT had become 'part and parcel of the capitalist state machine'[31].

Social Democratic Consensus, Partnership and Professional Autonomy

Teacher-state relations in Britain in the 1940s and 1950s were characterized by a development of that sense of partnership in education which had been present in the late 1930s. Whatever may have been the actual effect of organised teachers upon educational policy making and whatever may have been the actual balance of power between the partners (i.e., teachers, central state, and local state), organised teachers in the NUT had a strong sense that they were important partners in a great educational enterprise. That enterprise involved the reconstruction of the schooling system to realise the 'better future' universally looked-for after the war. The teachers were consulted in the planning for that reconstruction. They had the satisfaction of seeing the principle of equality of educational opportunity, which they had advocated, included in the political and policy-making language of the time. The 1944 Education Act, in abolishing the category of elementary education and replacing it by the accepted stages of primary and secondary education for all, had contributed significantly to the teachers' sense of dignity and respect. The membership of the NUT now consisted largely of primary and secondary modern teachers, the majority certificated but with a growing number of graduates. The derogatory association of the term 'elementary' had been left behind.

In the wider social, economic and political context of Britain in the 1940s and 1950s, education was perceived to be central to national regeneration. This was the period in which the social democratic consensus about the socio-political and economic potential of education in national life was formed. Modern schooling was seen to have the capacity to strengthen democracy through citizenship education; to reduce class divisiveness and promote social harmony through equal educational opportunity and to contribute to economic modernisation and growth through the more efficient cultivation of the reserves of talent in the nation. State policy in education, whether the elected government was Labour or Conservative, was shaped by this powerful ideology of transformation through education, although the mode of its realisation was the subject of political party differences. Given that publicly-provided education now stood so high in the nation's political priorities and given that the schoolteachers were the professional agents for the realisation of its potential, this seemed to imply an important change in teacher-state relations. The partnership which had been so much talked about between the state and organised teachers in the making of a new Britain was expected by the teachers to produce some obvious and tangible rewards for the profession. In fact these were not forthcoming either in terms and conditions of service or in greater measures of professional self-government. The contradictions in teacher-state relations were again apparent.

By the 1950s it was clear that the notion of partnership between the teachers and the central and local state lacked a power balance. The NUT, having embraced the ethic of legitimated professionalism so whole-heartedly and having distanced itself from the making of wider socio-political alliances, was now considerably less of a political force to be reckoned with. The moderate leadership of the Union, epitomised in Ronald Gould[32], adopted a classic position of liberalism in appearing to believe that rational argument alone would win the material benefits which the status of the teacher so obviously entailed. Tropp (1957, p. 253) records, with no apparent irony, that in the teacher-state salary disputes of the mid 1950s 'the NUT took an unparalleled step by asking all its members to cease collecting school savings. This obtained much publicity but had no apparent effect on the Minister or the local authorities'. Such professional 'action' was a long way from the sort of strategies which had brought down a President and a Permanent Secretary of the Board in 1911.

The agencies of the state in education in the 1950s found themselves able to deny the teachers the sort of salary increases which they expected and the greater professional self-government which they requested without any sense that a crisis situation would ensue. In the economic sector of teacher-state relations the power differential was in favour of the state and this applied whether the state in education was constituted by Labour or Conservative politicians. Although the teacher unions were able to secure equal pay in 1961, the relative position of teachers' salaries compared with those of skilled manual workers continued to decline in the 1960s. The white collar/white blouse respectability of schoolteaching and the sort of occupational ideology which it represented was literally becoming threadbare in the 1960s. In effect, the economic understanding implicit in the educational settlement between the teachers and the state in the 1930s had been reneged upon by the state, despite the existence of the social democratic consensus on the importance of education. While this was quite apparent and while it was apparent also that the National Union of Teachers was losing a section of its male membership to the more militant and aggressive National Association of Schoolmasters, the leaders of the NUT persisted in the stance of legitimated professionalism and the belief that liberal reason would ultimately win the day. Ronald Gould's statement to the salary arbitrators in 1965 stands as a classic expression of this position:

> 'We seek a revaluation of the teacher's position because we believe this to be essential to the development of the education service and the well-being of the country. Any salary increases awarded we suggest must do more than compensate for changes in the purchasing power of money and do more than maintain the teacher's position vis-à-vis others; to mark the importance of the education service in the modern world it should raise the teacher's position in relation to others. We ask the arbitrators to regard their task as an exercise in determining social priorities'[33].

This appeal did not in fact result in any significant evidence that the agencies of the state in education took seriously the call for a 'revaluation' of the teacher's position in British society. By the late 1960s, the weaknesses of the ethic of legitimated professionalism in the sphere of wage bargaining were now apparent to a large sector of the NUT membership. Against a background of general industrial and political unrest, and affected by the militancy of other unions, the stance of the NUT in the economic sector of teacher-state relations changed radically. A vigorous period of teacher militancy ensued between 1968 and 1974 which as Jones (1983, p. 113) has suggested, signalled a shift in an important category of NUT membership towards 'active trade unionism'. One of the historical alternatives to the ethic of legitimated professionalism for organised teachers in the state system of schooling had always been a strategy of active trades unionism. From the 1920s the teachers had increasingly followed the path of professionalism and had distanced themselves from trades unionism, from industrial action, from 'the political' and from the wider labour movement. Now at a time of general ideological ferment and with the weaknesses of legitimated professionalism fully exposed in the material sense, the opportunity for radical members within the NUT to re-activate that strategy had arrived. A national strike in 1969 (the first significant industrial action for fifty years) and, after a number of abortive attempts, the affiliation of the National Union of Teachers to the TUC in 1970, were unmistakable signs of a shift in teacher-state relations and the consciousness of organised teachers. Teacher militancy and industrial action especially by urban (particularly inner-city) NUT members continued in the early 1970s and added another dimension to the growing sense of crisis in education. The official leadership of the NUT found itself challenged by the explicit and militant trades unionism of sectional groups within the Union, particularly the Rank and File organisation which in its 'agitational' newspaper began to appear like a reborn Teachers' Labour League[34]. The total breakdown of the educational settlement between the teachers and the state in the economic sector of that relation was entirely visible by the early 1970s. Organised teachers in the NUT (despite internal strains and splits) had constituted themselves for a short period as a political and ideological force to be reckoned with, after decades of professional domestication and inaction. An informal leadership of young, radical men and women, largely urban teachers in inner-city comprehensive and junior schools, were at the centre of this transformation. Their activity forced the state in education to agree to a generous salary award in the Houghton settlement of 1974 (awarded significantly in 'the expectation of professional standards of performance'). In the long term, the transformation which had occurred in the public image of the teaching profession was to have profound consequences for the nature of teacher-state relations in the 1980s[35].

Of the two great principles of teacher-state relations in post-war Britain, i.e., partnership and autonomy for teachers, partnership by the early 1970s had lost much of its credibility. While it was retained in the formal and ideological language of consultation, policy discussion and advice in education, organised teachers had learned that it was a principle without power so far as they were concerned — a principle without a material reality. So far as their terms and conditions of service were concerned the teachers had not experienced the reality of partnership and they had been forced into confrontational politics and union action in order to gain an acceptable settlement in 1974.

This could not be said to the same extent about the other great principle, that of professional autonomy. Here was a principle which seemed to organised teachers to have a clear reality in the considerable freedom which teachers in the state system experienced in school and classroom autonomy[36]. From the 1950s to the early 1970s teachers in state schools in Britain experienced a sense of workplace autonomy which they could and did interpret as evidence that they were regarded as professionals of expertise and integrity[37]. In sharp contrast to their treatment in the economic sector of teacher-state relations, organised teachers in the cultural and pedagogic sector of those relations had a sense of relative power. The educational settlement of the 1930s and the social democratic consensus of the 1950s and 1960s had given to this particular facet of autonomy a highly legitimated status. In contrast to highly centralised and controlled systems of state schooling in other socio-political contexts, the de-centralised autonomy of British teachers with respect to curriculum selection and pedagogic methods was taken to be a distinctive feature of British democracy and schooling. Teachers felt themselves to be free in this sense from the influence of the central state and the local state in education and also from the influence of parents and employers. It was a theme repeated constantly in the pages of the NUT's journal, 'The Schoolmaster':

> 'I have heard it said that the existence in this country of 146 strong, vigorous LEAs safeguards democracy and lessens the risk of dictatorship. No doubt this is true but an even greater safeguard is the existence of a quarter of a million teachers who are free to decide what should be taught and how it should be taught'. (Ronald Gould, 10 September, 1954).

and

> 'The freedom of teachers in their classrooms is a strongly held professional value in England and Wales. It has always been a source of pride to the profession and a very proper one, that in this country the teacher has the inalienable right to decide what to teach and how to teach it'. (Editorial, 30 September 1960)[38]

As the Centre for Contemporary Cultural Studies Education Group (1981, p. 90) has put it, 'at the dead centre of autonomy lay the 'secret garden' of the curriculum. Politicians entered it at the risk of charges of totalitarianism (if in power) or subversion (if on the left)'. Throughout the period of the social democratic consensus the state in education respected this cultural power of organised teachers and actually facilitated it, as in 1963 when the teachers gained control of the Schools Council on Examinations and Curriculum[39].

The constant focus upon teachers' classroom autonomy in the 1950s and 1960s was in fact crucial both to the teachers' leaders and to the agency of the state in education. Without a conscious, conspiratorial intention, its existence served as a countervailing compensation in the cultural sector for the declining terms and conditions of service in the economic sector. Professional autonomy was a real source of pride and satisfaction to the teachers and it served to legitimate something qualitative about the professional/manual worker divide. From the viewpoint of both the teachers' leaders and the representatives of the state in education, an emphasis upon workplace autonomy served also to deflect attention from the lack of success in obtaining a greater measure of occupational autonomy or professional self-government. Organised teachers had no greater control over their own occupational group in terms of selection, training and administration through a professional council than they had had in the 1930s. The Royal Society of Teachers had proved to be ineffectual and had been abolished in 1949. Proposals for the formation of a Teachers' General Council had been rejected in 1959 by a Conservative Minister of Education (David Eccles) and again in 1965 by a Labour Secretary of State for Education (Anthony Crosland). The state in education, regardless of political persuasion, was not prepared to cede to the teachers an autonomy which had these sorts of power correlations. The unchanging resistance of the state to the teachers' long campaign for professional self-government can be seen as further evidence that the notion of partnership in education in the post-war period had a very restricted application.

In the context of the preoccupation of the time however, occupational autonomy remained a very muted theme when compared with workplace autonomy. Workplace autonomy was, for the great majority of organised teachers, *the* concept of professional autonomy. Its existence was taken to be evidence that they were professional experts trusted by the agencies of the state (and it was assumed by the parents and the employers) to produce those outcomes from schooling which were entailed in the social democratic consensus. In this sense at least the teachers felt themselves to be partners in delivering the promise of transformation through education. The promise of equal opportunity, of social justice, of economic efficiency and of talent utilization was to be delivered through the agency of teachers in the state system of schooling and the mode through which they would deliver was professional autonomy. This was the educational settlement of social democracy which dominated educational policy and practice in Britain throughout the 1950s and the 1960s. This was the central principle which mediated teacher-state relations at this time.

By the early 1970s this settlement was threatened. There seemed to be mounting evidence that the promises of social democracy were not being realised and that transformation through education had not achieved the objectives set for it[40]. The economic importance of education in particular was coming to be more closely questioned. Organised teachers were also being reappraised. Public perceptions of the teaching profession during the period of teacher militancy (1968–74) had changed and it was clear that the ethic of legitimated professionalism was no longer the unchallenged ideology of the occupational group. With the assistance of hostile media amplification[41] the image of the 'responsible' professional teacher was now being contrasted with that of the radical groups such as Rank and File. Radical teachers, especially in inner-city schools, were portrayed as militant trade unionists intent on industrial action and workplace democracy on the one hand and as cultural and ideological subversives intent on a politicisation of classroom practice on the other. These teachers, 'the trendies and the lefties', were, it was claimed, exploiting school and classroom autonomy to the full and for the wrong reasons. They were decisively breaking, in their classroom practice, the long social democratic and professional consensus that the curriculum and the social relations of schooling were neutral and apolitical. Encouraged by a new critical ('subversive') literature in the politics and sociology of education[42] these teachers were arguing that state schooling was deeply implicated in the reproduction of the class, race and gender divisions of existing capitalist society.

What was being constructed by the media and by ideological attacks from the Right (exemplified in the Black Papers in Education[43] and in Rhodes Boyson's book *The Crisis in Education*, 1975) was a picture of large-scale radical appropriation of teacher autonomy in Britain, especially in the inner-city working-class schools. The fears being constructed about the implications of this were not without some empirical substance[44], but the case was presented in populist and sensational terms. The ideological attacks from the Right exaggerated the extent of the radicalisation of the schools, but they were correct in their basic assumption that the granting of classroom autonomy to teachers in Britain had always been premised on the implicit understanding that teachers would use this autonomy conservatively and not radically. A fear of large-scale radical appropriation of teacher autonomy could be guaranteed to provoke a sense of cultural and political threat which resonated with a long historical preoccupation in the dominant social group in Britain. From Matthew Arnold's fears about working class anarchy in the 1860s to the panics about Bolshevism and subversion in the elementary schools of the 1920s, popular schooling had always been a site of potential crisis and if of potential crisis then also the site of potential reaction. By the mid 1970s at a number of levels and in a number of different sectors the period of social democratic consensus, of partnership and of professional autonomy as a stage in teacher-state relations in Britain had moved into crisis. Out of this crisis (partly real and partly constructed) a new mode of teacher-state relations was to emerge in the late 1970s and in the 1980s.

The Agencies of the State and the Reassertion of Explicit Control

In the most recent literature of teacher-state relations in Britain there is general agreement that the mechanisms of state control over organised teachers have once again become as visible and explicit as they were at the beginning of the century. As Lawn and Ozga (1986, p. 237) have put it, 'indirect rule has been replaced by direct rule'. From a perspective within the leadership of the National Union of Teachers, Roy (1983) has interpreted this change as an attack upon the relative autonomy of education and upon the professional freedom and integrity of organised teachers in Britain. In his book, *Teaching under Attack*, Roy argues that teachers have to face politicians and educational bureaucrats who have now adopted an interventionist central state philosophy in which 'schools exist to serve the interests of society as interpreted by those who hold political power and the purse strings and the teachers need to be made to toe the line' (p. 6). Roy's analysis which is written from a policy position within the ethic of legitimated teacher professionalism is characterized by a sense of moral outrage about the politicisation of contemporary schooling:

'There is no inalienable right given to politicians, no principle of democratic government, which support the notion that the educational process requires either political interpretation or a high degree of political control' (p. 17).

The socio-historical irony of a moderate teachers' leader having to insist, in a period of Conservative government in Britain, that education and politics ought to be kept separate, is considerable, and it is certainly evidence of a radical shift in teacher-state relations. From a 'rank and file' perspective within the NUT, Jones (1985, p. 280) sees that at the heart of the Union's current situation is:

'the combination of economic recession with a very marked shift in the relationship of major social forces to state education. The union's traditional pathways of advance are blocked. The assumption that educational expansion is synonymous with economic benefit is not widely shared. Governments no longer think that the teaching force can be relied upon to adjust itself to official perceptions of educational need . . . . The teaching force must not only contract. Just as important, it must be subject to increased control both of its educational work and its conditions of service'.

Although these two accounts vary in their analytical emphases and subsequently in their proposals for appropriate strategies for organised teachers in their changed circumstances, they are agreed that teacher-state relations in the 1980s have changed radically. As practising teachers and as union leaders, both writers are agreed that the state agencies in education have taken a series of initiatives which require organised teachers to re-think their occupational strategies with some urgency. Both writers see the present situation as a time of struggle between the teachers and the central state in education.

The breaking of the social democratic consensus and of the educational settlement between the state and the teachers (represented in notions of partnership and of autonomy) resulted from a conjunction of political, economic, ideological and bureaucratic forces whose significance became particularly salient from the mid 1970s. Of these, the most profound was the economic recession in Britain. This recession, signalled by a host of indicators (low growth rate, decline in profitability, rising unemployment, balance of payment deficits, recourse to the International Monetary Fund) had become highly visible and with this recession came the inevitable search for scapegoats. A major economic analysis of the mid 1970s which received wide publicity located the central cause of Britain's economic decline in the extensive growth of the public service sector — 'armies of teachers, social workers and civil servants' were putting pressure on the productive sector, causing exports to fall and investment to be diverted'[45].

Within a comparatively short space of time, the relation between publicly-provided education and the state of the economy was the subject of a severe reappraisal. Education, which had been expected to be a dynamic source of economic growth and prosperity in the 1960s, was now being cast in the role of the culprit for the economic failures of the 1970s. As these forms of analysis gained credibility, a legitimation was created for a whole series of ideological attacks upon teachers in the state system of schooling. The themes of earlier Black Paper critiques were resurrected and used as the basis of a campaign in the popular media which claimed that too many teachers were incompetent, slovenly, trendy, progressive and unable or unwilling to discipline the youth in their charge. In short, standards, both intellectual and personal, had been betrayed by a significant sector of teachers and therefore their claim to be regarded and treated as a profession was now seriously open to question. At the same time, leading industrialists associated themselves with these attacks, claiming, as did Arnold Weinstock (Managing Director of GEC) in 1976, that the shortage of skilled workers could be attributed to the anti-industry attitudes of many teachers. Weinstock's article, which was significantly entitled 'I blame the teachers', implied that the classroom autonomy of teachers needed to be limited and the links between education and industry strengthened[46]. Teachers had distanced themselves too much from the world of productive industry. Similar charges of unjustifiable distancing were made by the Conservative politicians (notably Rhodes Boyson) about the teachers' lack of rapport with 'the parents'. Teachers were characterized as keeping parents at arm's length and of refusing to regard themselves as accountable to the parents or the wider community. From this perspective, control of teachers, of curriculum and of standards had been lost by the excessive development of principles of teacher autonomy and the answers to the contemporary problems of state schooling could only be found in a reassertion of control. Thus Boyson argued:

> 'These problems can be solved only by making schools again accountable to some authority outside them. The necessary sanction is either a nationally enforced curriculum or parental choice or a combination of both' (1975, pp. 141–2).

These ideological attacks, which the CCCS Education Group have called 'the Conservative education offensive' (1981, p. 191) were highly effective in their constant repetition of a series of charges against the teachers, all of which had some historical substance. Collectively they provided a populist and simple explanation for Britain's contemporary social and economic ills. Although organised teachers attempted to answer these attacks and to show that the charges were exaggerated and the explanations were over-simplified, the ideological struggle was unequal. The teachers did not have the same media access or support nor were they generally able to present their case in the same clear-cut populist terms. A Marxist analysis of teachers in the early 1970s had referred to teachers as 'professional ideologists'[47]. The events of the mid-1970s in Britain were to show that teachers were in fact a relatively powerless category of professional ideologists. In what was a crucial struggle for popular and political consciousness about state education, the role of teachers and relations with the economy and the community, the teachers were outmanoeuvred by media ideologists and by the ideologists of the New Right[48]. The effects of this defeat were to be profound both at political and bureaucratic level in educational policy.

It is possible to chart from this time a series of initiatives from the state in education which have involved a steady reassertion of central and visible control over state schooling, and a steady erosion of teachers' professional autonomy, and certainly of any remaining sense of partnership in education[49]. This reorientation of teacher-state relations has in effect been a working-out of the agenda set for education policy originally by the Labour government of 1974–1979 and developed with more directness and vigour by Conservative governments since 1979. With a Labour central state in education the teachers have had to face moves towards a centralized curriculum or what James Callaghan described as 'the strong case for a so-called core curriculum of basic knowledge'[50]; proposals for greater parent power in the running of schools (Taylor Report, 1977) and the establishment of the Manpower Services Commission (1974) which, with its concepts of 'skill', 'training' and direct relation with industry, embodied a direct threat to the significance of conventional state schooling and to the significance of the schoolteacher's role.

With a Conservative central state in education, organised teachers have experienced an acceleration of centralized curriculum initiatives, of parent power initiatives and of the scale of the activities of the Manpower Services Commission in implementing what Salter and Tapper have called 'the new economic ideology of education' (1981, p. 220). Additionally, in the cultural and professional sector of teacher-state relations, the teachers have been obliged to accept the abolition of the Schools Council and the creation of a new form of direct state monitoring of teacher education and training in the Council for the Accreditation of Teacher Education.

In the economic sector of teacher-state relations, teachers have been faced with declining relative salary levels, declining job security with compulsory redeployment if necessary, and with proposals for career 'restructuring' and for compulsory teacher appraisal. The bitter and protracted teachers' dispute of 1985–86[51] has been the culmination of all these developments.

The policy of the state in education vis-à-vis the teachers has changed as political and economic developments have undermined the position of the teaching profession. The breaking of the social democratic consensus compelled the Labour Party when in power to take a new stance in its relation with organised teachers. For electoral and strategic reasons the Labour government of 1974–79 had to be seen to take seriously the much-propagated view that education needed 'tightening up', with a necessary reappraisal of the teachers' position. With the Conservative Party in government 'tightening up' became, especially under Sir Keith Joseph as Secretary of State for Education, the new ideological mission and was given new legislation and administrative forms.

However, the reorientation of state policy in education vis-à-vis the teachers in the 1970s and 1980s has not resulted solely from changed political priorities. Salter and Tapper (1981) have argued that the Department of Education and Science as the state bureaucracy in education has also been responsible for initiatives which have strengthened its control of education at the expense of organised teachers. Spurred on by the rapid expansion of the Manpower Services Commission as a new power centre in education, the DES has moved strongly towards an interventionist policy on curriculum matters. Thus teachers have had to face both political and bureaucratic imperatives in the 1970s and 1980s which have not only threatened but made serious inroads into their professional terrain (McNay and Ozga 1985).

The confidence with which the most recent initiatives have been made by the central state against the interests of organised teachers suggests something akin to the cultural and professional condescension of teacher-state relations at the beginning of the century. It suggests that the whole enterprise of state schooling is looked upon in a very different light from that of earlier periods and that a devaluation of the teacher's status is in progress. Unlike the early years of the century, there does not seem to be a sense among the agencies of the state in education that organised teachers in the NUT are any longer a political force to be reckoned with, so that even classroom autonomy (the heartland of teacher professionalism) can be proceeded against with impunity. In other words, there has been a major shift in the power differential of teacher-state relations in Britain in favour of the agencies of the central state[52].

The most obvious reasons for this shift in the power differential is the political and ideological strength of the central state and its sense of a radical-Conservative mission. A Conservative government with a large parliamentary majority and claiming a democratic mandate for cutting public expenditure and implementing the discipline of market forces and efficiency, is a formidable opponent for organised teachers in state schooling. When, in addition to this, the former Secretary of State for Education (Sir Keith Joseph) was one of the leading ideologists for such a policy then the teachers were faced at the political level with their greatest challenge this century.

Unlike the early years of the century the NUT in particular has faced this challenge in a much weaker situation and it seems likely that the perception of this weakness has added to the sense of policy confidence within both the political and the bureaucratic sectors of the state in education. Jones (1985) expresses the dilemma of the Union in this way:

'The Union has been accustomed to rising membership, educational expansion and increasing curricular influence. The accelerating revision of the (1944) settlement has shaken the NUT. Its membership falling, its influence lessened, the conditions of service of its members worsening, the Union is attempting to develop a new strategy ...' (p. 280).

The present acknowledged weakness of the NUT has arisen out of internal as well as out of external changes. The Union has lost membership, especially during its phases of militancy, with some headteachers withdrawing into their own organisations and a sector of ultra-professional teachers (committed never to strike) seceding to form the Professional Association of Teachers[53].

Whereas the NUT at the beginning of the century could claim to be *the* organisation for teachers in state schooling and was perceived as such, the contemporary situation of the NUT has a much reduced power significance:

'Only about half the teachers in England and Wales belong to the NUT — about 220,000. Of the rest, the National Association of Schoolmasters/ Union of Women Teachers claims 120,000 and the Assistant Masters and Mistresses Association, 80,000. Both organise mainly in secondary schools. The Professional Association of Teachers (23,000) and the head-teacher associations claim the rest[54]'.

These contemporary divisions among the total population of organised teachers in state schooling in Britain provide the central state in education with its greatest tactical advantage in both the cultural and the economic sectors of teacher-state relations. It is an advantage which the agencies of the state can constantly renew by ideological emphases upon the differences between professionalism and trades unionism among teachers and by financial policies which emphasize the significance of differentials ('management', 'responsibility', 'merit', 'status') in salary awards. The crucial importance of these divisions for the present nature of teacher-state relations in Britain is very clear.

But the disadvantages of the National Union of Teachers arise not only out of structural and ideological divisions among the total teaching force but also out of some failures in occupational strategies in the 1970s and 1980s. In a context which required new strategies appropriate to changed political, economic and ideological conditions, the leaders of the Union continued to assert the ideology of teacher professional autonomy in its classic form. They attempted to preserve the professional terrain of teachers from the 'interference' of the state, of industry and of parents. It was, in effect, a strategy of professional isolationism which made the making of any potential alliances with other groups, against the initiatives of the central state, very difficult.

In a commentary on this period, Salter and Tapper (1981) have made some strong criticisms of the teachers' leaders, claiming that they had 'a sense of their own importance which was rapidly becoming anachronistic' and that they did not appear 'to realise that the DES was making ideological alliances with everyone (industry, trade unions, LEAs, parents etc.)' (p. 210). The danger of this type of analysis is that it leads to a deficit and unsympathetic view of the teachers' situation and by contrast implies a high degree of central state-craft. It is wrong to suggest that this most recent period of teacher-state relations in Britain reveals some sort of superior political or strategic 'intelligence' possessed by the agencies of the central state over and against the leaders of organised teachers. The central state had in one sense to do nothing more than to exploit the possibilities arising from the crisis of the social democratic consensus and to exploit its own political and ideological advantages in a situation of economic recession. What organised teachers did was to use a defensive strategy which had never failed them in the past — a particular version of teacher professionalism. Such professionalism had a claim to curriculum and pedagogical autonomy, acknowledged expertise, professional integrity and trust — and therefore freedom from external agencies, inscribed at its heart. With this strategy the teachers had fought off the impositions of 'payment by results' in the nineteenth century and they had also fought off accusations of indoctrination and political bias in the 1920s. The NUT had seen this position legitimated and accepted by the central state in education in the concept of (limited) partnership from the 1930s and they had seen it become a celebrated and apparently immutable feature of British state schooling in the 1950s and 1960s. The whole historical consciousness and experience of organised teachers suggested that in the face of central state initiatives this version of professionalism would be their best defence. But this form of professionalism depended on another contextual element which was no longer there to the same degree.

Teacher professionalism in its classic form depended upon a political, economic and social valuing of the importance of state schooling and of its agents, the teachers. It was *this* which had changed radically. Perhaps, understandably, the teachers' leaders were slow to grasp an ideological and political change of such magnitude.

Teachers and the State: Theorising the History

The previous accounts have charted the shifts in teacher-state relations in Britain in four historical periods from the 1900s to the 1980s. They have attempted to show how these relations have changed as a consequence of wider political, economic, social and ideological developments; as a consequence of changes in state policy and in the operations of the educational bureaucracy and as a consequence of changes in the organisation and strategies of teachers in state schooling. It has been necessary to appreciate the complexities and the contradictions of policy 'on both sides'. But in addition to an appreciation of this complexity and of these contradictions it is also necessary to attempt a broader theoretical reading of these events, if socio-historical study is not to become 'just one damn thing after another'.

At the beginning of this paper, it was suggested that the whole story of teacher-state relations in Britain this century might be viewed as an extended war of position over the nature of teacher professionalism and its assumed correlates. The ethic of legitimated teacher professionalism has been a crucial theoretical notion which has permeated the previous socio-historical accounts and it is now claimed that this concept is central to the wider appreciation of teacher-state relations in Britain.

The ethic of legitimated teacher professionalism involves an implicit understanding between organised teachers and the agencies of the state in education in resolving their conflicting interests and concerns. In effect it is an understanding which involves, at the surface level, the idea that teachers will accept their legitimate realm, their sphere of 'proper' professional activity, as within the classroom and the school system and the state, for its part, will grant them a measure of trust and autonomy, professional salaries and occupational securities and professional respect and dignity.

For teachers, the ethic of legitimated professionalism provides, at the structural and economic level, only a partial realisation of their occupational aspirations but at the cultural level it provides a strong sense of professionalism through the experience of workplace autonomy. For the state, the ethic of legitimated teacher professionalism provides some sort of ideological guarantee that 'the teachers of the people' can be relied upon to be loyal professionals within the existing social order. The surface structure of this ethic can be discerned without too much difficulty.

At a deeper level, however, the ethic of legitimated professionalism has two effects which grow in significance over time. These effects are de-politicization and incorporation.

In the case of teachers in state schooling in Britain, de-politicization involves a cumulative process in which the occupational group comes to regard 'the political' as fundamentally a corruption of 'the educational'. It begins, in effect, with the response of teachers to external charges of indoctrination and political bias in schooling. In response to these charges a 'professional' defence is constructed which insists that party or class politics do not and cannot have any legitimate place in the classroom. As part of this response the occupational group distances itself from any explicit alliances with party or class organisations and constructs a position of neutrality within the political and social structure. What is argued here is that this process imperceptibly extends over time so that what begins as an inhibition of party or class politics develops into an *inhibition of the political per se*. The occupational group becomes progressively de-politicized both in its classroom practice (the political becomes invisible) and in its structural relations (its effective use of power declines). The ethic of legitimated professionalism through this mode of de-politicization 'domesticates' the occupational group so that it becomes, from the perspectives of the central state, a far less threatening entity[55].

At the same time and related to this de-politicization, processes of incorporation occur. The occupational group (*not* as a result of conscious state intention but arising out of a conjunction of forces) becomes increasingly incorporated within the existing social and cultural order. It is first 'accepted' and then, over time, achieves the status of apparent partner in the educational enterprise. This becomes a celebration of its professional influence. Both the process of de-politicization and the process of incorporation have the effect of attenuating alliances with other social and occupational groups. The occupational group has come to an understanding with the state in education and the ethic of legitimated teacher professionalism entails the distancing of all other groups. This is the deep structural weakness of the position. In a situation in which the central state in education *radically changes* its stance on the importance of state schooling within the social formation and on its evaluation of teachers within that system, the ethic of legitimated professionalism is rendered virtually impotent. The combination of occupational de-politicization and occupational incorporation provides the state with massive advantages in any ensuing struggle. Teacher-state relations in Britain have now reached that juncture.

Acknowledgements

I would like to thank Brian Simon, Paul Hirst, Neil Daglish, Felicity Hunt, John

Furlong and Martin Lawn for commenting on an earlier draft. Where I have taken their advice it has improved the paper. I am indebted to the Librarians of the NUT at Hamilton House and to the Sisters of St Augustine at Cambridge for research and writing facilities.

Notes

1 Gramsci uses the term 'war of position' to refer to wider popular struggles against State power which he describes as a form of trench warfare. See *Selections from Prison Notebooks* (1978, p. 243). The term seems to me to be also applicable to the nature of teacher-state relations in Britain this century. Teacher-state relations have been a long war of position about professionalism, autonomy, material conditions and control. See also Apple's (1982, pp. 16–17) use of the term to describe cultural and political struggles.

2 Education Group CCCS (1981) p. 18

3 McLellan, G. *et al.* (1984) p. 3

4 See Tropp, A. (1957) p. 148

5 See Simon, B. (1974) p. 216

6 See Gosden, P. (1972) p. 34 'The new pattern of local administration . . . in one way did not favour the teachers' cause. The new local authorities were multi-purpose bodies, education was only one of their functions and they had to meet the calls of many other public services . . . '

7 *Ibid.* pp. 201–202

8 *Ibid.* p. 334

9 It is not being claimed here that the political influence of the NUT was *alone* responsible for the fall of Runciman and of Morant. A complex set of political and other interests was involved. The Holmes-Morant circular provided a strategic opportunity for the Conservative opposition to embarrass the Liberal government with charges of elitism. It also provided radical Liberals with grounds for attacking the 'high-handed' bureaucracy of Morant. Nevertheless, the NUT clearly played a crucial role in sustaining a public and political outcry until the point at which both Runciman and Morant left the Board of Education. Perhaps most important in the context of the time was the fact that the national press *represented* the incident as evidence of the 'power' of the NUT (See extracts from The Saturday Review and The Morning Post, quoted in Tropp *op. cit.* p. 203) For a detailed discussion, see Tropp pp. 199–203 and M. Wilkinson, 'The Holmes Circular Affair', *Journal of Educational Administration and History* July 1980 pp. 29–38. I am grateful to Dr Felicity Hunt and to Dr Neil Daglish for comments on this issue.

10 There is no intention here to imply a conspiratorial policy on the part of the state in education. What is suggested is that L. A. Selby-Bigge, the Permanent Secretary of the Board of Education from 1911 to 1925, had learned much from the Holmes-Morant incident. The policy of the Board towards organised teachers was, so far as the permanent officials were concerned, one of conciliation and consultation.

11 *Ibid.* p. 36

12 See Tropp (1957) p. 211

13 See Gosden (1972) pp. 36–37

14 This is not to say that such a stance disappeared altogether but obvious condescension had played a large part in provoking the crisis of 1911.

15 See Dale, R. (1982) p. 137 for a discussion of this point.

16 The organisation started as the Equal Pay League and in 1909 became the National Federation of Women Teachers. This worked as a separate body although officially still part of the NUT. Dual membership of the NUT and the NUWT was not formally banned until 1932 but in effect the NUWT was independent in the 1920s (See Chapter 2 of this volume for a full discussion of the NUWT).

17 See Gosden (1972) p. 111

18 Gosden (1972, p. 113) suggests that the separate existence of the NUWT from the 1920s to 1961 was not 'a threat to the NUT . . . because of the apathy of many women teachers'. Quite apart from the problematic use of 'apathy' as an explanatory device, what this account overlooks is that the loss of committed and activist women teachers throughout this period undoubtedly weakened the NUT.

19 See Tropp *op. cit.* p. 215

20 See Barker, R. (1972) pp. 147–152 for a discussion of the Teachers' Labour League.

21 *Ibid.* p. 150

22 See Board of Education File 'Teacher's Oath of Allegiance (1922–1927)' PRO ED/24/1753

23 Between 1922 and 1930 various attempts were made by Conservative MPs to persuade the House of Commons to pass 'Seditious Teachings Bills' designed to 'prevent the teaching of seditious or anarchical doctrines or methods to the young' (See Simon, B., 1978, p. 73) See also National Union of Teachers Archive File E1151 'Blasphemous Teaching' which gives details of the Seditious and Blasphemous Teaching to Children Bill (1925) and NUT response to this published in 'The Schoolmaster', March 17 1927, under the title 'Painting the Schools Red'. 'The Schoolmaster' for December 18 1930, in reporting the talking-out of the Bill, noted that the proposer of the Bill had admitted 'that it was very difficult to find actual evidence of any widespread teaching of this kind'. (p. 993)

24 See Board of Education File 'Political activities of Teachers (1926–1934)' PRO ED/24/1761

25 See PRO ED/24/1753

26 Eustace Percy was prepared to make major speeches in which he warned of the dangers of political propaganda in schools and this was not well received by the National Union of Teachers, especially when he used phrases such as 'a constant and conscious effort among a large section of our fellow countrymen to conduct political propaganda, directly or indirectly, among children' (See Barker, R. 1972, p. 150). However, it seems clear that these references were directed to the Labour Party and not to organised teachers in general.

27 Lawn and Ozga suggest that Eustace Percy was influenced by models of indirect rule derived from British colonial administration (See p. 231)

28 'The Schoolmaster', May 21 1926

29 Simon, B. (1978) reports Lord Riddell, a newspaper proprietor and close associate of Lloyd George, arguing in relation to proposed cuts in teachers' salaries:-

'I strongly object to the teachers' salaries being cut down, they are not over-paid. Teaching is a hard job. Everything depends on it. If you cut down the teachers' salaries the result will be to turn them into Bolsheviks .... I look upon adequate payments for teachers as an insurance as well as an act of justice ...' (p. 46).

30 There was a considerable campaign in the pages of 'The Schoolmaster' in the early 1930s to persuade teachers to join the RST but as an organisation it had no power. For a full account of the teachers' attempts to achieve occupational autonomy see Parry, N. and Parry, J. (1974)

31 Quoted in Jones, K. (1983) p. 107

32 Ronald Gould (later Sir Ronald Gould) was General Secretary of the NUT from 1947 to 1970.

33 Quoted in Gosden, P. (1972) pp. 84–85

34 See Jones, K., *op. cit.* pp. 113–132 for a perceptive analysis of the significance of both the Rank and File organisation and of the Teachers' Labour League.

35 In the view of Ken Jones, *op. cit.* 'the relatively large 'Houghton' pay award at the end of 1974, which introduced wide and divisive differentials, was one sign of night regathering' (p. 116).

36 See for instance Grace, G. (1978) pp. 208–213.

37 See Grace, G. (1985) p. 130 for distinctions between occupational and workplace autonomy.

38 Quoted in Manzer, R. (1970) p. 83

39 Lawn and Ozga (1986) note that an attempt by the DES to take more initiative (and power) in the curriculum area in 1962 was forestalled by the joint action of the local authorities and the teachers. The creation of the Schools Council in place of these initiatives was 'hailed as a major victory for the teachers and a measure of their influence over the curriculum' (p. 236).

40 For a full account of the crisis of the social democratic project in education see Education Group CCCS (1981) Part 3.

41 *Ibid*, pp. 208–215

42 The 'new' sociology of education associated with the work of Michael F. D. Young *et al.* was consistently attacked.

43 The Black Papers in Education were a series of Conservative polemical attacks upon state education and upon a sector of state school teachers. They appeared between 1969 and 1977. For one discussion of their significance see Education Group CCCS pp. 200–207.

44 The events at the William Tyndale Junior School, Islington in 1975 gave considerable advantage to the Black Paper ideologists. For immediate discussion of these events see Ellis, T. *et al.* (1976), Gretton, J. and Jackson, M. (1976) and the Auld Report (1976). For later discussion see Dale, R. (1979) and (1980).

45 Quoted in Education Group *op. cit.* pp. 171–2.

46 Times Educational Supplement, January 23. For a discussion of the growing influence of 'industry' on education policy see Beck, J. (1983).

47 The term is that of Louis Althusser (1971).

48 The teachers' problems were only partly those of media 'style'. The main problem was

that the ideologists of the Right were in effect the controllers of a large sector of the media and it was in this sense that the teachers were outmanoeuvred.

49 The first stages of this process have been charted by Lawton, D. (1980).

50 Education Group *op. cit.*, p. 218

51 For a discussion of this dispute see Pietrasik, R. in this volume.

52 The shift in the power differential affects not only teacher-central state relations but also the relations between the central state and the local state in education. For a discussion of this see Hunter, C. (1983). See also Miller, H. (1985).

53 The Professional Association of Teachers seceded from the NUT following the affiliation to the TUC in 1970 and the period of teacher militancy 1968–1974.

54 Jones, K. (1985) p. 287

55 To this ideological factor must always be added the growing weakness arising out of the sectional division and structural fragmentation of organised teachers as a whole.

References

AHIER, J. and FLUDE, M. (1983) (Eds.) *Contemporary Education Policy*, London, Croom Helm.

ALTHUSSER, L. (1971) 'Ideology and Ideological State Apparatuses' in Cosin, B. (Ed.) *Education,Structure ad Society*, Harmondsworth, Penguin Books.

APPLE, M. (1982) (Ed.) *Cultural and Economic Reproduction in Education: essays on class, ideology and the state*, London, Routledge & Kegan Paul.

AULD, R. (1976) *William Tyndale School Public Inquiry* (Auld Report) London, ILEA.

BARKER, R. (1972) *Education and Politics 1900–1951*, Oxford, Oxford University Press.

BARTON, L. and WALKER, S. (1985) (Eds.) *Education and Social Change*, London, Croom Helm.

BECK, J. (1983) 'Accountability, Industry and Education' in Ahier, J. and Flude, M. (Eds.) *Contemporary Education Policy*, London, Croom Helm.

BOARD OF EDUCATION (1920s–1930s) Archives, Kew, Public Record Office.

BOYSON, R. (1975) *The Crisis in Education*, London, Woburn Press.

COATES, R. (1972) *The Teacher Unions and Interest Group Politics*, Cambridge, Cambridge University Press.

DALE, R. (1979) 'The politicization of deviance: responses to William Tyndale' in Barton, L. and Meighan, R. (Eds.) *Schools, Pupils and Deviance*, Driffield, Nafferton Books.

DALE, R. (1980) 'Control, accountability and William Tyndale' in Dale, R., Esland, G. and Macdonald M. (Eds.) *Education and the State*, Vol. 1, London, Routledge & Kegan Paul.

DALE, R. (1982) 'Education and the capitalist state' in Apple, M. (Ed.) *Cultural and Economic Reproduction in Education*, London, Routledge & Kegan Paul.

EDUCATION GROUP (1981) *Unpopular Education: schooling and social democracy in England since 1944*, London, Hutchinson/Centre for Contemporary Cultural Studies, Birmingham.

ELLIS, T. *et al.* (1976) *William Tyndale: the teachers' story*, London, Writers' and Readers' Publishing Cooperative.

GOSDEN, P. (1972) *The Evolution of A Profession*, Oxford, Blackwell.

GRACE, G. (1978) *Teachers, Ideology and Control*, London, Routledge & Kegan Paul.

GRACE, G. (1985) 'Judging teachers: the social and political contexts of teacher evaluation', in Barton, L. and Walker, S. (Eds.) *Education and Social Change*, London, Croom Helm.

GRAMSCI, A. (1978) *Selections from Prison Notebooks* (Ed. Hoare, Q. and Nowell Smith, G.), London, Lawrence and Wishart.

GRETTON, J. and JACKSON, M. (1976) *William Tyndale: collapse of a school or a system?* London, Allen and Unwin.

HUNTER, C. (1983) 'Education and local government in the light of central government policy', in Ahier, J. and Flude, M. (Eds.) *Contemporary Education Policy*, London, Croom Helm.

JOHNSON, R. (1976) 'Notes on the schooling of the English working class 1780–1850' in Dale, R. *et al.* (Eds.) *Schooling and Capitalism*, London, Routledge & Kegan Paul/Open University Press.

JONES, K. (1983) *Beyond Progressive Education*, London, Macmillan.

JONES, K. (1985) 'The National Union of Teachers (England and Wales)' in Lawn, M. (Ed.) *The Politics of Teacher Unionism*, London, Croom Helm.

LAWN, M. (1985) (Ed.) *The Politics of Teacher Unionism*, London, Croom Helm.

LAWN, M. and OZGA, J. (1981) 'The educational worker? A re-assessment of teachers', in Barton, L. and Walker, S. (Eds.) *Schools, Teachers and Teaching*, Lewes, Falmer Press.

LAWN, M. and OZGA, J. (1986) 'Unequal partners: teachers under indirect rule', *British Journal of Sociology of Education*, 7,2.

LAWTON, D. (1980) *The Politics of the School Curriculum*, London, Routledge & Kegan Paul.

MANZER, R. (1970) *Teachers and Politics*, Manchester, Manchester University Press.

McLENNAN, G. *et al.* (1984) *State and Society in Contemporary Britain*, Cambridge, Polity Press.

McNAY, I. and OZGA, J. (1985) *Policy-making in Education: the breakdown of consensus.* Oxford, Pergamon Press/Open University.

MILLER, H. (1985) 'The local state and teachers: the case of Liverpool' in Barton, L. and Walker, S., (Eds.) *Education and Social Change*, London, Croom Helm.

NATIONAL UNION of TEACHERS (1920s–1930s) Archives, London, Hamilton House.

OZGA, J. and LAWN, M. (1981) *Teachers, Professionalism and Class*, Lewes, Falmer Press.

PARRY, N. and PARRY, J. (1974) 'The teachers and professionalism: the failure of an occupational strategy' in Flude, M. and Ahier, J. (Eds.) *Educability, Schools and Ideology*, London, Croom Helm.

ROY, W. (1983) *Teaching under Attack*, London, Croom Helm.

SALTER, B. and TAPPER, T. (1981) *Education, Politics and the State*, London, Grant McIntyre.

SIMON, B. (1974) *Education and the Labour Movement 1870–1920*, London, Lawrence and Wishart.

SIMON, B. (1978) *The Politics of Educational Reform 1920–1940*, London, Lawrence and Wishart.

THOMPSON, E. P. (1963) *The Making of the English Working Class*, London, Gollancz.

THOMPSON, E. P. (1978) *The Poverty of Theory*, London, Merlin Press.

TROPP, A. (1957) *The Schoolteachers: the growth of the teaching profession in England and Wales from 1800 to the present day*, London, Heinemann.

WEINSTOCK, A. (1976) 'I blame the teachers', *Times Educational Supplement*, January 23.

WHITE, J. (1975) 'The end of the compulsory curriculum', in *The Curriculum: the Doris Lee Lectures*, London, University of London Institute of Education.

List of Contributors

Geraldine Clifford	is Professor in the School of Education, University of California at Berkeley.
Gerald Grace	is Professor of Education at the Victoria University of Wellington, New Zealand.
Marilyn Joyce	teaches in an Inner London Education Authority Infant School and is a member of the M.A. Women and Education Course at the University of Sussex.
Sarah King	is a Research Assistant in the School of Humanities at Thames Polytechnic.
Martin Lawn	is a Senior Lecturer in Teaching Studies in Westhill College.
Jan Lee	is a Lecturer in Primary Education at the University of London, Goldsmiths' College.
Jenny Ozga	is a Lecturer in the Centre for Educational Policy and Management in the School of Education at the Open University.
Richard Pietrasik	is a maths teacher in a London Comprehensive School and editor of 'Socialist Teacher'.
Carolyn Steedman	is a Lecturer in Arts Education at the University of Warwick
Kieron Walsh	is a Lecturer in the Institute of Local Government Studies at the University of Birmingham.

Index